D1527023

Valerius Maximus & the Rhetoric of the New Nobility

The
University
of North
Carolina
Press
Chapel Hill
and
London

Valerius Maximus

& the Rhetoric of
the New Nobility

W. MARTIN BLOOMER

PA
6791
.V7
B58
1992

© 1992 The University of

North Carolina Press

All rights reserved

Manufactured in the United States of America

The paper in this book meets the guidelines for permanence and

durability of the Committee on Production Guidelines for Book

Longevity of the Council on Library Resources.

96 95 94 93 92   5 4 3 2 1

Library of Congress Cataloging-in-Publication Data

Bloomer, W. Martin.

   Valerius Maximus and the rhetoric of the new nobility / Martin

Bloomer.

      p.   cm.

   Includes bibliographical references and index.

   ISBN 0-8078-2047-4 (alk. paper)

   1. Valerius Maximus. Factorum et dictorum memorabilium libri IX.

2. Rome—History—Republic, 265–30 B.C.—Historiography.

3. Rome—History—Tiberius, 14–37—Historiography.   4. Authors

and readers—Rome.   5. Rhetoric, Ancient.   6. Nobility—Rome.

I. Title.

PA6791.V7B58   1992

937'.02'072—dc20   92-53628

                          CIP

CANISIUS COLLEGE LIBRARY
BUFFALO, N.Y.

Contents

Preface

My aim in this book is in part to reveal the distinctive
qualities of a neglected and maligned author. I will not enter into apologies for a highly mannered rhetorical and ethical handbook written
in a period of significant social, political, and literary changes. The interest of Valerius' work should now elicit a new readership—of social
and literary historians, to say nothing of those professionally concerned with ancient history, rhetoric, and their transmission. In particular I hope to have made Valerius Maximus more accessible and
comprehensible, and so I have emphasized his methods of research and
principles of composition, his aesthetic desiderata, his peculiar transformation of "history," and his cultural milieu.

My hope is that students of Silver Latin and students of the Renaissance canon will be encouraged to read and use Valerius Maximus,
although this is still hampered by the lack of an English translation
(Samuel Speed's translation of 1678 is the only English version), the
lack of a modern commentary, and by an inadequate text (Kempf 1888,
which I have used). Consequently, I have translated all passages discussed except some of those in the final chapter where the argument
(on style and rhetoric) seemed to demand the original.

I fondly acknowledge my continuing debt to George P. Goold and
Gordon W. Williams, my teachers at Yale University and advisers of my
1987 dissertation on Valerius. For their valued contributions and support I thank Joseph Solodow, Elizabeth Meyer, and Thomas Habinek,
who read the manuscript at varying points and each suggested paths
of revision.

1 Introduction

Culling 967 stories from various authors and arranging them under categorical headings is a peculiar way to write a book. Valerius Maximus drew only one of the stories from personal experience: he observed the suicide of an old woman on the island of Ceos while traveling to Asia with Sextus Pompeius. His book, *Memorable Deeds and Sayings,* compiled during the reign of Tiberius, the second Roman emperor, narrates this dramatic and unsettling event as proof of the Greek origin of publicly administered poison. The preceding example in this chapter on foreign institutions had related the similar practice among the citizens of Marseilles. The strange subject and the bizarre reason for telling it are typical of Valerius Maximus. An author so little present in his own work also attracted little attention of any other type: this fact, that he once accompanied the Roman magistrate Sextus Pompeius on a trip to the East, is the only one known about Valerius' life.[1]

This work was clearly meant for specific audiences and uses; a collection of anecdotes organized under general rubrics was of most service for students and practitioners of declamation, a form of oral performance that constituted both the final stage in Roman education and, for the professional performer and the Romans who thronged the recital halls, the preeminent public art form of the early Principate.[2]

---

1. The story (2.6.8) relates the suicide and her words to Sextus Pompeius (proconsul A.D. 24/25 as Syme has argued, 1978, 161–62). Valerius was in the course of writing his final book in A.D. 31 as is indicated by the condemnation (9.11.ext.4) of Sejanus, the emperor Tiberius' one time favorite who perhaps conspired against the emperor and at any rate was denounced in the senate and executed in that year.

2. The closest analogy to declamation is the modern concert, widely attended and with its own coterie of experts and a certain snob appeal. The concert by and large is more self-contained: the performer's distinction merits advance-

Valerius' *Memorable Deeds and Sayings* provided a stock of rhetorical illustrations and in its treatment of this material demonstrated the various rhetorical shapes an exemplum could take and the ways to introduce, join, and conclude such stories. The common appeal to all readers of Valerius has not, however, been his strong rhetoric but the myriad anecdotes themselves. His brief narratives offer the proper subject of study—the classical past—but in a most accessible form with tantalizing touches of detail, just a hint of historical context, and the sensation of human nature observed, condensed, and communicated, all in an elevated if at times abstract Latin prose style.

Valerius' mercurial literary fortune has confounded the appreciation of his contemporary purposes, sources, and audience. He is nearly unread today, every now and again appearing in a learned footnote to tell a story or detail unknown from Livy or Cassius Dio, Suetonius or Plutarch. Although he would never have boasted of being a historian, the Middle Ages and the Renaissance prized him as such. He has for many generations been Rome's most popular historian. His popularity is unmistakable: more manuscripts of the *Memorable Deeds and Sayings* survive than of any other Latin prose text, save the Bible.[3] The subsequent loss of readers should elicit no lament; it is rather testimony to a change in taste and to developments in the modern practice of reading, scholarship, and printing. Valerius has lost readers to Livy, whose lengthy narrative the former's discrete anecdotes had once eclipsed. Livy came to be deemed the model for style as well as the source for history, and so the traditional classicists' uncomplimentary stylistic comparison of the handbook maker with the golden Augustan historian joined the historians' charges of error, distortion, and fabrication.[4] This was in-

---

ment in the musical world. The declaimer could aim at a career in the courts or in the emperor's service. The political dimension of declamation is for the most part unparalleled.

3. Carter 1975, 39. For the most recent list of manuscripts, see Schullian 1981, 695–728.

4. See the harsh judgment of Norden 1973, 303. Historians had taken as springboard for criticism the list of historical "errors" compiled by Kempf in the introduction to his first edition. For Valerius as a source for contemporary historians, see Maslakov's appendix, 1984, 484–96.

direct acknowledgment that Valerius' stylistic aims, like his audience, were far different from the preceding generation's, the late republican and Augustan writers enshrined by scholars as the single model for prose and poetry.

The irony here lies not with the change in estimation of different eras but with the charge against Valerius, irrefutable and inconsequential, that he was not doing what Cicero and Livy had done. For the literary and cultural historian, Valerius Maximus remains of great interest as a figure and document of Tiberian Rome, of a city and culture faced not so much with the transition from republic to dictatorship as with the first peaceful succession of an autocrat. This new imperial reality has fascinated historians from Tacitus on. The coupling of political change with a "decline" in literature has an obvious ideological appeal for the enthusiasts of the old political, social, and literary order. Yet the writing of this period has drawn little attention. Even those intent on the anatomy of intellectual and cultural decline pass it by, as if a dormant art, in their haste to prove decline. Thus the Augustan and Neronian periods and literatures often figure as apogee and attempted revival whereas the intervening Julio-Claudians must stand as barren backdrop.

Valerius, however, provides an insight into the manner and the material of the final stage of Roman education in the early first century A.D. His work also illuminates a culture that presented itself as derivative, in part by taking the Augustans as models and reflecting self-consciously on their own distance from those models. At the same time this imperial literature, in seeking and reflecting the emperor's patronage, strove to maintain an allegiance and continuity with the republican past. Like his contemporary, the historian Velleius Paterculus, Valerius presents his peers' culture as one with the past; the emperors' supporters did not present autocracy as an ideological alternative. The Republic and its culture continue but with the Caesars as leading and saving family.

Finally, Valerius represents a particular step in the cultural phenomenon of declamation. He has not offered a history of it, as Seneca would, or a critique of its vices as so many have. His is a document from and for declamation, and specifically for those who wished to learn the proper illustration for public speech. This last consideration suggests two possibilities: Valerius' work codifies material that had grown too large for memory, and—or—codifies material for those not familiar either with the works of Roman history and oratory or with their traditional content. As his work supplants familiarity with these texts, it attests the success of declamation and declamatory training. These, and not careful study of the literary classics, have become the vehicle of instruction, of acculturation into the elite of Tiberian Rome.

The antecedents for the technique of rhetorical illustration are quite clear in the ancient world. In all types of speeches, Greek and Roman orators had long used historical anecdotes as an aid to argument. The historical example, for Aristotle (*Rhet.* A 2 1356 a35–b6), is peculiar to rhetorical prose, which unlike philosophical writing has as its means of persuasion not syllogism and induction but enthymeme and example. In truth, Aristotle here excludes Plato's closer parallel to the historical example, philosophic myth. Later rhetorical theorists refined analysis of the exemplum's proper role in oratory.[5] In particular they were concerned with what constituted, and where to employ, a historical allusion. The injunctions of the second-century A.D. Greek grammarian Aspines are typical: "Examples must be familiar, clear, not too old nor mythic but in accord with the audience" and "every example takes its subject from actual occurrences and is drawn either from native or foreign events. Domestic examples are more striking and appropriate."[6] Rome's debt to and continuation of Hellenistic rhetorical theory need not be restated here. Discussion of the exemplum is found both in Cicero's *De inventione* (1.49) and the contemporary *Rhetorica ad Herennium* (4.62). Rome's (and Cicero's) special contribution was the extended use of the historical example. In Aristotle enthymeme might rank with paradeigma as a means of proof, but in Roman practice national *exempla virtutis* overwhelmed any abstract argument.[7] No theorist

5. The best description of ancient theory of the rhetorical example remains Alewell 1913.

6. Aspines 1.2, 281.1 (Spengel), χρὴ δὲ τὰ παραδείγματα γνώριμα εἶναι καὶ σαφῆ καὶ μη πάνυ ἀρχαῖα μηδὲ μυθώδη, συνάδοντα δὲ τοῖς ὑποκειμένοις, and 280.6, πᾶν παράδειγμα ἔχει μὲν τὴν ὕλην ἐκ τῶν γεγονότων, λαμβάνεται δὲ ἢ ἐξ οἰκείων ἢ ἐξ ἀλλοτρίων. τὰ μὲν ἐξ οἰκείων ἀγωνιστικώτερα καὶ προσεχέστερα, cited in Alewell 1913, 32–33.

7. Roman practice is described in Haight 1940.

is as important for Roman prose as Cicero, and no theoretical statement is as important as his practice. He laid down as theoretical prescription his own practice at *Orator* 132 where he jokes with his interlocuter Brutus that to prove his present point, "I would use examples from my own speeches if you had not read them; I would use foreign examples— Latin if I could find any, Greek if it were appropriate."[8] The hierarchy is most important. Suitability (τὸ πρέπον) is the constant guide and criterion for the Hellenistic literary scholar; for the practical Cicero the theorists' criteria, suitability and domesticity, coalesce: a subject appropriate for his listeners is a Roman subject. Only a lack of *inventio* could drive him to a Greek example.

Cicero, not Livy, is Valerius' methodological predecessor; Valerius' practice, like Cicero's, follows this statement from the *Orator*. More accurately, this ethnic preference describes the practice of Cicero in his speeches. Cicero's fondness for Greek culture is not in question; he does cite Greek anecdotes, but these are found in the theoretical works, especially the philosophical dialogues, and in his correspondence.[9] That the Greek Stoic Panaetius is not mentioned in the speeches tells nothing of Cicero's philosophical expertise but reflects only Cicero's differing audiences.

The subordination of Greek to Roman examples is not the only important influence of Cicero's practice. His speeches and theoretical works provided a wealth of information for a host of historical figures, and his name and classical style ensured that these were the descriptions read and remembered. The eventual standardness of Cicero's passages should not obscure their innovation at the time.[10] For Cicero changed the schools' scheme of personages and thereby canonized a new and fuller list of heroes and villains, whose treatment Valerius among others would follow. In the course of the speeches, Cicero came to cite the older generals (such as the Decii) less and less and instead used names from more recent Roman history. Generally, the historical

---

8. *uterer exemplis domesticis, nisi ea legisses, uterer alienis, vel Latinis, si ulla reperirem, vel Graecis, si deceret.*

9. Schoenberger 1910, 33–41; Schoenberger 1914, 33.

10. For an account of Cicero's preferred subjects and groupings and his evolving practice, see Schoenberger 1910.

examples in Cicero's speeches cluster around the time and circle of the two Scipios. An index to his swift influence on the new gallery of heroes is *Aeneid* 6. 818–46 where Virgil has almost the same names as in Cicero's speeches. (Marius makes no epic appearance and is thus the exception; Cicero, though, had restricted his praise to celebration of his fellow townsman's military prowess.)

The most striking feature of Cicero's use of historical exempla is that the names are always the same. Again and again the Gracchi and the Scipios are invoked, albeit for shifting reasons and in different lights. The Gracchi, for instance, are positively portrayed in speeches to the people (*De leg. agr.* 2.10 and *Pro Rabir. perd.* 12–15). Their commemoration is altogether negative when Cicero speaks to the senate or writes for the aristocrats. The use and reuse of the same historical figures for a variety of purposes also characterize Valerius' work.

In a number of cases Cicero had used the same exempla or even series of exempla in different works but with close verbal similarity. This affords a clue to the role of memory (hardly intertextuality) for the practicing orator and prolific writer. This practice reveals the genesis of some of Valerius' series; it also prefigures the basic structural unit of his work: the chapter as an individual series of exempla. Cicero's technique of connecting exempla also provides an important precedent for Valerius' practice. In lists of exempla Cicero often follows chronological order and puts the domestic examples first, the Greek second—as do Valerius' chapters. Thus the subjects of Valerius' exempla and the structures of their presentation owe a major debt to Cicero. Cicero's technique had been calculated and controlled, as the far different practice of his letters reveals. The exempla of his correspondence exhibit a philhellenism banished from the speeches.[11] Atticus no doubt appreciated the allusions, but this more familiar style would not influence Valerius Maximus or subsequent speakers. And once Cicero's speeches—and not Livy or any rhetorical theorist—are seen as the background for Valerius' practice, both the charges of historical inaccuracy and some of the peculiarities of employment recede.

Even here Cicero offers some clue to Valerius' practice. In retailing incidents from early history Cicero displays what at first seems mod-

---

11. Schoenberger 1914, 33.

esty: rather than asserting his own learned authority, he downplays his knowledge with "we are told" or "tradition has it."[12] The story is meant to be understood as having its own authority; traditional history is not an area for speculation, certainly not in a public speech. This context explains both his diffidence toward foreign examples and his uncritical reception of the native. Valerius does not repeat Cicero's formulas of introduction, but this stylistic habit (which distances the author from the material) partially explains Valerius' disinterest in authenticating the stories. The Tiberian author is operating in a sphere now doubly traditional: the material after all had been deemed venerable more than a generation ago and now the medium for that traditional fare was a canonical authority. If Cicero approved, Valerius would not dissent.

The untechnical, practical nature of Valerius' collection has put it on the margin of studies of ancient rhetoric. Neither "real" political prose nor academic theorizing, *Memorable Deeds and Sayings* has been, like declamation itself, judged a peculiarity of what was at best a narrow educational curriculum. The alleged narrowness itself should fascinate us: how and why does a culture restrict its studies and its common symbols of persuasion and dissuasion? The unease that scholars feel with a work that falls into neither of their categories, literature or theory, is evident also in treatments of Valerius' contemporary, Seneca the Elder. In the absence of any clear-cut affiliation of his vocabulary with Hellenistic or Roman theorists, his interpreters have labeled him a descriptive, not a theoretical critic.[13] His use of critical terms is said to be indiscriminate, the happenstance learning of a fan of the recital halls. Valerius and Seneca can be better understood by shifting the focus and categories of investigation. These two contemporary sources for Roman declamation were not engaged in producing theoretical works. A critical vocabulary for such works was current: Cicero's dialogues attest to it, Quintilian's great work would soon organize it, and Valerius' and Seneca's contemporary, Rutilius Lupus, provided a most technical trea-

---

12. Schoenberger 1910, Panaetius: 26–27; older generals and Cicero's practice: 17; Virgil and Marius: 18; recurrent names: 18; the Gracchi: 19–20; role of memory: 29–31; series of exempla: 31–32; *accepimus and scimus*: 57.

13. Fairweather 1981, 59.

tise by translating into Latin a list of Greek rhetorical figures complete with definitions. Like Seneca, however, Valerius offers not theory but a piece of declamation itself. Seneca has distorted the picture of declamation by his collection of *sententiae* and *colores*—declamation at its most epigrammatic and most fabricated—but Valerius' work also gives a skewed picture, for it preserves only the historical anecdotes, bound together on a scale no speaker or listener could have endured.

Despite this distortion, *Memorable Deeds and Sayings* offers a glimpse into what was actually said about, and thought of, the republican past in a particular social and cultural milieu in Rome in the 20s and 30s A.D.; it is also the product of that most occasional oral genre, declamation, worked out on a grand, written scale. Declamation is, then, product and source for Valerius. Like Seneca the Elder he had no doubt heard countless speakers give their versions of Cicero's last words, their advice to Hannibal or Alexander, or their solution to the quasi-legal dilemmas presented by the *controversiae*. Yet if he reflects a culture of speakers, he also represents a crucial moment in that culture, the moment of recording what had been oral. Tiberian Rome is not a likely candidate for discussions of orality, as those are mainly concerned with the evolution and consequences of writing and literacy. The situation at Rome does not mirror archaic Greece: Seneca and Valerius do not simply represent a shift to writing down what had been oral, nor had a cultural phenomenon somehow become "too oral" in a tradition-bound society. Rather, the recent vintage had grown too large to consume, or its consumers had grown too many. At this moment in Rome, declamation offered too much to remember, while the audience had outgrown the recital hall. Seneca had been moved to write, he maintains (*Contr.* 1.pr.10–11), because declamation was becoming too oral. Its antecedents were being forgotten as plagiarism went undetected. This authorial statement implies a change in audience, perhaps of size and origin as well as generation. Men of Seneca's day would have remembered the great declaimers; he seeks to preserve the past and its great speakers, to extend declamation to school fare, school reading. Valerius moves to take advantage of a still fluid declamation to establish himself and also to give enduring form to what had been an oral genre, to make declamation into reading. He thus testifies to the scale and orality of declamation. Like the declaimers Seneca criticized, he hoped his reworkings of classical *loci* would displace the originals in his audience's memory and become paradigms themselves.

Both Valerius and Seneca had a pedagogic purpose: to provide models of proper declamation. But both were concerned with a set of stylistic and substantial paradigms. This book centers around the qualities and implications of those paradigms. To collect exempla is necessarily to canonize and to exclude. To organize and reshape exempla goes far beyond reporting what one has heard or read. Valerius' collection does not simply offer what a first-century declaimer thought memorable, effective, or merely possible rhetorical illustration. The means of persuasion constitute a common language, a language of resonant emblems, a hierarchy not just of villains and heroes but of values, behavior, and ethics.

But first the principles of Valerius' composition must be plumbed. Chapter 2 of this book treats the structure and design of Valerius' long work and the implications these have for his audience. Chapter 3 surveys his methods of research and composition (in particular the pattern and scope of his reading). Then we may approach his particular vision of the past (chapter 4) and, in that light, the influence of recent and contemporary history as revealed through the family of the Caesars (chapter 5): here Valerius faces his greatest challenge, his most resistant material, and he attempts a political fusion of the republican traditions to the new imperial reality. The final chapter draws together Valerius' various ideologies, his entwined political, historical, and stylistic programs, to suggest how and why he memorialized the past in a fashion that would prove so popular to some readers and be so castigated by more recent scholars.

The peculiar and unseasonable charm of Valerius Maximus should be apparent throughout, for anecdote has an unmistakable, universal fascination. In Valerius' cases the reader does not find simple anecdotes but paradoxical and even bizarre stories communicated in a compressed and overwrought form. The historian will always bridle at anecdotal and traditional history, at the Greek world reduced to stories of Marathon, Thermopylae, and Alexander's near execution of an ass driver; but readers have not. The appeal of Valerius, though not quite of a storyteller, is that of a story binder. He rambles on like a sententious conversationalist who cannot stop stringing anecdotes together and yet never tells all the details, or never builds his stories to full yarns, but darts along to another instance while the listener entertained, if a little put upon, tries to catch the thread.

2 Audience and Design

From what Valerius tells his reader *Memorable Deeds and Sayings* is a time-saving, smooth, and seamless collection. In his proem and the prooemia to the various chapters Valerius is concerned to ease transition so as to maintain his reader's interest, to ensure that the reader keeps reading. Assiduous and self-conscious transitions mark, of course, the difficulty of joining two sections and, at the same time, draw attention to the person and skill of the joiner. Valerius' notices of his work's organization attempt to make whole and connected what is disparate. In part this is inevitable for one whose program is to assert the connection of the present with the past. The difference of the past must be downplayed for a number of reasons: to have events in the past serve as models of conduct; to have the emperors as supporters and continuators of the Republic. The design of this presentation of the past is important, for it reveals the structural and thematic connections Valerius found and imposed on the past.

The organization of the book explains in large part Valerius' later popularity. For those who would compose, *Memorable Deeds and Sayings* is easier of access than any historical narrative. The structures of Valerius' book also reveal contemporary concerns; these divisions of subjects and signals of structure indicate what Valerius deemed worthy of record, and why. The latter is particularly interesting: Valerius was not content to retail stories, but provides his reader with proper interpretation. The categories by which we are to understand the past and judge its actions and values are laid down in the chapter headings and chapter introductions. Valerius has written a book of aristocratic culture: he gives most space and prominence to the institutions and code of conduct of the Roman noble families. So too, it is easily argued, does Cicero, but in retelling and reshaping stories from Cicero and Livy, Valerius has lost the optimate and republican program. Factionalism and indeed nearly all political motivation recede under the pressure of

an understanding insistently moral and abstract. Valerius is not simply
"rhetoricizing" what were originally political and historical texts. He is,
rather, engaged in communicating these texts and especially their leading actors as the culture for a new age. Part of that new culture is to
deny the break from the past, the innovations of the present.

Literature of the Julio-Claudian period is often examined as a response to the social and political innovations of the Principate—as critical dissent or sycophantic accommodation, both of which positions
presuppose the recognition in the writer of a distance from the past
and seem to insist that literature is a direct response to politics. Valerius' work will not be examined in this book in this way but instead
as a creation and communicator of the new culture of the Principate.
Valerius' work displays a new generation's appropriation of Roman noble culture.

The categories, difficulties, and failures of that comprehension are
first and best examined in Valerius' structures, themes, and their connections. These in turn have significant indications of Valerius' contemporary audience. Clearly, declaimers and schoolboys—apprentice
declaimers—found this book useful and in all likelihood contributed
to its form and contents, but we can be more exact in defining who was
learning of Roman culture through Valerius' work and through declamation in general.[1] This is not a work for Roman nobles; it may not
have been a work primarily for the traditionally literate classes of the
city of Rome. Provincials and Italians were coming to Rome; and
though there is nothing novel in the city's pull, the immigrants' ambitions were novel. The Roman senators certainly resented the emperors' new favorites. Sejanus' humble origin (though exaggerated by his
critics) was a topic of abuse in Valerius' day just as Claudius' employ of
freedmen in governmental positions would anger those whose families

1. Like the public performances of the declaimers, the cases of the lawyers
have not been preserved. Still the model school exercises of Pseudo-Quintilian
(the *Minor Declamations*) attest at the least to the use of historical exempla in
practice declamations. Caesar, the Catos, Scipios, and Gracchi appear with
some frequency (e.g., 268.19–20, 338.21, 377.9, 379.3). Certain historical figures provide the theme for declamation: Alexander is afflicted with an illness
after burning an Athenian temple (323).

had traditionally conducted Roman public affairs.[2] Ever since Julius Caesar had packed the senate house with provincials loyal to him, the Romanness of the senate was felt to be in decline.[3] Most the provincials who came to Rome did not of course reach the senate, but such access now had precedent.

The Empire did have great need of bureaucrats, soldiers, and men of letters. The allegiance of these men would be uncomplicated by traditional family and factional ties if this staff were drawn from men outside the traditional ruling classes, outside the capital. Success depended first on recognition from above, and letters if not literature was a tried and safe field of contest and distinction. The bureaucracy, the army, and the courts were the great opportunities for those without noble birth. Even the soldier at Rome could profit from literary ability; for the line between soldier and administrator was never distinct, and the Roman patron, high-ranking officer, magistrate, or administrator, always had need of competent men of letters. Velleius Paterculus, Valerius' contemporary, is remembered as the author of a breviary history that he dedicated to his old commanding officer. His success in gaining patronage, of course, came before he wrote the history, which has survived, and his literary competence—we can scarcely call his ability anything more—may well have helped this Italian in his ambitious rise. For those who would be lawyer, administrator, and even soldier, a classical education was the first step. Such an education was different in kind and purposes from the same first step for the careerist in the British Empire. The Roman was not simply competing with his peers for the grade that qualified entrance to civil service. The product of the ancient education was not training in the mechanics of imperial government or in the fundamentals of law but a "Romanness" of speech (including, no doubt for some, morphology and pronunciation) and of the subjects of speech. Valerius' work appealed to such an audience of imperial supporters and beneficiaries. His serviceable design provided the topics of speech and sample demonstrations.

The present chapter begins and ends with consideration of Valerius'

2. For the restoration and reconstruction of Sejanus' family connections, see Adams 1955, Sealey 1961, Stewart 1953, and Sumner 1965.

3. Syme 1939, 78–96.

definition and intimation of his audience. The interconnections of this audience with Valerius' methodology and purposes are of paramount importance if we are to advance beyond dismissal of the literature of Valerius and his generation as "rhetorical." The chapter proceeds by examination of Valerius' divisions and order of his material. The general sequence of Valerius' subjects leads to some conclusions about the history of the text's composition and more importantly elucidates the nature of his interests. Examination of the chapter as unit of structure and composition offers the most concrete insight into what Valerius found memorable and how he presented this. An extreme of his presentation then concerns us. Valerius' inclusion of recalcitrant material—subjects and figures of noble culture enshrined by canonical prose masters—exhibits the most distorting qualities of his composition and also his and his generation's particular anxieties. These anxieties, the difficulties that the canonical, republican stories offered, betray themselves again in Valerius' prefaces to certain chapters where he imports the conditions and status of his audience.

The Proem and Valerius' Audience

Valerius declares his purpose, methods, and audience from the very start.

> The memorable deeds and sayings of the city of Rome and of foreign nations, which have been so scattered in the works of authors that they cannot conveniently be learned, I have resolved to select from outstanding authors so as to spare those who want concrete evidence the tedious task of research. I have not succumbed to the desire to treat all things. For who can consider the history of the world in a few volumes? Or who in his right mind would hope that he could write Roman and foreign history with greater accuracy or eloquence, so polished as it has been by our elders?[4]

4. *Urbis Romae exterarumque gentium facta simul ac dicta memoratu digna, quae apud alios latius diffusa sunt quam ut breviter cognosci possint, ab inlustribus electa auctoribus digerere constitui, ut documenta sumere volentibus longae inquisitionis labor*

The proem promises that he has selected exempla from illustrious authors as a shortcut for his readers. Valerius' words have not, however, found many believers. Indeed, the proem is most often cited so as to be dismissed, for Valerius' whole enterprise has been judged plagiarism of another collector.[5] Valerius' statement of method is thus said to be the author's pretense of scholarship. In fact, the proem is more interesting and complex than such skepticism implies. Further, this extreme skepticism is unwarranted. Valerius has done just what he says; in particular he has read the works of Cicero and Livy and drawn from this reading historical anecdotes that illustrate some abstract category such as "Friendship" or "Luxury and Lust" or "Cruelty" or "Illustrious Men Who Dressed Somewhat Outlandishly." Once Valerius' statement of method is credited, the remainder of the proem may be reconsidered.

In particular, Valerius' definition of his subject and intimation of his audience demand attention. Nowhere in this proem does he mention the term exempla, although this is clearly his subject. Valerius is being quite careful to elevate and delineate his subject. At the same time he offers a sort of *recusatio* for not writing history. What then is he doing? The proem begins grandly: any remotely historical work that begins *Urbis Romae* cannot fail to echo Livy's massive *Ab urbe condita*. The diction of this first sentence has led to speculation that Sallust is being recalled here.[6] The historian at Rome is always engaged in *memoria rerum,* in the commemoration of the worthy. Valerius' subject at first seems lofty; he proposes treatment of all the world and not simply Rome. Valerius draws his project up short with a brief and Sallustian

---

absit. Nec mihi cuncta conplectendi cupido incessit: quis enim omnis aevi gesta modico voluminum numero conprehenderit, aut quis compos mentis domesticae peregrinaeque historiae seriem felici superiorum stilo conditam vel adtentiore cura vel praestantiore facundia traditurum se speraverit?

5. Alfred Klotz first advanced this thesis in 1909; Clemens Bosch 1929 was its next champion. For analysis of these and other source critics and demonstration that Valerius was reading and excerpting directly, see my discussion in chapter 3.

6. Guerrini (1979, 154) maintains that Valerius' wording (*facta simul ac dicta memoratu digna . . . digerere constitui*) echoes Sallust's *Catiline* 4 (*statui . . . memoria digna . . . perscribere*). See my discussion, in chapter 3, of Valerius' alleged borrowings from Sallust.

second sentence (*nec mihi cuncta complectendi cupido incessit*)—though Sallust would not have been as fond of alliteration. Two rhetorical questions follow, each with a specific contemporary or near contemporary target. The first asks who would write the history of the world in a few volumes. The reader need not turn to the slim volumes of Nepos lost to us but praised by Catullus. Valerius' contemporary Velleius Paterculus was writing a universal history in two books. The second possibility for historical writing seems even remoter to Valerius. He asks, "Or who in his right mind would hope that he could write Roman and foreign history with greater accuracy or eloquence, so polished as it has been by our elders?" That is, who can compete with Livy or with the Augustan encyclopedic historians Dionysius of Halicarnassus or Diodorus of Sicily? This two-sentence negative definition of the book's program is strongly colored by a sense of the inferiority of the present. Perhaps Valerius means to reprove his contemporary Velleius Paterculus for his very slim two books on all the world's history.

But what justifies or distinguishes Valerius' project? The author advances no claim to originality: originality in style or substance or even in historical genre has been denied with these rhetorical questions, which suggest not so much *dubitatio* as *aporia,* not the author's hesitation over alternatives but a complete writing block. The narrator does not hesitate on which authorial road to follow but whether to write at all. This is a peculiar *recusatio,* which implies not the author's unwillingness to write history but the impossibility of other historical writing. Valerius can engage in such an exclusive and polemical rhetoric because he has already made his positive case in his first sentence, and here the audience and not genre, subject, or treatment constitutes originality. The needs of his readers, he maintains, have motivated the personal act of composition. Valerius describes his audience, literally, as those who want to take proofs—that is, those who would read so as to cull instances of memorable deeds and sayings, Roman and foreign. While this may seem a most expansive category, among his contemporaries those who used and wanted historical anecdotes with an authoritative literary pedigree were public speakers, lawyers, and declaimers.

This is clearly Valerius' audience, and their needs justify Valerius' writing. The declaimers' *controversiae* and *suasoriae* had Greek and Roman contexts ripe for rhetorical exemplification, and their categories have clearly influenced Valerius' chapter headings. The interaction of the declaimers' contests and Valerius' work involves far more than coincidence of individual anecdote or the correspondence of some of the headings for those examples. The structure and organization of Valerius' book arise from and seek to direct declamatory composition.

The Organization of the Collection

Book Divisions and Subjects

Valerius' collection of rhetorical exempla is divided into nine books of, on the average, nine chapters, each with some categorical heading and a number of rhetorical examples. These examples are divided into two categories: the Roman and the foreign. Most often these headings are abstract categories—types of morality or immorality—for example, "Religion," "Pretended Religion," "Parental Love," "Constancy," "Luxury and Lust." Frequently, the incongruous or paradoxical interests Valerius—stories that involve a reversal of fortune such as his very last chapter: "The Lowborn Who Tried through Deceit to Enter Others' Families."

The individual story has most often been taken from a classical Latin author, placed under a heading, and stylistically reworked so as to be suitable for insertion into a declamation. A system of verbal classification forms the heart of Valerius' scheme of organization. First, anecdotes are subsumed in a broad category. Within this generalizing category individual events are listed without narrative expansion or indeed often without narrative explanation. The date is summarily indicated—we are told that the particular person under consideration was consul or, as in 1.6.5, that a cow spoke "in the Second Punic War." Figures are sometimes given (e.g., troop numbers derived from Livy), but without a systematic attempt to date the years, either by giving an absolute year-number from Rome's foundation or by reference to the consuls. The transitions, the short introductions to each exemplum, are the key to the groupings within the chapters. Without an index, table of contents, or footnotes, the reader needs some guide to this mass of heterogeneous material, and the rubrics, these chapter headings, provide the needed direction. Then, Valerius gives his reader brief introductions and transitions, which often contain the key words of the chapter titles.[7] For instance, Valerius begins the chapter 4.7, entitled "Friendship," "Let us now consider the bond of friendship," and as transition from "Ingrates" to a string of chapters on piety Valerius' proem is "But let us leave off ingrates and speak rather of the pious."[8]

The various prose genres of Latin literature, especially the works of Cicero and Livy, were mined for rhetorical illustrations. Valerius was not the first to gather rhetorical exempla; any speaker would accumulate exempla, although theoretical treatises on rhetoric did not. Written collections of exempla arose late in the history of rhetoric, and like biography itself (to which they are clearly related) they first appeared in late republican and Augustan Rome. The biographer and historian Cornelius Nepos wrote a work entitled *Exempla,* as did the prolific Greek freedman of Augustus, Hyginus. The *Hebdomades* of Varro was an illustrated account of famous men. Valerius himself made use of a prior collection at least once, for he refers to the otherwise unknown "Collecta" of Pomponius Rufus (4.4.pr.). Unquestionably, his work does profit from the antiquarian investigations of scholars of the late Republic. His book, however, has more in common with the functional world chronology of Atticus and the universal history of his contemporary Velleius Paterculus than the scholarly productions of Varro. For declaimers did not retail the recondite; in order to be hortatory, in order to be paradigmatic, examples had to be readily comprehensible and familiar. And the familiar was to a great extent that narrated or immortalized by Cicero and Livy, both of whom are responsible for the commemoration and canonization of the protagonists of the Roman Republic and of foreign history. Valerius most often took as his sources the explicit exempla he found in Cicero's works and those he could glean from Livy's and Pompeius Trogus' narratives. He was not a scrupulous scholar; he did not use a fraction of the sources available to him,

7. The authenticity of the chapter headings has been disputed. See Helm 1955, 97–98. It is hard to imagine an author not including such rubrics. Certainly any reader would, especially if he wished to read the text again.

8. Valerius 4.7, *De amicitia: Contemplemur nunc amicitiae vinculum.* Valerius 5.4, *De pietate in parentes* follows *De ingratis* and begins, *Sed omittamus ingratos, et potius de piis loquamur.*

which to the historians' regret have perished. And as he worked, he excised anecdotes from their historical surroundings, from the patterns and details that give a particular event its individuality. Great men doing great things and the despicable doing the reverse swiftly become moral categories, not historical events. Analogy and even invention do not lag far behind when historical figures are served up to the declaimers. One Scipio can easily be granted the feats of another (7.5.2), just as a Roman replacement must be found for a Marathonian hero (3.2.22). These practices are the occasion for the charges of historical inaccuracy leveled against the handbook maker by those who wanted a historian.

These compositional practices explain, therefore, the unhistorical quality of certain exempla—to work as exempla events had to be to a certain extent "dehistoricized." Up to now a preoccupation with Valerius' shortcomings as historical source has narrowed scholarly attention to the individual exemplum, its relation to a single source, and its historical reality. This has obscured the nature of Valerius' composition. Valerius' choice of themes and his connections of these themes reveal his methods, interests, indeed his preoccupations. The choice of material and statements of the relations of those materials divulge the principles of exclusion and inclusion, what to Valerius' mind made a person or action worthy of memory. Further, his organization, including the juxtaposition of certain stories, provides insight into the terms in which he understood the past and into the connections he saw in the most disparate material. Valerius' indications of his organization, the chapter headings and prefaces, provide insights into how and why he juxtaposed certain stories, under what terms he understood the past, and what connections he saw in the most disparate material. Not only should the general subjects themselves be examined, but Valerius' composition should be scrutinized at a level intermediate between the general consideration of subjects and their divisions, on the one hand, and a minute consideration of a particular exemplum and its literary antecedents, on the other. Individual sources, the study of which has so preoccupied Valerian scholars, will not explain his choice and arrangement of material. Valerius did create a certain structure for his work; he chose to communicate a connected structure with his references (often in the first person and in the prefaces to individual chapters) to the *propositum* that guides him, and to his deviations from and recall to this program.

At the outset the *propositum* is quite clear. The thematic development and cohesion of the first three books are obvious: their subject—religion most broadly conceived—moves from formal state ceremonies at the beginning of book 1 to, in book 3, those personal moral qualities that rendered the Roman noble "religious," pious and estimable in the eyes of his peers and clients. Valerius offers no systematic account of Roman or foreign religion but instead a list of precedents, what the Romans would have called *exempla* or *documenta* of the *mos maiorum*. The first book, for example, presents famous Romans and some Greeks who are exemplars of religion, specifically types and antitypes of performers of public religious ritual and of religious revelation. A snake appears at the altar while Sulla is sacrificing, who then, on the haruspex's urging, immediately leads out his army to conquer the Samnites (1.6.4). The ghost of Tiberius Gracchus appears in a dream to his brother to warn him of the coming catastrophe (1.7.6). These examples belong to the public sphere; they depict the observance, flaunting, and revelation of the divine will by the leading men of the Roman Republic. No story of the individual devotion of an otherwise unknown Roman is told. Piety alone does not ensure commemoration, as Valerius' subject is not private *pietas* but the instances of the *pietas* offered the state by the *mos maiorum*, literally the custom of the ancestors.

Book 1 begins with religion observed, neglected, pretended, and rejected and then moves to auspices, omens, prodigies, dreams, and miracles. These latter categories again relate events of public importance. Indeed, this is the sort of fantastic material that the priests had recorded in their annals, the predecessor to Roman historical writing. Even the chapter on dreams, a favorite figure for the declaimers, relates only those whose contents were of public importance. The chapter begins with the dream of Augustus' physician before the Battle of Philippi (Athena advised that the ailing Octavian be on hand) and proceeds to the admonitory dream of Calpurnia, Caesar's wife, on the eve of the Ides of March (1.7.1 and 2). The transition to the fourth example openly declares this criterion for inclusion: "The following dream is equally relevant to public religion."[9] Valerius seems to have found this

9. Valerius 1.7.4: *Sequitur aeque ad publicam religionem pertinens somnium.*

assertion necessary because the historical figure, the dreamer, was a plebeian. The man's rank is excused since his dream averted disaster from the Republic.

In these final two chapters of book 1, on dreams and miracles, the foreign examples do outnumber the Roman. The Roman continue to be oriented toward civic matters, whereas the foreign examples attest heaven's favor or warning to famous individuals (Hannibal, Croesus, Cyrus, Alexander the Great, Alcibiades, the poet Simonides). The contrast of national and individual greatness and divine favor is inescapable as the memorial of foreign men moves from individual to individual without regard for chronology or national origin. The effect of these foreign examples is not, like the Roman, a careful marshaling of praise but a disconnected series of unusual events.

Book 2 constitutes the juncture between the public and the individual. The first five chapters narrate the offices and practices of the Roman magistracies with foreign examples reserved for the sixth chapter. This division reflects the preponderance of Roman material characteristic of the first three books. A patriotic bias runs throughout Valerius' work, but the first part of *Memorable Deeds and Sayings* particularly celebrates Rome's ancestral religious institutions. The course of Valerius' program remains clear throughout the second book: following the foreign institutions comes a treatment of military practices (2.7 and 2.8). Valerius has moved from the civic to the military side of the magistracies. But chapters 1–5, 7, and 8 do not treat Roman political institutions systematically. Only the first five chapters were a unity. The remaining seem to fill in some of the gaps—the foreign, the military, and the extraordinary. For at 2.8 and 2.9 he treats two extraordinary Roman magistracies, the triumphator and the censor. He is once again not interested in the office itself, or even in those who triumphed, for this chapter considers the cases of those who do not triumph—either because the senate or the courts denied them the honor or, in the singular case of Cn. Fulvius Flaccus (2.8.3), because he refused it. The only details we learn of the office is the number of slain needed to earn a triumph (2.8.1) and the triumphator's practice of inviting and then disinviting the consuls to dinner on the eve of the triumph (2.8.6). Valerius is characteristically interested in the exceptional and the paradoxical, those whose exclusion defines the office and the chapter title.

Similarly, the final instance of the next chapter, "Censorial Severity," lists those who gained the censorship after having been expelled from the senate by the censors (2.9.9).

The final chapter of the book makes the juncture to a new type of religious theme; here again Valerius reveals his guiding principle. The topic of 2.10 is *maiestas,* a word hard to translate: the English majesty has too much of the later Latin imperial, royal ring to it. In Valerius' exempla it necessarily involves an audience (a jury, the senate, the Roman people, a king) and is that audience's publicly manifested respect for a man of the highest station. No king has *maiestas* in Valerius, although Xerxes does show it to the Athenian tyrannicides, Harmodius and Aristogeiton. In the preface to this chapter Valerius justifies his inclusion of the topic by likening majesty to a private censorship (*quasi privata censura*—an oxymoron: "as if a private individual held the censorship"). Valerius imagines the show of respect to a private man the equivalent of election to the Roman office charged with maintaining morals. His concern is both to find the proper praise and to rank the praiseworthy.[10] His task is not simply one of invention, to find instances of a category, but of hierarchy and equivalency. Valerius' work presents the process and the product of that ordering.

The third book moves to abstract personal moral qualities: "Bravery" (3.2), "Patience" (3.3), "Constancy" (3.8). The transition to the private or personal realm has been made with *maiestas* at 2.10, where the private qualities of the men make the office and not the other way around. The formally religious has receded as his subject. A movement from divine to human institutions recalls Varro's works of those titles, but Valerius has not been treating these spheres as separate subjects nor

10. On this theme in particular Valerius had a distinguished predecessor. Cicero sought to equate private status with public office in the case of the murder of Tiberius Gracchus by Scipio Nasica, who in so doing defied the consul or, as Cicero would have it, acted the proper part of consul (*Tusc.* 4.51). This highly charged optimate point of view has lost its factional volatility for Valerius (1.7.6) who does not justify the action by reference to the good of the Republic; he is concerned with respect and status. Indeed, for Valerius the office is of less importance than the public deference granted it.

does his work reflect antiquarian concerns or the antiquarian's precision. Book 2 had not been without categories of personal qualities; the two chapters that have as titles abstract nouns denoting personal virtues—"Frugality and Innocence" (2.5—this is clearly the theme for this chapter although the title is one supplied by later manuscripts), "Majesty" (2.10)—seem the spillover of the prior chapters, as if Valerius had had more material than the original category could embrace. Thus in 2.10 men of majesty as private censors follow the chapter devoted to "Censorial Severity," and similarly at 2.5.1 the first golden statue of the city is a natural successor to the final example of the preceding chapter, at 2.4.7, the first gladiatorial contest at Rome; and so 2.4, "Spectacles" (public games), gives way to 2.5, "Frugality and Innocence." Both preceding chapters in these pairs involved a Roman magistracy; the foils that follow in the second chapters underscore the quality of Valerius' interest in these subjects. The offices do not hold him in themselves; rather the men do. He chooses to commemorate the qualities of these men that define them and their category, especially in some paradoxical fashion like those denied a triumph or those who had the honor of the censorship without the office. Valerius is celebrating the character and achievements exhibited by magistrates and those worthy of magistracies.

The shift from the public to the individual has been made by the beginning of the third book, although the move is not absolute. He has exhausted the subject of Roman state traditions as exemplified in Roman nobles. From book 2 through book 6 Valerius presents individual moral exemplars; that is, his chapter headings are predominantly the names of virtues: "Moderation" (4.1), "Friendship" (4.7), "Justice" (6.5). Valerius writes of virtues made manifest in the lives of famous Romans and foreigners. The divisions after book 6 are clear. Book 7 begins with a chapter that is clearly meant to join the new book with the preceding; "Felicity" (constancy of fortune) (7.1) is the opposite half of the prior chapter, "The Mutability of Customs and Fortune" (6.9). Valerius has several such pairs of chapters. Book 7 differs in that after 7.2 and 7.3, which are a pair of opposites (wise and foolish, respectively, deeds and sayings) and a chapter on military stratagems (mental cleverness seems the slim connection), Valerius turns to the law, to the forensic world. "Necessity" at 7.6 is an interloper, but Valerius justifies its inclusion as it is a law unto itself.[11]

The legal sections, 7.5 and 7.7–8.6, have no foreign examples. This is significant: Valerius' treatment of wills, witnesses, and the courts reflects the concerns of the orator. No doubt the orator who would benefit from these exempla is more academic than professional. Significantly, however, Roman declamation has been criticized as reflecting Greek or even fictional legal practice; but no matter how farfetched the case of a *controversia* in Seneca may seem, the argument is conducted as if at Rome.[12] Foreign precedents are of no service to the pleader-in-training. The world of fantasy and of historical recreation belongs to *suasoriae*, not *controversiae*. Foreign examples recur with the change in subject at 8.7, which begins a series of six chapters on the arts. The fine arts are not being canvassed; rather Valerius has written of the arts ancillary to practical oratory, whose legal concerns constitute the prior section. Admittedly, these chapters wander from the forensic, but their connection with the preceding is clear. "Study and Industry" (8.7) is one of the rare chapters in which the foreign material outweighs the domestic; as with "Wise Deeds and Sayings" the foreign majority is due to Greece's wealth of philosophers, poets, and statesmen. Valerius then considers "Proper Leisure" (8.8) the balancing opposite to "Study and Industry." The role of *studium* in eloquence is a commonplace; Valerius has begun here and then, as he often does, has considered the opposite in a separate chapter. Eloquence and its art, a proper continuation of his forensic theme, then become the subject again at 8.9 and 8.10.

11. This metonymic connection may indeed seem slim, but the declaimer often had to pit the spirit against the letter of the law (*aequitas* and *ius*). Necessity provides a similar conflict—a condition where legal formula failed to direct action. Valerius is interested not in Roman law but in declamatory training for the aspirant lawyer. For discussion of the conflict of *ius* and *aequitas* and the more general issue of law and declamation, see Parks 1945 and Bonner 1949, 45–48 (rhetorical schools as preparation for the bar) and 84–132 (analysis of the Romanness of declamatory law).

12. Bonner (1949, 131) has noted the suitability of declamatory training in argument: "arguments used were often parallel to those of the advocates in Roman courts."

Yet the exempla afforded by foreign artists led him from his proper subject: just as with 8.7, "Study and Industry," the foreign examples constitute a majority at 8.11, "The Rare Effects of Art," and 8.12, "Artistic Virtuosi." The end of this book is discursive. Valerius seems emboldened by these artistic digressions, for the final three chapters of book 8 are a hodgepodge; disparate material—"Famous Cases of Longevity" (8.13), "The Love of Glory" (8.14), "Outstanding Things Which Happened to Individuals" (8.15)—cluster at the end of the book. Perhaps these were the residue of Valerius' inquiries. The ninth book could not receive them, for this final book offers a different class of exempla—vices. The titles are, familiarly, abstract nouns denoting personal qualities such as "Cruelty" (9.2) or "Avarice" (9.4).

From the religious and institutional subjects of books 1 and 2 to the vicious of the final book, the most obvious common thread is the format, the subordination of human action to a series of discrete anecdotes, moral and immoral, comprehended by a unifying rubric, the chapter heading. Valerius' own entries into the text, the references in the proems to his program, his first-person statements of transition and even of temporary disjuncture and then recall, all reinforce this formal cognitive system. Valerius' work communicates a way of understanding and relating events. A structured understanding of the whole of history or of religion or of rhetoric is neither the purpose nor the outcome. Transition, the ability to display verbal connection, which involves the choice and deft use of a subsuming rubric and the ordering of instances under that rubric, is the prized figure and structure. Such a technique is almost naive in its reliance and faith in rhetorical structures; it draws attention to itself and, more to the point, to the virtuosity of the speaker who employs it. Such a rhetoric when compared with that of Cicero seems distracting. Clearly, it is meant to be. The listener now is trained to hear familiar matter but to listen for the novel figure, connection, or treatment.

When the overt structures that purport to tie a work together are the author's entries into the text and various rhetorical junctures, often metonymic, the structure of the whole will not seem organic. A highly subordinated, compact structure is not Valerius' aim. When transition, the verbal display of connection, is especially prized, the two parts to be joined will come to be more and more disparate. The reader is not simply being instructed in some antithetical mode of thought—having been told of one subject, be ready to entertain the opposite. Certain of Valerius' chapters do work this way, and the suitability of opposite examples for debate is obvious. But when the display of transition becomes a valued oral skill, the course of subjects is necessarily more and more discursive. The ability to move from one exemplum to the next is not a narrow talent; it is essential to the declaimer who must hold an audience by surprise and paradox. It is also essential to the use of an exemplum, to argument by example since the speaker and adviser must always assert the relevance and connection of the paradigm to the present circumstances. Ovid is the greatest late Augustan and Tiberian master of transition, but Valerius too learned and taught the joining of the opposite, the paradoxical, and the discursive.

Valerius' work is a showpiece in many ways, including its use of transition, the sophisticated signaling of shift of topic. Book divisions are thus not arbitrary or random: the division of subjects between books 1, 2, and 3 and between 8 and 9 are striking. Book length and number of chapters are fairly uniform (the final book has the most chapters; perhaps a final book on a different tack, vices, was an afterthought, though one with plenty of material).[13] The book divisions then are original; their length is appropriate for a single papyrus roll.[14] These divisions and structures reveal the concerns of Valerius and his audience and explain why his work has been serviceable for so many audiences. We are bent on discovering the structure of Valerius' organization and understanding. These are not primarily those of the book but of the chapter. For the chapter is the unit that Valerius has in particular organized to be understood together.

13. Valerius' epitomator Julius Paris refers in his prologue to ten books of Valerius. His manuscripts include another work (not by Valerius) after *Memorable Deeds and Sayings*. There would then be no difficulty about the number of Valerius' books except that Aulus Gellius (12.7.8) cites 8.1.amb.2 as from the ninth book of Valerius. Perhaps a table of contents constituted a first book. See Helm 1955, 115.

14. Reynolds and Wilson (1974, 2–4) describe as a very long book (papyrus roll) P. Oxy. 843, which contains the text of Plato's *Symposium*, about seventy pages. Valerius' fifty-page books would have taken a full roll each.

Chapter Division and Chapter Titles

Valerius' chapter titles have much to reveal. Not simply an index to the subjects of his or his audience's interest or a clue to the system of symbols and categories from the contemporary intellectual pursuit of declamation, these chapter titles betray certain gaps. These are hiatuses in his program, the categories of his interest that depart from traditional material and indicate the elision, the attempted juncture of competing ideologies. The form of these chapters has not changed: all titles are prepositional phrases (about x or y); the object of the preposition and subject of the chapter are either an abstract noun, occasionally a pair of such nouns, or a relative clause. The favored title is the single abstract noun; the relative clause is used where Latin afforded no nominal abstraction. This is made quite clear by the proem to the single chapter that has a Greek title, "Stratagems" (7.4: "[examples of this category] have virtually no satisfactory expression in our language; in Greek they are called Stratagems").[15] No traditional virtue could embrace instances of "The Humble Born Who Rose to Prominence" (3.4) or "Women Who Pleaded Their Own and Others' Cases before Magistrates" (8.3) or "The Lowborn Who Tried through Deceit to Enter Others' Families" (9.15). Moreover, the relative clause at times allows Valerius to append a category clearly related to the prior chapter. The second chapter may be the opposite category: so 3.5, "Those Who Degenerated from Their Noble Birth," follows the humble born of 3.4; and 5.9, "Those Who Showed Restraint to Their Suspected Children," follows on "The Severity of Fathers toward Their Children," itself a response to the prior chapter (5.7) "Paternal Love and Indulgence." The difference of form does not of itself imply a different sort of subject; each chapter deals with a class of men; where possible Valerius provides an abstract quality as the common category for the men whose behavior has made them memorable.

Even so, the set of what Valerius finds memorable is finite. While on occasion his most immediate principle of composition is the juxtaposition of contrary chapters, every virtue is not followed by its

---

15. *appellatione nostra vix apte exprimi possunt, Graeca pronuntiatione Stratege-mata dicuntur.*

corresponding vice. Indeed, vices are reserved for the final book. Similarly, the virtues commemorated, while they may seem eclectic, are not indiscriminate. The long series of virtues from books 3 through 5 are notable not, as in the first two books, for a concern with the proper demeanor and behavior of the magistrate, but for the concern with the proper conduct of the individual within the family. This concern with birth, achievement, and behavior is signaled at the outset of the third book (3.1, "Inborn Talent"). Chapters 3.4 and 3.5 have titles in the form of relative clauses ("The Humble Born Who Rose to Prominence" and "Those Who Degenerated from Their Noble Birth") because these were not part of Rome's traditional, aristocratic virtues. Here the contrast in title type serves to emphasize legitimacy and propriety.[16] Similarly, from 4.4 to the first example of book 6 Valerius' subject is proper kin relations, orderly behavior within the family. This subject recurs in the extended treatment of fidelity (6.6, "The Republic's Fidelity"; 6.7, "Wives' Fidelity to Their Husbands"; 6.8, "Slaves' Fidelity to Their Masters"). This last topic leads to "The Mutability of Customs and Fortune," a transition remarkable not for its admonitory originality but, like all these chapters, for its concern with status and the behavior proper to each status and role.

Within a chapter exempla are joined in a sort of hierarchy as if the individual anecdotes were steps leading to the perfect manifestation of the quality in question. Valerius is concerned that his reader realize the ranking; thus one exemplum is said to be equal to another or one is said to surpass another or one is simply said to be the best or greatest of the category. The sequence of exempla is most often chronological, so the structure alone does not indicate relative merit; rather the hierarchy is indicated in Valerius' transitions, the lead-in sentences for each exemplum. In brief, this is how Valerius presents the fruit of his labor. Those interested in proofs need only select from the graded series. As Cicero advised, Roman examples precede and dominate.

16. The emphasis on legitimacy in Valerius is quite striking; an interest in wills and their correct execution and a more general insistence on the legitimate connection of the present to the past reflect in great measure Augustus' own legislation and preoccupation.

Composition by Chapter: The Construction of 1.6

Much of Valerius' treatment of an individual story thus depends on the choice of chapter title and the manner of composition within the chapter. Valerius' manner of composition and structure of presentation are best appreciated by an example, by the examination of a particular chapter. In the introduction to 1.6, "Prodigies," Valerius justifies the inclusion of the subjects and sketches briefly an organizational principle: "An account of prodigies as well, both the favorable and the adverse, is owed to our undertaking."[17] This undertaking is the whole section of book 1, which, in canvassing religion and religious institutions, succeeds especially in celebrating the Roman examples. In this chapter Valerius generally follows chronology: miraculous signs are surveyed, beginning with the kings and culminating with the Caesars. As an apologetic afterthought come the three foreign examples: Xerxes, Midas, and Plato. The chronology at second glance seems far less than strict (see table 1).

Chronological order is not followed, so it seems, until the episodes are divided (as Valerius indirectly posited in his introductory sentence) into the favorable and the adverse. Numbers one to four are felicitous events; five to thirteen augur ill to Rome. Within each of these two groupings there still remains one exception to the temporal sequence. An omen, or properly a *prodigium* (what we might call miraculous omens—distinguished from an omen that could be a single ordinary event with prophetic importance), following the defeat of P. and Cn. Scipio in Spain (211) intervenes between the seventh-century king Servius Tullius (1.6.1) and the miraculous overflow before the capture of Veii in 397. In the adverse prodigies, the folly of C. Hostilius Mancinus (cos. 137) does not come between Marcellus and Octavius (cos. 87), but is placed too early, coming between Flaminius and Tiberius Gracchus (proconsul 212). Valerius' sense of history is not at issue here—he knew perfectly well that the Punic Wars followed Veii—but he has with 1.6.1 and 1.6.2 joined two like prodigies. His motivation is the easy verbal link, "of equally fortunate outcome was that flame"

---

17. *Prodigiorum quoque, quae aut secunda aut adversa acciderunt, debita proposito nostro relatio est.*

TABLE 1. *Order of the Roman Examples in 1.6*

	Character and Date	Prodigy
1.6.1	Servius Tullius ("as a young boy")	a flame about his head
1.6.2	L. Marcius (211)	a flame about his head
1.6.3	The siege of Veii (396)	overflow of the Alban Lake
1.6.4	L. Sulla (cos. 88)	snake at a sacrifice
	*****	*****
1.6.5	Volumnius and Servius Sulpicius (coss. 461)	a cow speaks
	Cn. Domitius (Second Punic War)	(similar prodigies)
1.6.6	Flaminius before Lake Trasimene (217)	falls from horse, immobile standards
1.6.7	C. Hostilius Mancinus (cos. 137)	chickens, prophetic voice, snake
1.6.8	Ti. Gracchus (pro cos. 212)	snakes
1.6.9	M. Marcellus (208)	first no liver, then double
1.6.10	Octavius (cos. 87)	immobile head of Apollo's statue
1.6.11	Crassus at Carrhae (53)	wrong cloak, immobile standards
1.6.12	Pompey vs. Caesar (48)	bees, miscellaneous prodigies
1.6.13	Caesar (Ides of March 44)	no heart in the sacrificial cow, Spurinna's prophecy

(*aeque felicis eventus illa flamma*), which ties the anecdote of the young man who would be king to the story of Lucius Marcius, leader of the fractured forces of the Scipios. Chronological order has been sacrificed for verbal point. The third exemplum is introduced solely with "Likewise" and then immediately turns to the narration of the divine favor shown the Romans in their siege of Veii: "Likewise, when in a bitter and lengthy conflict the citizens of Veii . . ." (*item, cum bello acri et diutino Veientes*). The fact of temporal sequence, Valerius feels, need not be pointed out.

As for Mancinus interrupting the flow of history, Valerius has again juxtaposed like events. In both the disaster of Lake Trasimene and this setback from the Numantine Wars, the consul ignored prodigies, with the immediate consequence of a signal Roman defeat. By removing Mancinus from his correct position and placing him between Flaminius and Gracchus, Valerius can then also present together a series of three consuls who met their own deaths (but without the loss of their Roman armies). The first two of these, Gracchus and Marcellus, met chance deaths after ignoring prodigies. Valerius then turns to Octavius, who feared but could not avoid his fate (1.6.10). Ever eager to ease his transitions from one exemplum to the next, Valerius follows an underlying scheme that is temporal, but this he violates in order to join like events and to comment on this likeness, to draw attention to similarity but not just any similarity. In these chapters of book 1 that embrace dreams, miracles, omens, and prodigies, he is not interested in the sciences of the astrologer, haruspex, or augur. Thus in 1.6 the events are not organized by grouping all the like omens together. An exception is 1.6.5, where the stuff of the magistrates' annals (cows talking, stones raining, etc.) is appended to the like prodigies of 461 B.C., but this sequence is added as an afterthought (and, as we shall see, because Valerius found it in the passage of Livy from which he has culled other parts of this chapter). The priests' records and the Etruscan science do not hold him in themselves; cases of chickens ignored or the various epiphanies of snakes or lobeless livers are not the organizing categories. Rather a series of great men is split into good and bad examples; chronological order is thereafter observed except where the similar fortunes of men allow Valerius to group them together and to draw some generalizing, often moral connection.

To bind the stories further, he makes use of transitions that depend on verbal and not historical connections. So the "headlong audacity" (*praeceps audacia*, 1.6.6) of Flaminius is followed by the "mad obduracy" (*vesana perseverantia*, 1.6.7) of Hostilius Mancinus whose "rashness" (*temeritas*, 1.6.8) is joined to Gracchus'. The stringing together of exempla—familiar stories incongruously, that is imaginatively, joined— is a feature of the rhetorical schools and of Roman declamation in general.[18] Valerius' fondness for abstraction is not simply a mannerism of

18. See Seneca's criticism of Ovid (*Contr.* 2.2.12) and also Bornecque 1967, 98–99.

style. In this chapter, for example, a progress of abstract qualities leads to the crowning example of the chapter heading—here, the worst of the disastrous prodigies. Abstraction enables transition, just as, more generally, it groups disparate events into the various chapters of Valerius' work. Valerius communicates a moral understanding of the events of this chapter through a steady emphasis on abstract qualities and on their relation.

He did not find his material in this form or even in these combinations. In this chapter Valerius does give the impression of a composer skipping from one book to another while dictating. The sixth exemplum of this chapter provides a test case for examination of his method of inquiry and of composition. At 1.6.6 Valerius recounts the infamous episode of the Roman consul Flaminius at Lake Trasimene—uniquely memorable and commemorated by Polybius, Coelius Antipater, Cicero, and Livy. Coelius' work was abridged by Brutus (whose epitome may have been Cicero's source).[19] Valerius had, it is clear, sources far greater in number and different in character from those extant. Where Valerius is choosing between Livy and Cicero, we may gain no insight about these additional sources but, at least, can learn about his methods and purposes of research. The exemplum about Flaminius offers some light here:

> Moreover, C. Flaminius—the consul who took office without consulting the auspices—just before joining in battle with Hannibal at Lake Trasimene, ordered the assembly of the standards, was thrown to the ground over his fallen horse's head, and, undaunted by this prodigy, threatened to punish the standard bearers (who maintained that the standards could not be moved) if they did not dig them up that instant. If only this folly had had as recompense his death alone and not the greatest slaughter of the Roman people! In that battle fifteen thousand Romans were killed, six thousand captured, and ten thousand put to flight. Hannibal, who had entombed Rome's power as much as he could, sought out for burial the butchered body of the consul. (1.6.6)[20]

19. See Pease 1963, 179, who cites Zingler, *De Cicerone Historico Quaestiones*, 24–25.

20. *C. autem Flaminius inauspicato consul creatus cum apud lacum Trasimennum*

That Valerius can be determined to have followed any source at all would be remarkable. The details of the story (the fall from the horse, the immobile standards, the ensuing defeat) were well known. Perhaps we are to imagine Valerius the excerptor working in haste—using his written sources' phrasing with some of the mechanical stylistic variation described by Bliss.[21] The verbal parallels make clear that Valerius had the twenty-second book of Livy before him: *equus repente corruit consulemque lapsum super caput effudit* (22.3.11), which is "declined" by Valerius as *lapso equo super caput*. This change in case, rather than a feature of a peculiar aesthetic, is the natural result of having the subject at hand (here Flaminius) the grammatical subject of the exemplum, a common practice for Valerius. He has begun in the briefest manner possible—indicating name, rank, and historical context—and narrates nearly the entire episode in a single sentence that subordinates (convolutedly) the material of the source. Direct speech is eliminated—for example, Flaminius' words before his fall and his command to the standard bearer. In Valerius this soldier has been expanded to *signiferis negantibus*. Livy, however, had reported Flaminius' words as "Go tell them to dig up the standards" (*Abi, nuntia, effodiant signum*), for which Valerius has substituted "he threatened punishment if they did not dig them up that instant" (*malum, ni ea continuo effodissent, minatus est*). In simplifying the situation (i.e., not narrating the one standard bearer's difficulties and the order for *men* to uproot the standards), Valerius has eliminated the extraneous agent. Thus all can be told in one period.

An even stronger tie between the two passages is that Valerius has

---

cum Hannibale conflicturus convelli signa iussisset, lapso equo super caput eius humi prostratus est nihilque eo prodigio inhibitus, signiferis negantibus signa moveri sua sede posse, malum, ni ea continuo effodissent, minatus est. verum huius temeritatis utinam sua tantum, non etiam populi Romani maxima clade poenas pependisset! in ea namque acie $\bar{X}\bar{V}$ Romanorum caesa, $\bar{V}\bar{I}$ capta, $\bar{X}$ fugata sunt. consulis obtruncati corpus ad funerandum ab Hannibale quaesitum, qui, quantum in ipso fuerat, Romanum sepelierat imperium.

21. Bliss (1951, 56) established that Valerius had modified his sources deliberately with a finite number of types of verbal transformations (e.g., changes in word order or the substitution of compound for simple words of the same stem and vice versa).

repeated the prodigies narrated by Livy at 22.1.8–13. These Valerius
has appended to 1.6.5, the preceding exemplum. Finally, the numbers
of casualties, prisoners, and fugitives (found at Livy 22.6.8–7.3) he has
used to round off 1.6.6. Valerius has, then, certainly read this particular section of Livy. He has taken a famous, major episode from the
narrative and has, in all probability, been led astray from his proposed
scheme by the additional prodigies that Livy had to tell, in an adjacent
section, of Cn. Domitius.

At first glance, Valerius does not seem to have needed or known Cicero's version of Flaminius' disaster. At *De natura deorum* 2.8, Cicero
mentions Coelius Antipater's writing about Flaminius "at Trasimene"
(Valerius has "at Lake Trasimene").[22] This is the closest thing to an echo
or parallel. In *De divinatione* 1.77, Cicero again follows Coelius who, it
would seem, differed from Livy, for Flaminius is said to have neglected
(i.e., abandoned) the intractable standards, as he seems not to have
done in Valerius. The evidence that Valerius did have Cicero's *De divinatione* before him while composing 1.6 comes from the foreign exempla of that chapter. There are to be found miraculous stories of
Midas and Plato. Cicero writes of these marvels in the *De divinatione*,
immediately after Flaminius at Trasimene and the dire portents of this
disaster. Valerius' passage is as follows:

> Ants deposited grains of wheat in the mouth of Midas, the con-
> queror of Phrygia, while asleep as a child. When his parents won-
> dered what this prodigy presaged, the augurs answered that he
> would be the richest of all mortals. Nor was this an empty proph-
> ecy: for Midas excelled all kings in wealth. He recompensed the
> swaddling clothes of his infancy, given as a cheap present of the
> gods, with treasures heavy with gold and silver. (1.6.ext.2.)[23]

22. Cicero: *apud Trasumenum*; Valerius: *apud lacum Trasimennum*. The different spellings of this name are immaterial as the manuscripts differ. See Pease
1955 on *De natura deorum* 2.8.

23. *Midae vero, cuius imperio Phrygia fuit subiecta, puero dormienti formicae in os
grana tritici congesserunt. parentibus deinde eius corsus prodigium tenderet exploran-
tibus augures responderunt omnium illum mortalium futurum ditissimum. nec vana
praedictio extitit: nam Midas cunctorum paene regum opes abundantia pecuniae an-
tecessit infantiaeque incunabula vili deorum munere donata onustis auro atque argento
gazis pensavit.*

It is a full but manifest expansion of the first two sentences of Cicero's passage:

> Ants deposited grains of wheat in the mouth of the Phrygian Midas, asleep while a boy. It was predicted that he would be the richest of men, which happened. But when bees settled on the lips of the young Plato sleeping in his cradle, the response was that he would have singular sweetness of eloquence. So was future eloquence foretold in infancy. (*De div.* 1.78)[24]

Valerius makes the latter two sentences the core of the concluding exemplum of this chapter:

> Rightly and justly would I prefer the bees of Plato to the ants of Midas; the latter presage a frail and perishable, the former a firm and eternal happiness, by putting honey in the lips of the child sleeping in his cradle. When the seers heard this, they said that a singular sweetness of eloquence would flow from his mouth. And indeed in my opinion those bees, fed not on Mount Hymettus fragrant with thyme but on the Heliconian hills of the Muses, which teem by the goddesses' inspiration with every kind of learning, seem to have instilled the sweetest nourishment of highest eloquence upon the greatest genius. (1.6.ext.3)[25]

Once Valerius' reading of both the *De divinatione* and a section of the *Ab urbe condita* has been established, the composition of the entire chapter can be reassessed. Source identification is the beginning of such

---

24. *Midae illi Phrygi, cum puer esset, dormienti formicae in os tritici grana congesserunt. divitissimum fore praedictum est; quod evenit. at Platoni cum in cunis parvulo dormienti apes in labellis consedissent responsum est singulari illum suavitate orationis fore. ita futura eloquentia provisa in infante est.*

25. *formicis Midae iure meritoque apes Platonis praetulerim: illae enim caducae ac fragilis, hae solidae et aeternae felicitatis indices extiterunt, dormientis in cunis parvuli labellis mel inserendo. qua re audita prodigiorum interpretes singularem eloquii suavitatem ore eius emanaturam dixerunt. ac mihi quidem illae apes non montem Hymettium tymi flore redolentem, sed Musarum Heliconios colles omni genere doctrinae virentis dearum instinctu depastae maximo ingenio dulcissima summae eloquentiae instillasse videntur alimenta.*

analysis. The case of the first exemplum is very like that of Flaminius: the *De divinatione* has a brief mention of the episode of the flame about the head of the young Servius Tullius, whereas Livy provides a sustained anecdote complete with Queen Tanaquil's speech. Valerius' treatment is nearly too brief to allow identification of the model chosen. Indeed, no model was necessary, at least according to Cicero: "What history has not written of the flame about the head of the sleeping Servius Tullius?" (*Caput arsisse Servio Tullio dormienti quae historia non prodidit?*). The lack of verbal parallels prevents any sure conclusion. However, Valerius certainly has more than Cicero tells; and though, as Cicero indicates, the subject was familiar and the sources many, the use of Livy in other exempla of this chapter, together with Livy's and Valerius' emphasis on Tanaquil's role, suggests that Livy is being abridged here. Again, the *De divinatione* seems to have suggested a subject while the *Ab urbe condita* provided a fuller account. In this case, perhaps because the topic was a commonplace, Valerius does not dwell on Servius Tullius.

Valerius is clearly following Livy for his second example of the chapter. Here too Livy is not simply copied out. Various details are selected or suppressed so as to make a coherent, consistent anecdote. (This is the exemplum that Valerius has imported from its proper chronological place in order to join the same prodigies.) For the modern Latinist the most famous instance of a prophetic flame is the fire about Ascanius' head, which so worried the onlookers. Valerius does not take stories from Virgil; poetry seems off limits, as if Valerius dealt only in "facts." More to the point, he chose his models from Latin prose. The story of Marcius is not told in the *De divinatione*, but, among other direct verbal echoes, the casualty figures mentioned in the exemplum demonstrate that Livy 25.39.12–16 was Valerius' source. This passage is not taken over entire, for in Livy the details of the battle or battles are far from clear. The Augustan historian reports the variant accounts and figures of Claudius Quadrigarius (said to be following the *Annals* of C. Acilius), Valerius Antias, and Piso.[26] The versions of the latter two, along with

26. Valerius reports the number of Carthaginians slain as thirty-eight thousand (*octo et triginta milibus hostium caesis*). Livy begins his account with the number as given by Claudius Quadrigarius (*Ad triginta septem milia hostium caesa*).

all discussion of booty, are omitted by Valerius. In fact, he has jumped from the beginning of the Livian passage to the point where narration of the prodigy begins. Thus no hint of historical uncertainty is allowed to punctuate the exemplum. Valerius Antias reported that only one camp was taken; Valerius like Livy mentions two camps. Valerius is not concerned with variant accounts; he takes (or mistakes) the first figure reported by Livy, omits the annalists' conflicting reports, and moves to the prodigy where he again borrows and varies Livy's diction.

A preference for Livy guides Valerius also at 1.6.3, the miraculous overflow of the Alban Lake with the Romans' consequent embassy to Delphi. Cicero mentions this prodigy at *De divinatione* 1.100. Here too Cicero begins by drawing attention to his source ("annals"), but unlike the other notices from the *De divinatione* this offers a full account. Valerius, however, has used Livy 5.15.2–4. In addition to Valerius' echoes of Livy (e.g., *neque caelestibus auctus imbribus, neque inundatione ullius amnis adiutus, solitum* after *sine ullis caelestibus aquis causave qua alia quae rem miraculo eximeret, in altitudinem insolitam*), Valerius' version follows Livy and not Cicero, who has no embassy to the Delphic oracle and makes the prophet a deserter from Veii. Valerius and Livy have the haruspex captured by Roman soldiers after which the senate is doubly advised.

Valerius did use Cicero's work for the next example: 1.6.4, Sulla sees a snake, is drawn from *De divinatione* 1.72. The remainder of the chapter, with the exception of the foreign examples and perhaps the examples treating the Caesars, is from Livy. The passage 1.6.5 joins like prodigies from Livy 3.10.6 and 22.1.8–13. The diction of 1.6.8 and 9 follows Livy 25.16 and 27.26.13–14 respectively. For 1.6.7 and 11 the parallel texts in Livy are not extant, but comparison with the epitome (*Periochae* 55 and 106 respectively) strongly suggests that Livy was the source for the first exemplum. The epitome records no prodigies for Crassus before the disaster of Carrhae. Parallels are also wanting for the prodigies before Pharsalus and the Ides of March (1.6.12 and 13).

This might be Valerius' (and not some scribe's) error: the next figure given, in the same sentence, is *captos ad mille octingentos triginta*. If this "error" is not simply the loss of a stroke, it might have arisen from an eye jumping from *ad triginta* to *ad . . . oct . . . triginta*, which would account for Valerius' word order *octo et triginta*.

Our purpose is not to posit use of Livy wherever a parallel of substance might allow but to describe the origins of Valerius' material in a single chapter. The pattern of this use can be discerned in table 2.

TABLE 2. *The Sources of 1.6*

	Character and Date	Source	Parallel
1.6.1	Servius Tullius ("as a young boy")	Livy 1.39.1–2	Cic., *De div.* 1.121
1.6.2	L. Marcius (211)	Livy 25.39.12–16	
1.6.3	The siege of Veii (397)	Livy 5.15–17	Cic., *De div.* 1.100
1.6.4	L. Sulla (cos. 88)	Cic., *De div.* 1.72	
	*****		
1.6.5	Volumnius and Servius Sulpicius (coss. 461)	Livy 3.10.5–6	
	"another conflict" (the winter before and spring of Flaminius' consulship)	Livy 21.62.2–5 and 22.1.8–13	
	Cn. Domitius ("in the Second Punic War" [192 B.C.])	Livy 35.21.4	
1.6.6	Flaminius before Lake Trasimene (217)	Livy 22.3.11–14 and 22.7.1–5	Cic., *De div.* 1.77
1.6.7	C. Hostilius Mancinus (cos. 137)	Livy (*Periochae*) 55	
1.6.8	Ti. Gracchus (cos. 212)	Livy 25.16	
1.6.9	M. Marcellus (208)	Livy 27.26–27	
1.6.10	Octavius (cos. 87)		
1.6.11	Crassus at Carrhae (53)	Livy (*Periochae*) 106	
1.6.12	Pompey vs. Caesar (48)		
1.6.13	Caesar (Ides of March 44)		
1.6.ext.1	Xerxes		
1.6.ext.2	Plato	Cic., *De div.* 1.78	
1.6.ext.3	Midas	Cic., *De div.* 1.78	

With this overview, Valerius' method of composition becomes clearer. First, he is writing a section on prodigies. A natural and easy method might have been to read through Livy in order to cull examples or to check one's notes (these would be the results of wide reading). Valerius, however, seems to have worked from a more suitable text, one filled with omens and prodigies. Cicero's brief notices of prodigies in the first book of the *De divinatione* were Valerius' departure point; in particular he has read from 1.72 through 1.121. The foreign examples receive rhetorical amplification. The Roman figures had been famously treated, at considerable length, in an Augustan classic. So Livy's wording lies behind the portents of 1.6.5 and the battle at Trasimene of 1.6.6. The modern scholar, had he wanted to know more than Cicero told, would have gone to Cicero's source, Coelius Antipater. Valerius, on the other hand, is interested in the preeminent, classical, and so canonical stylistic treatment of a story. Cicero's notices, when they are too brief, do not allow the sort of stylistic modification that is Valerius' method of composition.

The stylistic and substantial characteristics that disqualify Valerius as a historian should be attributed to these same interests. Valerius does not compare accounts in order to weigh conflicting reports. Reported variants are suppressed as Valerius strives to make his material and especially its message unequivocal. Lack of narrative and of historical exegesis are not here the marks of a poor historian. Actual historical errors are far from legion. In this section can be singled out the slip of *C.* for *P.* Volumnius (though who can say this is not a copyist's error?) and the compression of time in 1.6.9 where Marcellus meets his death after the capture of Syracuse. The Sicilian city fell in 211, but the general did not fall into the Carthaginians' hands until 208. Valerius is not guilty of historical error, only of omission, with the result that an unwary reader might suppose Marcellus' death followed shortly on Syracuse's fall. History can be grandly declared to be serving rhetorical demands, but this ignores and distorts the manner of Valerius' composition. He is engaged in the selection of a series of exempla; for the theme of this chapter he finds his guide in a classical theoretical work of Cicero. Livy then provided the material of these anecdotes worked out at greater length but still with venerable, canonical style. Valerius' work does, on close inspection, display consistent criteria in the selection and emulation of models, but these criteria are not those of a historian or an antiquarian.

The Process of Arrangement

A brief review of three other chapters, where again Cicero or Livy offers a vantage point, reveals similar criteria of selection and combination. These chapters on the ancient practices of the senate and the magistrates (2.2), "Friendship" (4.7), and "Cruelty" (9.2), however, admit of much greater variety. Their subjects are not so narrowly Roman; indeed, the Roman instances of two of these are problematic for the imperial enthusiast. The historical matter is not so safe or so removed as the sober and solemn subjects of book 1. Valerius' inclusion of material that could be interpreted as critical of Rome or the Caesars provides a window into the course of his composition, for these subjects require apology or reclassification, a reunderstanding of the past, which in turn reveals the margins of his subject, the limits of what is acceptable, and the limits of his technique of making all the past acceptable.

Molo, Cicero, and Marius

Valerius handles such difficult material by a technique of apologetic transition. In the second chapter of book 2 Valerius employs this to join the venerable instances of the early days of the Republic to the looser standards of the late Republic. Valerius does not offer much on concrete practices of the old senate. Instead in 2.2 he has started with an anecdote of the senators' former tight-lipped discretion and then moved to their steadfast habit of speaking and hearing Latin alone. The third exemplum recounts the first violation of this practice: the rhetor Molo addressed the Roman senate in Greek. This, anyway, is the element of the third exemplum that has most to do with the preceding example and with the general theme of this section of book 2 (ancient institutions and specifically the old republican senate). Valerius has, however, developed Molo into a full-fledged entry in his own right. Molo was Cicero's teacher, and this fact Valerius proffers as justification for the break with precedent: "[Molo] not undeservedly reaped this distinction, since he had aided the greatest force of Roman eloquence." That other native of Arpinum, Marius, who had no Greek, actually begins this exemplum; indeed, he is directly addressed and given pardon for his Greekless state:

> Therefore you ought not to be found guilty on the charge of rustic severity, C. Marius, because as conqueror you did not want your old age, crowned with the double laurel of your German and Numidian triumphs, to become more refined by the eloquence of a conquered tongue lest, I believe, the practice of a foreign talent make you a late fugitive from your fathers' customs. Who opened the door to the present practice by which the senate's ears are deafened by Greek pleadings? In my opinion, it was the rhetorician Molo, the one who improved M. Cicero's technique, for it is well known that first of all foreigners, he addressed the senate without an interpreter. This distinction he earned quite rightly since he had aided the greatest power of Roman eloquence. Arpinum is a town of outstanding fortune, whether you wish to look upon the most famous contemner or the richest source of letters. (2.2.3)[27]

A most peculiar aspect of this exemplum, itself an addendum to the preceding, is its form—the apostrophe to Marius. Certainly, this gives a lively air to the digression. But the distinctive quality of this exemplum is not so much the behavior or presence of Marius as that of Valerius Maximus. The author supports his statements and justifies their inclusion by assertions in his own person: "I believe" and "in my opinion" are the authorities advanced for Marius' disdain for Greek and

---

27. *quapropter non es damnandus rustici rigoris crimine, C. Mari, quia gemina lauru coronatam senectutem tuam, Numidicis et Germanicis inlustrem tropaeis, victor devictae gentis facundia politiorem fieri noluisti, credo, ne alienigena ingenii exercitatione patrii ritus serus transfuga existeres. quis ergo huic consuetudini, qua nunc Graecis actionibus aures curiae exurdantur, ianuam patefecit? ut opinor, Molo rhetor, qui studia M. Ciceronis acuit: eum namque ante omnes exterarum gentium in senatu sine interprete auditum constat. quem honorem non inmerito cepit, quoniam summam vim Romanae eloquentiae adiuverat. conspicuae felicitatis Arpinas municipium, sive litterarum gloriossisimum contemptorem sive abundantissimum fontem intueri velis.*

Molo's use of that language in the curia. The rhetorical and original nature of this exemplum grows more distinct at the close, which addresses the reader while joining Marius and Cicero, antithetical in attitude to Greek culture, common in their origin. Marius is a difficult figure to praise, here in particular for his disdain for education but generally as a type of civil strife and autocracy. The contemporary of Tiberius, faced with an increasingly provincial senate, would make a virtue of Marius' homespun ways. To follow the thread of Valerius' connections is not an exercise in untangling the superficial if bizarre web of a declamatory stylist; Valerius proffers a rhetoric of association whose transitions and apologies reveal what he found difficult or almost intractable in his subject.

The contrast of Valerius' treatment of this particular subject, Marius, with that of earlier prose authors does not intend criticism but elucidation of his methods. Valerius' "defense" here of Marius has little to do with partisan spirit or even with admiration for the man. Sallust had shown how such encomium could be made: "But he, born and raised in Arpinum, when youth first endures military training, devoted himself to active service, and not to Greek eloquence or the refinements of the city." A little later in the same work, he has Marius defend his own ignorance: "and I did not learn Greek; for it pleased me little to learn what benefited its teachers nothing in the pursuit of virtue. But I did learn the things of far greater advantage to the Republic."[28] Valerius' compliment of rustic rigor is, after all, the very Roman way to praise an uneducated man; and, for the Roman encomiast, if his subject lacks illustrious ancestors, in their stead he must celebrate signal personal service. Much like Cato in Plutarch, Sallust's Marius has in place of *imagines* weapons and scars.[29] Valerius has the Roman defense for not knowing Greek, the sort of thing that had been fully developed by Sallust and which Plutarch would put in terser, more epigrammatic form:

28. Sallust, *B.I.* 63: *sed is natus et omnem pueritiam Arpini altus, ubi primum aetas militiae patiens fuit, stipendiis faciundis, non Graeca facundia neque urbanis munditiis sese exercuit. B.I.* 85: *neque litteras Graecas didici; parum placebat eas discere, quippe quae ad virtutem doctoribus nihil profuerant. at illa multo optuma rei publicae doctus sum.*

29. Plutarch, *Cato* 1.5.

"it is ridiculous to learn ABC's from teachers who are enslaved by other men."[30] Valerius, remarkably, does not overindulge his rhetoric here. Similarly, he does not develop the contrast, rich in rhetorical possibilities, of Marius and Cicero. The present theme, the Romans' ancient institutions, will not permit that.

The rhetor Molo is the figure relevant to the theme; his connection with Cicero brings mention of that son of Arpinum. The development of a single fact, Molo speaking Greek to the senate, to a full exemplum also serves an ancillary, incidental theme: the importance of speech (and its opposite). The preceding and following exempla fit the chapter heading; they relate Fabius Maximus' mistake of telling a nonsenator of the senate's business and his scrupulous adherence to protocol while advancing with his son the consul to parley with the Samnites. That is, both illustrate ancient customs (while in truly Valerian manner they are further joined as actions of the same man). But they have also developed and illustrated this subtheme of the importance of speech. One senator's unintentional breaking of the senate's taciturnity leads to a second peculiarity of the senate's speech and its violation. Molo, the violator, leads to Cicero, and he to Marius. Divergence from the set theme has occurred. With the next exemplum (Fabius Maximus and his son, 2.2.4) the connection to the initial themes becomes even more distant. The senate is no longer the subject—the great general is. Properly, such a story should belong to a chapter on *pietas*, specifically on the preference of *patria* to family or personal glory. Yet Valerius tells the story here, depending for his continuity on the identity of the agent (introduced two exempla earlier) and on the reference to his impending converse (*conloquium*) with the enemy. Such divergences, returns, and new directions are an understandable result of a method of composition whose digression can be metonymic, prosopographic, (sub)-thematic, or some mixture of these.

Neither theme nor the ideal of a "historian's accuracy" or "fullness of explanation," then, exercises a tyranny over Valerius' arrangement of a chapter. Consistency of viewpoint can and will be found, but often in these likenings of great men, the quality being compared outweighs

---

30. *Marius* 2.2: ὡς γελοῖον γράμματα μανθάνειν ὧν οἱ διδάσκαλοι δουλεύοιεν ἑτέροις.

and does no justice to the substance of the persons involved. The comparisons of Marius and Molo with Cicero are tidy, effective ways to flesh out an exemplum, but not particularly insightful or significant. Valerius will on occasion admit an unsavory subject—at 2.8.7 and 9.2.2, for example, Marius is condemned for the civil strife he brought to Rome— but the pattern of Valerius' composition in a single chapter does not follow from abstract questions of politics.

Praise of Defeated Partisans

The second chapter on a difficult or dangerous subject to be considered here likewise reveals in a positive light a historical figure Valerius otherwise censures. In 4.7 too the course of composition can be glimpsed by reference to other ancient treatments and in particular by comparison with Valerius' source, Cicero's *De amicitia*. Valerius' subject is not all of friendship but rather the public, melodramatic proof of fidelity, friendship unto death. Noble deaths and the deaths of famous men make good reading, and good exempla. Such tales were in general circulation and encouraged embellishment—for instance, the versions of the end of Cicero in Seneca the Elder; so it is small wonder if authors do not agree on the names of the lesser participants. This particular chapter in Valerius displays well his historiographical method or lack thereof. His technique of variation is not limited to minor embellishment of name, scene, or detail. Whereas a technique of apologetic transition enabled him to write of and praise Marius, a technique of abstraction makes commemorable the defeated partisans of Rome's various civil conflicts.[31]

At 4.7.2 the friendship of Pomponius and Laetorius for C. Gracchus follows that of Blossius for Tiberius Gracchus (4.7.1). The variety of ancient report on the two friends of Gaius who fought to the death trying to protect him is great. The author of the *De viris illustribus* like Valerius places Pomponius at the Porta Trigemina, Laetorius (as a sec-

31. Compare Valerius' judgments of the negative Roman exempla of 1.6, "Prodigies." For this pejorative material, abstraction enabled transition: see my previous comments on the "audacity" of Flaminius giving way to the "mad obduracy" of Hostilius Mancinus.

ond Horatius Cocles) at the Pons Sublicius (65.5). Plutarch has in place of the latter Gaius' well-known slave Licinius (*C. Gracchus,* 16.4). Orosius knows only of Laetorius (5.12.7). In Valerius, Laetorius is a knight; in Velleius, Pomponius is the knight (2.6.6). Not even the subtlest connoisseur of sources would dare disentangle this web—the threads are too crossed. Heroic models may have worked their distortion: in some popularist account, the Gracchan faction has been granted its own Horatius at the Bridge. Perhaps in ignorance of such a source, Orosius knows of one courageous friend only, whereas other authors confound the name of the Horatius imitator.

The theme of this example and chapter is "Friendship," and it is from Cicero's work of the same name that Valerius drew the prior example (4.7.1) of the Stoic philosopher C. Blossius Cumanus and his patron T. Gracchus. In this anecdote the characters are all of the most famous and distinguished sort, so no confusion of names. Cicero is most responsible for the lack of any conflicting details. His work differs from the like-named chapter in Valerius in that it is analytic (even if there is a certain polemical undertone): he asks, "What limit should there be in devotion to a friend" (*quatenus amor in amicitia progredi debeat*) and, having dispensed with Coriolanus, turns to the radical tribune.

> We were observing the abandonment of Tiberius Gracchus, while he troubled the Republic, by Q. Tubero and his friends. But, Scaevola, when that guest friend of your family, C. Blossius Cumanus, came to plead for pardon from me (since I was in consultation with the consuls Laenas and Rupilius), he offered as excuse that he thought he should do whatever Gracchus wished because he had valued Tiberius Gracchus so highly. Then I said, "Even if he wanted you to set fire to the Capitol?" "He never would have wanted that," he said, "but if he had, I would have done it." (*De amic.* 37)[32]

32. *Tib. quidem Gracchum rem publicam vexantem a Q. Tuberone aequalibusque amicis derelictum videbamus. at C. Blossius Cumanus, hospes familiae vestrae, Scaevola, cum ad me, quod aderam Laenati et Rupilio consulibus in consilio, deprecatum venisset, hanc, ut sibi ignoscerem, causam afferebat, quod tanti Tib. Gracchum fecisset, ut, quidquid ille vellet, sibi faciendum putaret. tum ego: "etiamne, si te in Capitolium faces ferre vellet?" "numquam," inquit, "voluisset id quidem; sed si voluisset, paruissem."*

Cicero does not have much time for this as a touching testimony of true devotion, nor for the preference, like E. M. Forster's, of friend to country. He argues rather the opposite: "Therefore it is not an excuse for wrongdoing, if you have done wrong for the sake of a friend; for, since a judgment of virtue is what joins friends, it is difficult for friendship to endure if there is defection from virtue."[33] Valerius shows more sympathy for Blossius; he does not feel, strongly and personally as Cicero, the political objection. Rather, his topic required instances of devotion regardless of political allegiance. Blossius' politics are not objectionable for Valerius; they simply throw his actions into better relief.

A second signal difference, which also contributes to the amplification and expansion of the source's material, is Valerius' dramatization of the verbal interchange. The inquisitor Laelius and his intended victim do not as swiftly reach their conclusion:

> Tiberius Gracchus was thought to have been an enemy of the fatherland—not without reason, since he had preferred his power to her safety. Nonetheless, the unswerving, loyal friend Gracchus had in C. Blossius Cumanus even in this criminal undertaking merits recognition. Judged a public enemy, afflicted with capital punishment, stripped of the final office of burial, nevertheless he did not lack the goodwill of this man: for when the senate ordered the consuls Rupilius and Laenas to exercise the ancient practice on the Gracchan sympathizers, and Blossius came to Laelius, on whose consultations the consuls especially relied, to plead for himself on the grounds of friendship, Laelius asked, "What? If Gracchus had ordered you to burn the temple of Jupiter, would you have complied with his will from the friendship of which you boast?" He replied, "Gracchus would never have bade that." Enough, no, too much! He dared to defend practices condemned by the consensus of the entire senate. But the next is even more daring and more dangerous: hemmed in by Laelius' continued questioning, he stuck at the same level of fidelity and even said he

---

33. *De amic.* 37: *nulla est igitur excusatio peccati, si amici causa peccaveris; nam, cum conciliatrix amicitiae virtutis opinio fuerit, difficile est amicitiam manere, si a virtute defeceris.*

would have done it if only Gracchus had given him the signal. Who would have thought him wrong to keep silent? Who would not even have thought him prudent to speak as circumstance and necessity demanded? But Blossius was unwilling to let an honorable silence or prudent tongue guard his own safety, lest he abandon to any degree the memory of this unfortunate friendship. (4.7.1)[34]

Valerius actively draws his readers' attention to the events and, in so doing, punctuates Cicero's version of Blossius' words. He is sure to alert his reader to the significance of what is happening and to the imminent climax, and, once this is reached, he piles on two rhetorical questions, lest anyone miss the point. A new context for understanding the story has been provided. Further, Valerius is not interested in narrating a piece of history (like Livy) or in using the piece as rhetorical argument (like Cicero). The declaimer's art lies in giving new twists to the familiar—thus redundancy in itself is not only not to be avoided but is in part inevitable. He achieves his novelty at some cost to good storytelling—that is, the narrative suffers for the rhetoricization of the source. Cicero had presented Tiberius "abandoned by his friends"; Valerius replaces this with the tricolon crescendo: "judged a public enemy, af-

---

34. *inimicus patriae fuisse Ti. Gracchus existimatus est, nec inmerito, quia potentiam suam saluti eius praetulerat. quam constantis tamen fidei amicum etiam in hoc tam pravo proposito C. Blossium Cumanum habuerit operae pretium est cognoscere. hostis iudicatus, ultimo supplicio adfectus, sepulturae honore spoliatus benivolentia tamen eius non caruit: nam cum senatus Rupilio et Laenati consulibus mandasset ut in eos, qui cum Graccho consenserant, more maiorum animadverterent, et ad Laelium, cuius consilio praecipue consules utebantur, pro se Blossius deprecatum venisset familiaritatisque excusatione uteretur, atque is dixisset: "quid? si te Gracchus templo Iovis optimi maximi faces subdere iussisset, obsecuturusne illius voluntati propter istam, quam iactas, familiaritatem fuisti?" "numquam istud," inquit, "Gracchus imperasset." satis, immo etiam nimium: totius namque senatus consensu damnatos eius mores defendere ausus est. verum quod sequitur multo audacius multoque periculosius: conpressus enim perseveranti interrogatione Laeli in eodem constantiae gradu stetit seque etiam hoc, si modo Gracchus annuisset, facturum respondit. quis illum sceleratum putasset fuisse, si tacuisset? quis non etiam sapientem, si pro necessitate temporis locutus esset? at Blossius nec silentio honesto nec prudenti sermone salutem suam, ne qua ex parte infelicis amicitiae memoriam desereret, tueri voluit.*

flicted with capital punishment, stripped of the final office of burial."
After this rhetorical amplification, Valerius paraphrases Cicero's concrete phrase with "nonetheless Tiberius did not lack Blossius' benevolence." He uses a second abstract noun, "familiarity" (i.e., the intimacy
and tie of friendship and family), for Cicero's "because he valued Tiberius Gracchus so highly." Does a change in the wording of this excuse
matter at all? It is not of great moment, even to the telling of a story,
but the change does make the point less emphatic. The reader no
longer hears an echo of Blossius' speech; instead, an abstract noun is
substituted. Even the separate elements of the story have been reduced
to moral categories. The general theme, as the chapter heading declares, is "Friendship." Within this sphere, "Familiarity" motivates a
final "Benevolence" without regard for "Salvation" or "Safety."

Valerius is composing from Cicero, but clearly his rewriting constitutes no simple inversion of word order, no mechanical system of stylization. He is composing from Cicero to the extent that he drew the
subject and diction of an exemplum and perhaps the chapter title from
the most famous Latin work on friendship. But this was a departure
point, a place from which to move to other stories, from Tiberius to
Gaius Gracchus and on to other partisans of different causes. The
chapter topic and no single source or issue of political allegiance constitutes the criterion of inclusion, and so by the end of the chapter the
enemies of the Caesars have been included.

The Cruelty of Sulla

Chapters such as "Friendship" or "Cruelty" are remarkable for their
proposed scope; they are meant to survey all of human experience.
Valerius' treatment of "Cruelty" is on a grand scale, and here too famous Romans from literary works illustrate his chosen subject. This
chapter has been chosen as the concluding illustration of Valerius'
manner of composition, since it reveals him in considerable difficulty
as he strives to balance the Roman and the foreign and to hold his
chapter together without any hint of criticism of the present day.

Within this chapter the customary division of exempla into Roman
and foreign is tactfully, patriotically handled: the Romans abuse themselves only; the provincials and foreigners are spared. That is, the Ro-

man exempla are all civil. The first three foreign exempla describe instances of cruelty toward the Romans; in the remaining, non-Romans act heinously toward other foreigners and Romans. The progression of internecine acts spans the civil wars, reaching as end point Julius Caesar, but with no discredit to the imperial line. After an unusually lengthy recounting of Sulla's victims, Valerius narrows his focus; the whole chapter seems a diminuendo from Sulla, who has assumed the preeminent position in the list of cruelties. Marius' proscriptions are seen as less severe; the second exemplum explicitly compares Marius with Sulla, "The odium of whose cruelty Marius lightens" (9.2.2: *Cuius tamen crudelitatis C. Marius invidiam levat*). This is faint praise, but Marius does manage to escape with mention of only two of his victims. Valerius is careful not to suggest the ongoing and culminating collapse of morals; he suppresses the customary praise of the ancients and despair for the present decline. Damasippus, in the following exemplum, is credited with but a single named murder (that of Carbo Arvina) though Valerius alludes to others ("the heads of the chiefs of state"). Scaevola the Pontifex was among these illustrious senatorial casualties; but Valerius has no time, it seems, for such details. He is moving away from the horrors of Roman examples. Thus, no Caesarians are mentioned by name in the fourth and final Roman example; instead Munatius Flaccus wreaks his cruelty on Caesar's Spanish sympathizers. At the head of the list of Rome's martyrs to foreign cruelty comes, naturally, Atilius Regulus. Hannibal and his outrages follow at 9.2.ext.2; Mithridates is next. The first three external examples simply offer the greatest villains Rome had known: the Carthaginians generally, Hannibal in particular, and then the man who was nearly a second Hannibal for the Romans, Mithridates.

After developing on these patriotic lines, the chapter turns to purely foreign examples. This Greek and barbarian material is more what one would expect: tales of tyrants and their loathsome tortures. Yet only the final two exempla (9.2.ext.10 and 11) lack a political context. This is significant, since the theme—*De crudelitate*—does not denote or presuppose this context, and yet, except for these final two, each case in this chapter is an act of war or of tyranny. Even in this last pair of examples, nations and not individuals are involved (the Etruscans and an unnamed tribe of barbarians). This is perfectly consistent with Valerius' patriotism: Rome is never faulted for national cruelty; the remaining nations of the world are all culpable. Positive praise of Rome is not possible in this chapter on cruelty; vituperation of Rome's enemies is. Thus, the ethnic "flaws" of the Carthaginians and the Greeks are paraded forth; Rome's cruelty is, in contrast, never national but individual, aberrant, and in decline. Consequently, Damasippus is not tied to a cause, that is, called a Marian; he seems by Valerius' account a solitary manifestation of vice. Even Munatius Flaccus is set at some distance from his proper faction: Valerius calls him "a more bitter than just defender of Pompey's name" (9.2.4: *Pompeiani nominis acrior quam probabilior defensor*). This slender comment rids Pompey of blame. Valerius, generally, prefers to exonerate by silence. Discussion of partisan politics might lead to questions of legitimacy of one-man rule in Rome but, more to the point, has nothing to do with "Cruelty." Further, such historical examination would only complicate the example and so undermine its validity as a moral or, as here, immoral type.

Sulla and Valerius' emphasis on him in this chapter are the exception that proves the rule. The variety and length of this exemplum are quite astonishing, but for all this detail of treatment no clear image of the partisans or the issues emerges. Valerius' introduction of Sulla is more elaborate than usual. First, he explains Sulla's fecundity for praise and blame. He continues by maintaining the essential divorce in the general's character: in military affairs he was a second Scipio, in civil another Hannibal (*dum quaerit victorias, Scipionem populo Romano, dum exercet, Hannibalem repraesentavit*). This antithetical representation may seem peculiar but is typical of Valerius. The reversals of customs or fortune have been replaced with schizophrenic historical exempla. Sulla the dissipated youth and Sulla the able general are no longer the contrast, but the manner of depiction is the same, again with no effort to explain the development or difference. A rhetoric communicating an antithesis over time has inspired Valerius' rhetoric of antithesis of domestic and foreign action. The picture created by Valerius from his historical sources remains simple and personal. The reader sees no development of character as he has seen no picture of factional strife; instead, one man follows two exempla.

Valerius' explanation by exemplum, by reference to Scipio and Hannibal, remains essentially unhistorical. This is all the more remarkable and a strong indication of Valerius' hand at work since the substance of this exemplum was lifted from Livy. The parallels of this passage and the epitome of Livy's book 88 are set forth in table 3.

First, some clarification or disclaimer is necessary to interpret and

TABLE 3. *Parallels between Valerius 9.2.11 and Livy 88*

VALERIUS	PERIOCHAE
a. L. Sulla . . . —egregie namque auctoritate nobilitatis defensa	Sulla Carbonem, eius exercitu ad Clusium ad Faventiam Fidentiamque caeso, Italia expulit . . . reciperataque republica
b. crudeliter totam urbem atque omnes Italiae partes civilis sanguinis fluminibus inundavit—	pulcherrimam victoriam crudelitate . . . inquinavit . . . urbem ac totam Italiam caedibus replevit
c. quattuor legiones contrariae partis fidem suam secutas in publica villa, quae in Martio campo erat, nequiquam fallacis dexterae misericordiam implorantes obtruncari iussit	octo milia dediticiorum in villa publica trucidavit
d. V milia Praenestinorum . . . cum abiectis armis humi corpora prostravissent, interficienda . . . curavit.	omnes Praenestinos inermes concidi iussit.
e. quattuor milia et DCC dirae proscriptionis edicto iugulatos in tabulas publicas retulit . . .	tabulam proscriptionis posuit
f. M. Mario praetore . . . non prior vita privavit quam oculos infelices erueret et singulas corporis partes confringeret.	Marium, senatorī ordinis virum, cruribus bracchiisque fractis auribus praesectis et oculis effossis necavit.

CANISIUS COLLEGE LIBRARY
BUFFALO, N.Y.

not to overemphasize this table. In the left column the order of Valerius' text has been followed; the right column has been arranged and selected solely to illustrate the (ultimately Livian) parallels. Much that is in the epitome is not in Valerius. The actual sequence of elements, in the story according to the *Periochae*, is: a, b to *inquinavit*, c, then the remainder of b, d, e, f. Thus the order of Livy (presuming the epitome preserves this) is the more natural, since, in narrative fashion, it follows chronology: Sulla's victories north of Rome (a), the cruel dispatch of the Samnites before the city (c), and then the civil atrocity—the proscriptions (b). Valerius has in typical wise compressed the introductory, historical material; the setting of the scene is achieved in a more compact, self-contained form. Instead of listing the battle sites and naming the defeated (and for this exemplum unimportant) Carbo, Valerius has replaced this and the concluding ablative absolute ("the Republic restored") with the vague though all-embracing "the authority of the nobility defended" (another ablative absolute). The compression worked on the Livian material is again evident in the introduction of the first instance of Sulla's cruelty. The epitome identified those Valerius is content to call "of opposing side" as "Samnites, who alone of the Italians had not yet laid down arms." Indeed, Valerius' has so effectively blurred the picture that the reader has no idea where the scene is taking place. Unlike Livy, who is narrating the final battle in a sequence of struggles and who places the contest before the very walls of Rome, Valerius has so stripped the episode of context that he must interrupt his story to orient the action and his reader: the villa, he says, was in the Campus Martius. All of this seems quite familiar—Valerius as usual abridging and splicing his model, occasionally falling into some difficulty from the ensuing obscurity. Valerius casts the slaughter of the Samnites into indirect speech; the verb required by such a subordination is imported from the subsequent sentence in Livy (*iussit*). Indirect discourse and a contamination of diction are joined, at the passage's end, by a third, characteristically Valerian feature: the gruesome details of the praetor M. Marius Gratidianus' torture, no doubt compressed by the epitomator, are rendered in full, periodic form. Valerius' sentence is no more graphic—indeed it is less specific—but is slower-moving, putting off death while piling torture upon torture.

This is the usual manner of Valerius' closure: the return to a high-flown rhetorical style signals the end of the exemplum.

This particular exemplum is exceptional in that it continues. Valerius tries to smooth over the digressive, disjointed, and extraordinary quality of his exemplum by personally entering the text: "I think that I am narrating what is barely credible." What does follow are two further incidents of Sulla's cruelty. Cicero too tells of Sulla's desecration of Marius' ashes (an event not found in the epitome of Livy) though the passage in the *Laws* (2.56) is not Valerius' model. The movement of the exemplum has to this point been straightforward: Valerius has culled material from a single, classical source. But the juncture, which may mark Valerius' turn to a different source, was bridged by the personal intervention of the author, while unity of theme and person buttresses the connection to the preceding episodes. Livy's words have provided the incidents for the greater part of this exemplum and the theme for the whole chapter. The chapter heading is to be found in Livy's text, for the epitome relates, "by cruelty, the greatest of any man, did Sulla defile the most beautiful victory."[35] This clause, with its joining of the abstract noun and the figure of Sulla, was surely Valerius' point of departure. One classical locus did not exhaust this theme's richness, and so Valerius has tacked on two additional deeds of cruelty.

In this chapter Valerius has treated the most difficult of his subjects, the horrors of Roman civil war. Elsewhere he apologizes for or excludes commemoration of these times. His chapter on triumphs (2.8), for example, refuses to list civil war victors. Notably, he does not altogether exclude the abuses of these times and the murders of the proscribed, but he does shape these stories so as to preclude comparison with the present. The times of Sulla have no link to more recent history, in particular to the proscriptions of the triumvirs. In this chapter the Romans

---

35. *Periochae* 88: *pulcherrimam victoriam crudelitate quanta in nullo hominum fuit, inquinavit.* Valerius' method of composition here is not unique. Reading Cicero's account of Sulla's approval of the rightful slaying of his nephew (*Pro Milone* 9), Valerius noted the abstract noun Cicero used for this event, employed this as his chapter heading (*De pudicitia*), and modeled his exemplum (6.1.12) on this passage.

remain innocent of cruelty. The agents of cruelty are foreign nations and individuals or aberrant individuals, like Sulla, animated by personal vice or enmity. The construction of his chapter is noteworthy for this control of subject and for the emphasis on Sulla as peak of Roman cruelty. Techniques of moralization and abstraction help to contain the material, to restrain it from spilling over to the present day. This peculiar rehabilitation avoids synthesis of character or period. Historical explanation and connection are not so much denied as replaced by rhetorical classification and transition.

Prooemia and the Reinforcement of Design

In combination with the chapter titles, the prooemia signal Valerius' design. The prooemia inform the material that they announce, since they both declare the change of topic and provide the new category, often in terms that echo and augment the chapter title. In addition, the language of the prooemia asserts continuity of general theme and of reading as they try to pull the reader along. Further, while they refer back to the general design, the prooemia to individual chapters reveal Valerius' specific concerns; in these introductions Valerius' apologies belie novel or problematic chapters. In these cases, Valerius' first-person assurances of importance and of relation are far more than a rhetorical technique that hopes to hold the reader or listener in a long, unsubordinated series of subjects.

At 6.2, for instance, Valerius notes the ambivalent nature of his present subject, "Liberty" (freedom of speech, independence of action).

> Lady Liberty, whom I should not call but still could not bar, comes of her own accord, tried and proved by audacious words and deeds. Midway virtue and vice, when she has restrained herself, let me praise her; when she has spilled over where she ought not, she deserves censure. She finds greater favor in the ears of the mob than approval in the eyes of the wise, seeing as the indulgence of others saves her more often than her own foresight. But since our proposal covers the departments of human life, in keeping with our program let this be recounted with its proper assessment. (6.2.pr.)[36]

36. *Libertatem autem vehementis spiritus dictis pariter et factis testatam ut non in-*

The stated difficulty with this quality is that it is as liable to be a vice as a virtue (*inter virtutem vitiumque posita*). Further, it appeals to the mob, not to the wise. Valerius finally justifies the inclusion of this subject by reference to his general program: "But since our proposal covers the departments of human life, in keeping with our program let this be recounted with its proper assessment." Are his chapters then to be taken as the various departments of human life? Perhaps this is why his material seems difficult to contain; perhaps, much like Pliny the Elder in his massive *Natural History,* Valerius is presenting a totality that can barely be contained by words. Yet whatever the affinities of Valerius' and Pliny's works, certainly Valerius' cannot be said to represent and reflect the parts of human life. Valerius is not aiming at an encyclopedic totality as Pliny, at least, would understand it. For "human life" has a much narrower meaning here. Valerius is intent on representing the precedents for civic life, for an audience that would participate in Roman rule or in declamatory display of the republican traditions. Freedom of speech is a republican tradition even if the sentiments and criticisms expressed by the republican Romans of the exempla were no longer possible in Tiberian Rome.

These chapters on civic setbacks and on freedom of speech can constitute only problematic paradigms for Valerius and his readers. The republican jurist A. Cascellius (6.2.12) refuses to legitimize the triumvirs' actions with his legal authority and, when warned by his friends not to speak so freely of Julius Caesar's times, answers that he has two sources for his freedom of speech: old age and childlessness. Very much like 2.6.5 (Cato's dismissal as evidence of a letter of recommendation from the contemporary autocrat, Pompey), this story of a slight toward Julius Caesar can no longer apply directly to Roman life; they may be parables but not paradigms. No longer to be understood as the pattern for direct imitation, such stories are on their way to becoming antiquarian curiosities. Clearly troubled by these famous liberties, Va-

---

vitaverim, ita ultro venientem non excluserim. quae inter virtutem vitiumque posita, si salubri modo se temperavit, laudem: si, quo non debuit, profudit, reprehensionem meretur. ac vulgi sic auribus gratior, quam sapientissimi cuiusque animo probabilior est utpote frequentius aliena venia quam sua providentia tuta. sed quia humanae vitae partes persequi propositum est, nostra fide propria aestimatione referatur.

lerius has inserted a paradigm for judgment into the proem of "Liberty." He has defined laudable liberty and the reverse and likewise contrasted the judgment of the crowd and of the wise.

A perilous subject seems to require the careful instruction of interpretation and redefinition of audience. As so often Valerius' rhetoric provides the correct reaction, dictating rather than evoking the emotions and response of the audience. Valerius' anecdotes quite obviously commemorate correct behavior and become problematic when the inherited paradigms jar with contemporary codes. The ideologically correct behavior of a society's subordinate members is an increasing concern of a society undergoing not revolution but accommodation to a new order. Valerius of course tells stories that had been told for centuries. The presence and prominence of stories that celebrate social concord or subordination are not striking. For example, the obvious function of anecdotes about old-time Roman women, whether they are told by Valerius, Varro, or Pliny the Elder, remains the commemoration of behavior deemed ideal and has next to nothing to do with contemporary practice and little to do with social change. In a remarkable proem to the last chapter of the sixth book, which follows immediately two chapters that recount the proper behavior of wives toward husbands and slaves toward masters (6.7 and 8), Valerius reveals his and his intended audience's more particular anxieties.

A realization that outstanding men of old underwent reversal of character and fortune can add great self-confidence to and remove much despair from the spirits of men, whether we look on our own status or that of our neighbors. For when we see, by observing the fortunes of others, fame and distinction have emerged from a humble and contemptible beginning, how should we not always think that better is in store for ourselves? Remembering it is foolish to presentence ourselves to perpetual misery and to exchange for despair a hope (which should be entertained even when dubious) that is at times certain. (6.9.pr.)[37]

37. *Multum animis hominum et fiduciae adicere et sollicitudinis detrahere potest morum ac fortunae in claris viris recognita mutatio, sive nostros status sive proximorum [ingenia] contemplemur: nam cum aliorum fortunas spectando ex condicione abiecta*

Valerius' explanation for the inclusion of this chapter on the whims of Fortune posits the contrast between the *clari viri* of the example and us. The readers' ("our") envy is introduced as a theme with *sive nostros status, sive proximorum contemplemur.* The envy is not directed against the famous men of old but against contemporaries whose talents, but notably not birth, have raised them above "our" status. The visual quality of this resentment is suggestive: it is public recognition, perhaps the symbols of office and rank, that the readers of low station covet. In the chapter on "Electoral Defeats" (7.5), too, the *clari viri* are contrasted with "us." Valerius draws a general moral that we should accomplish by patience what we miss by *gratia,* "favor." This is the favor others should grant us as the people should have elected Cato (7.5.6). The gap between birth and achievement is becoming a paradigm for ambitious men of a status quite removed from Cato's. The opposition of the famous men of old and men of the present day is unusual because it is not simply a *laudatio temporis acti,* which is what a reader of Cato the Elder or Cicero or Livy expects. But the issue in Valerius is not a contrast of morals but of status. Specifically, Valerius is concerned with his generation and himself becoming "clarus," acting in the fashion memorialized by earlier Romans of noble status and being recognized as their peer or descendant. Cato's story recounted honor denied to status. Valerius has used this as consolation for honor denied to talent. In particular, the frustration of Cato as candidate for office has undergone a metamorphosis. The story of achievement (election to the praetorship) denied to birth and moral worth (the noble Stoic) has been reinterpreted in terms pertinent to Valerius; it becomes a story of recognition denied to achievement. Birth is the element being elided or reconstituted as Valerius communicates the birthright of the Roman upper classes—the aristocratic culture founded on the *imagines* of the nobles—to the nonaristocrat. Quite revealingly, Valerius has voiced his hopes, most clearly and at greatest length, for a change in status in the chapter that immediately followed "The Fidelity of Slaves toward Their Masters." Like the faithful slave he advocates patience and condemns

---

atque contempta emersisse claritatem videamus, quid aberit quin et ipsi meliora de nobis semper cogitemus, memores stultum esse perpetuae infelicitatis se praedamnare spemque, quae etiam incerta recte fovetur, interdum certam in desperationem convertere?

the sources of illegitimacy (9.15, "The Lowborn Who Tried through Deceit to Enter Others' Families"). Birth has not been forgotten; it worries the men of talent who seek recognition from men of birth—directly as their patrons and indirectly as the font of their paradigms.

Valerius has composed *Memorable Deeds and Sayings* by a process of association. Instances of a particular abstract quality, provided they have as pedigree a classical source, are grouped together. These groupings are in themselves most important for understanding Valerius' project and audience. This is not the work of a haphazard compiler or of an overly "rhetorical" plagiarist. Valerius' reading and rewriting of traditional culture reflects not only one man's knowledge of the Republic's past in the early first century A.D. or what declaimers found paradigmatic from the extant knowledge of that past but the constitution of that paradigmatic knowledge. The present chapter has investigated the categories and relations of Valerius' associations. In the next chapter, Valerius' relation to his sources will illumine the preferences and patterns of his reading and also his peculiar use of the classic Latin texts. This more exact study of Valerius' reading is the necessary prolegomena to the analysis of his reconstitution of the past, which for Valerius involves both the appropriation of republican history and the stylistic emulation of canonical literary passages.

3 Sources and Reading

Reading, Writing, and "Originality"

The Picture of the Ancient Research Scholar

How did Valerius assemble this collection? The picture of the research scholar in antiquity is not flattering. Our picture of research methods remains hazy, and skeptical; it is most influenced by two criteria: the supposed difficulty of reading[1] and the alleged preference of reading to any form of autopsy. This skepticism is nowhere stronger than in the field of ancient historiography, whose modern study begins with analysis of the reliability of the *logoi* of the first two major historians, Herodotus and Thucydides. Analysis of reported speech and of the rhetorics alleging autopsy and the direct retailing of word and deed remains the preoccupation of classical historiographers. In Valerius' case extreme skepticism raised doubt that an otherwise unknown author, whose versions of anecdotes did not exactly follow the Augustan and late republican classics, could have produced this work; the solution was to posit a lost intermediate source that had essentially done Valerius' work for him. His contribution was to obscure the relation to the ultimate sources by his introduction of "rhetoric." The falsity of this hypothesis has been adequately demonstrated, but this scholarly fancy has more interest than the mistaken conjecture of an outmoded methodology; it attests the reluctance to believe in autopsy, the examination of individual authors and works, and the pre-

---

1. Reynolds and Wilson (1974, 4–5) describe the difficulty of the ancient papyrus roll (minimal punctuation, no indices, scribal errors, the task of covering and uncovering a particular passage). Notably, Cicero only complained (to Atticus) of the copyists' errors. These alone slaves' labor could not easily mitigate, though the learned Tiro must have been considerable help.

dilection to see composition as a scribal exercise, with one particular source and little extraneous or nonliterary influences.

In Valerius' case a modified skepticism is warranted: he has not seen every source he cites yet has clearly read widely in the Latin prose authors. The difficulty of reading in the ancient world is an argument often used to suggest that an author has from memory the material he quotes. With no index a reader could not easily find the passage that interested him and further would have to unroll the papyrus *volumen*.

We do however have a picture of the ancient research scholar at work. Pliny the Younger tells us that his uncle wasted no time; he read or was read to continuously; what interested him he had a slave jot down.[2] The crucial element of this evidence is not the eccentricity the nephew strives to commemorate but slave labor. The uncle's act of scholarship, which involved so many books, was not the work of one man but of a coterie of readers and notetakers. Scholars have heretofore conjectured about the system Valerius followed without taking into account that he may not have written a word but, like Virgil and Pliny, dictated his composition. This would then require neither a memory so powerful as to recall all of Livy and most of Cicero nor the duplicity of Valerius copying out a prior collection. It would explain how Valerius has at times combined sources in the same exemplum; and though it is not necessary to imagine that one man could not have done the work, the theory of collaborative effort, besides being in accord with the little known of scholarship at Rome, explains how a series of texts could be conveniently read and their versions then compared. It need not imply a composition of a single moment. Valerius was familiar with the needs of speakers and with the works of Cicero and Livy. A list of categories, the chapter titles, would precede the reading or more likely rereading of the texts. Valerius was not working from scratch; declamation and the rhetorical schools were an oral tradition of category and instance. He had to take these, the various dreams inserted into speeches, the severe behavior of old Roman fathers conjured up in a set piece on the decline of morals, and make of them a systematic, complete work. The augmentation of category and instance required the direct inspection

2. *Ep.* 3.5. Mejer (1978, 16–29) has discussed the ancient technique of excerpting and its consequences for composition.

of Cicero's or Livy's wording and entailed the deliberate variation of their style.

Traditional Approaches to the Problem of "Originality": Valerius as Copybook

Scholars and scholarship on Valerius Maximus have, for the most part, been devoted to assessing his sources. This is unfortunate, for it has meant not the belittling of Valerius, but the miscasting of this author and the misunderstanding of his materials, interest, and manner of composition. Moreover, the only rival to source criticism among Valerian experts has always been textual criticism. This rival too has not fared well. Since Kempf's misunderstanding of the stemma and of the importance of various manuscripts and his numerous errors of collation, the state of the text has not been significantly improved, with the sole and notable exception of C. J. Carter's dissertation on the manuscript tradition.[3] Meanwhile, the vast effort expended on Valerius by the avid investigators of sources had until the time of Helm advanced little beyond the contributions of the nameless scribes and early scholars who, in the margins of manuscripts, jotted down the parallel passages of Livy and Cicero, Plutarch and Cassius Dio. Helm, the leading expert on Valerius in the first half of this century, was preoccupied in refuting a misguided theory, still assumed occasionally today, of a lost source between Valerius and his Augustan models.[4]

Consequently, before any further consideration of the design and purpose of *Memorable Deeds and Sayings,* the chief premises of the source critics must be challenged. Again and again, a single source has been posited for a single exemplum; then arguments are advanced either to demonstrate a close verbal dependence or to reveal variation of event or style, which indicates a different source. The possibility of contamination, from another written source or from the halls of declamation or from general knowledge, is seldom considered. Even more infrequent is discussion of the use of a book by Valerius. I shall argue that

3. Carter 1968.

4. Helm in two studies (Helm 1939 and 1940) attempted to refute Klotz's theory of a lost intermediary (Klotz 1909). Klotz persisted (1942).

in order to understand Valerius' composition we must first investigate his range and pattern of reading. Potential sources must not simply be canvassed, but the actual use of individual authors and particular books—*volumina* read by Valerius—must be examined in the various chapters of *Memorable Deeds and Sayings*. The chapter and not the single exemplum will be seen the more natural focus of research, as it was no doubt for Valerius.[5] This examination discerns in Valerius' composition a much more fluid and shifting process than the older source critics imagined. One author may provide material for a chapter, but another's treatment of an individual figure or event may have greater appeal to Valerius, for reason of detail or style. Valerius' composition is ultimately the result of wide reading and of wide listening; not only Seneca took from the declamation hall a stock of characters, events, twists of plot, and *sententiae*.

Valerius gives two direct indications of his reading; his preface refers to "illustrious authors" whom he has read to spare his reader the toil, while scattered throughout the nine books are references to individual authors (see table 4). The Greek references outweigh the Latin (eleven to ten), but no one should be misled into believing Valerius actually used Greek sources more than Roman, or for that matter that he used them much at all. The reference to Plato, borrowed from Cicero,[6] is the sole Greek citation outside of the thirteenth and fourteenth chapters of book 8. Moreover, a mere count of authors tells nothing: to consider only the author first cited, Valerius has clearly lifted the name of Coelius Antipater from the pages of Cicero (*De div.* 1.56). Scholars have long distrusted Valerius' citations of authority, but the more serious charge of plagiarism no doubt reflects a little of the frustration they felt in not finding more of the junior annalists, for example, embedded in the exempla of Valerius Maximus. In fact, his references to others

5. See chapter 2. Of the source critics Bosch (1929, 5) especially sought to derive entire chapters from earlier works.

6. Valerius has not taken the myth of Er from its proper place in the tenth book on Plato's *Republic* (614b). Verbal parallel (e.g., Cicero's *qui rogo impositus*) demonstrates that Valerius' 1.8.ext.1 is drawn from Cicero's *Republic* (6.3.1). Although Cicero's work is fragmentary and Er is not mentioned by name here, he is clearly Cicero's subject (see Macrobius, *Comm.* 1.1.9).

are not outright lies. They are simply misleading: like the "borrowed" footnote, they suggest a familiarity with the stated source. With a reference, Valerius is not saying "I have read Coelius," only "Coelius says."

If the list of authorities cited by Valerius (and casuistry in his defense) does not inspire much confidence, the parade of authors proposed by

TABLE 4. *Valerius' References to Classical Authors*

LATIN AUTHORS	GREEK AUTHORS
Direct references	
Coelius Antipater (1.7.6)	Alexander Polyhistor (8.13.ext.7)
Cato the Elder (8.1.2)	Aristoxenus Musicus (8.13.ext.3)
Cicero (8.10.3, 8.13.ext.1)	Ctesius of Cnidos (8.13.ext.5)
C. Gracchus (9.5.ext.4)	Damastes (8.13.ext.6)
Livy (1.8.ext.19)	Hellanicus (8.13.ext.6)
Asinius Pollio (8.13.ext.4)	Herodotus (8.13.ext.5)
Munatius Rufus (4.3.2)	Plato (1.8.ext.1)
Pomponius Rufus (4.4.pref.)	Theodectes of Phaselis (8.14.ext.3)
M. Scaurus (4.4.11)	Theophanes of Mytiline (8.14.3)
Varro (3.2.24)	Theopompus (8.13.ext.5, 8.14.ext.5)
	Xenophon of Lampsacus (8.13.ext.7)
Attributed by modern scholars	
Valerius Antias	Diodorus Siculus
Verrius Flaccus	
C. Julius Hyginus	
Cornelius Nepos	
Valerius Messalla	
Sallust	
Velleius Paterculus	
Pompeius Trogus	
A collection of *exempla externa*	
An epitome of Livy	
A list of long-lived men	

critics is similarly confusing. Livy and Cicero have been declared his main source; their use has been categorically denied; reasserted; and, in the dissertation of F. R. Bliss, systematically propounded. In addition to the authors named by Valerius, scholars have proposed several sources (see table 4). These names are all but irrelevant if the thesis first advanced by Klotz, and championed by Bosch, is true. Klotz denied that Valerius had used Cicero and Livy. Discrepancies in, for instance, Pliny the Elder's and Valerius' account of a story were attributed to a lost source that had drawn its material from Livy and Cicero. Bosch maintained that there were two collection books—one that Cicero himself had used and one dated to Augustan times, which he tentatively declared was the work not of Verrius Flaccus (*sic* Rabenhorst) but Hyginus. Klotz had already, in his studies of 1909 and 1942, credited Valerius' variations to lost handbooks of rhetorical exempla.[7] Klotz marked an unfortunate extreme in source criticism, but at the same time he represented a new perception of Valerius' difference. Earlier scholars had labored to demonstrate Valerius' dependence on Livy and Cicero, but Klotz's basic observation that Valerius is not simply transcribing Cicero and Livy is undeniable. Upon this observation the peculiarities of his school of criticism took over, and any differences of content or style were explained not in terms of a particular man writing in Rome in the days of Tiberius but by means of the ahistorical vacuum of model and apograph. Klotz did more than label Valerius' innovations and departures the debased peculiarities of a Silver style. His work should not be summarily dismissed even if it is wrongheaded, for he was a keen discerner of variation.

7. Bosch (1929, 10) declares his presupposition magisterially "die Quellen einer Exempelsammlung sind vornehmlich ältere Exempelsammlungen." After demonstrating, as he believes, the common use of a lost source by Valerius and Cicero (e.g., p. 6 citing 6.1.1 and 6.1.2), Bosch devoted his second chapter (13–56) to reconstructing the lost collection of Augustan times. After discounting Rabenhorst's suggestion of Verrius Flaccus as the author of the lost collection (43), Bosch supports the candidacy of Hyginus (first alleged by Klotz). Helm strove to disentangle the web of their arguments, though he too resisted the possibility that Valerius was Pliny's or Plutarch's or Lactantius' source—that is, he too was bent on the reconstruction of lost versions.

In coming to his conclusions, Klotz did however make errors. In addition to a fundamentally flawed approach—seeking a separate source for every variant of information and diction—Klotz's thesis was built on uncertain practice. A comparison of Valerius with a later author (in his first article, primarily with Seneca the Younger) was said to demonstrate that Valerius and the later work, since they were closer to each other than either is to Livy, derived from a lost common source. This particular methodology made two false suppositions: first, that Valerius was not using Livy; second, that Seneca was not using Valerius. Klotz's method, for example, followed from the observation that Valerius and Seneca had the same sequence of exempla: Aemilius Paullus, Horatius Pulvillus, and Marcius Rex (Valerius 5.10.1–3; Seneca *Dial.* 6.13 names the first two and presents the situation of the last; compare *Ep.* 99.6). When in this and similar cases Seneca's diction seemed distant from Valerius', the lost source was responsible. Klotz began his first article with the case of Horatius Pulvillus, who never flinched—so Livy, Valerius, and Seneca tell—when his son's death was told him as he dedicated the temple of Capitoline Jupiter.

> The temple of Jupiter on the Capitoline had not yet been dedicated. The consuls Valerius and Horatius drew lots to decide who was to be the dedicator. The lot fell to Horatius; Publicola set out for the war against Veii. The dependents of Valerius resented, far more than is right, that Horatius should dedicate so famous a temple. After they had tried to block the dedication by every means and all in vain, while the consul was holding the temple column and reciting the prayer to the gods, they brought the bad news that his son was dead and since he was in mourning he could not dedicate the temple. History does not hand down nor can we easily determine whether Horatius disbelieved the news or was simply of an iron constitution. Unmoved from his duty by this report he ordered only that the body be buried; holding the temple column he concluded the prayer and dedicated the temple. (Livy 2.8.6–8)[8]

8. *Nondum dedicata erat in Capitolio Iovis aedes; Valerius Horatiusque consules sortiti uter dedicaret. Horatio sorte evenit: Publicola ad Veientium bellum profectus. aegrius quam dignum erat tulere Valeri necessarii dedicationem tam incliti templi Horatio dari.*

Horatius Pulvillus, as pontifex dedicating the temple of Jupiter Optimus Maximus on the Capitoline, with his hand upon the temple column heard amid the solemn recitation that his son was dead. Neither did he lift his hand from the temple column lest he interrupt the dedication of so great a temple nor did he change his demeanor from that of public rite to private grief lest he seem to have discharged the role of father rather than priest. (Valerius 5.10.1)[9]

The pontifex Pulvillus, whose son's death was announced while he held the temple column and dedicated the Capitoline, has secured that Greece may not glory too much in that father who in mid sacrifice, on the announcement of his son's death, only ordered the flute player to be still and removed the garland from his head, then finished the rite in proper, full fashion. Pulvillus feigned that he had not heard and took up the solemn recital of the pontifical chant without a groan interrupting the prayer and with Jupiter propitiated on the mention of his son's name. Do you think there ought to be some limit to his grief whose first moment and first attack did not lead a father from the public altars and the sacred service? . . . Nevertheless on returning home he wept and cried out, but once the customary rites had been paid the dead, he returned to that Capitoline demeanor. (Seneca, *Dialogus* 6.13.1–2)[10]

---

id omnibus modis impedire conati, postquam alia frustra temptata erant, postem iam tenenti consuli foedum inter precationem deum nuntium incutiunt, mortuum eius filium esse, funestaque familia dedicare eum templum non posse. non crediderit factum an tantum animo roboris fuerit, nec traditur certum nec interpretatio est facilis. nihil aliud ad eum nuntium a proposito aversus quam ut cadaver efferri iuberet, tenens postem precationem peragit et dedicat templum.

9. *Horatius Pulvillus, cum in Capitolio Iovi optimo maximo aedem pontifex dedicaret interque nuncupationem sollemnium verborum postem tenens mortuum esse filium suum audisset, neque manum a poste removit, ne tanti templi dedicationem interrumperet, neque vultum a publica religione ad privatum dolorem deflexit, ne patris magis quam pontificis partes egisse videretur.*

10. *Ne nimis admiretur Graecia illum patrem qui in ipso sacrificio nuntiata filii morte tibicinem tantum tacere iussit et coronam capiti detraxit, cetera rite perfecit, Pulvillus effecit pontifex, cui postem tenenti et Capitolium dedicanti mors filii nuntiata est. quam*

Klotz has chosen a case where the lines of dependence are unusually unclear.[11] As if he were seeking to isolate a family of manuscripts, he cites a common mistake—the appellation of Horatius as pontifex, not consul—to group Valerius and Seneca together against Livy. But Livy is not so easily excluded. Valerius' simplification of the events is typical; the number of agents is reduced (no mention of Horatius' fellow consul Valerius and his henchman) and all reference to factional politics and to any doubt about Horatius' motivation (*non crederit . . . fuerit*) is missing. True historical context and variety of interpretation do not suit a patriotic, rhetorical exemplum. The point to be illustrated must be clear; Valerius' rubric (Horatius' fortitude) allows no ambiguity.[12] The detail of the disqualification of a priest for reason of domestic pollution will not be included by Valerius. His use of Livy cannot be denied, therefore, because there is found wanting a complexity of plot or motive that is proper to historical narrative but foreign to a historical exemplum. Klotz, however, simply seized upon the "mistake" of calling the consul pontifex so as to deny use of Livy. Valerius may be faulted for historical error here, perhaps for a slip of memory, but his reading of Livy is clear. Whole phrases from Livy are reused or rearranged to make one grand sentence (e.g., *dedicata . . . in Captolio Iovis aedes . . . Horatius . . . postem . . . tenenti*). *Nuncupationem sollemnium verborum* is Va-

---

ille exaudisse dissimulavit et sollemnia pontificii carminis verba concepit gemitu non interrumpente precationem et ad filii sui nomen Iove propitiato. putasne eius luctus aliquem finem esse debere, cuius primus dies et primus impetus ab altaribus publicis et fausta nuncupatione non abduxit patrem? . . . idem tamen ut redit domum, et implevit oculos et aliquas voces flebiles misit; sed peractis quae mos erat praestare defunctis ad Capitolinum illum redit vultum.

11. This example was not idly selected: Klotz was attempting to refute Schendel, who had used it to argue Seneca's dependence on Livy (H. Schendel, "Quibus auctoribus Romanis L. Annaeus Seneca in rebus patriis usus sit" [dissertation, Gryphiae, 1908] cited in Klotz 1909, 198). Helm, in refuting Klotz by advancing the case for Cicero's *Consolatio*, followed the observation of Krieger and especially the detailed arguments of Münzer (Helm 1939, 132, acknowledging Baiter and Kaiser *Cic.* vol. II, 74; Krieger 1888, 26; and Münzer 1963, 383).

12. The appeal to the schools of rhetoric of this sort of story, which pitted public and private ethics against each other, is clear from the popularity of the Torquati and the Horatii.

lerius' rather vague if high-sounding variation for *precationem deum*.
Livy's question, *non crediderit factum an tantum animo roboris fuerit, nec
traditur certum nec interpretatio est facilis,* has been answered by Valerius'
chapter heading, *De parentibus, qui obitum liberorum forti animo tulerunt,*
and by the wording of his preface, *qui mortem aequo animo tolerarunt.*
The significant differences between Livy and Valerius, which Klotz
deemed so obvious as not to merit discussion, are the results of Valerius'
refashioning of an event into an exemplum.

Helm, though the first to take issue with Klotz's specific conclusion
here and with his general thesis of a lost collection book, shared Klotz's
belief that Livy had not been used for the story of Horatius Pulvillus.
His solution was to posit another lost source. The argument is more
convincing, in part no doubt because, unlike a hypothetical collection
book that has affected no other author, the source proposed is an in-
fluential work and a major loss to Latin letters, the *Consolatio* of Cicero.[13] Like Klotz, Helm has here relied on the observation of the same
sequence of exempla in Valerius and a later source. Klotz had used this
technique to assert that parallel series in Valerius and Seneca pointed
to the original order in the lost collection book. Helm as well denied
the use of Valerius by the later author but substituted the *Consolatio* for
the supposed work of Hyginus.

Following Krieger and Münzer, Helm attributed the sequence of the
three fathers bereaved but ungrieving—Aemilius Paullus, Horatius
Pulvillus, and Marcius Rex—to Cicero's *Consolatio*. The evidence for
this claim is the testimony of Cicero himself and of Jerome. In the *Tusculans* (3.70) Cicero names as fathers who did not grieve for their sons
Q. Maximus, L. Paulus, and M. Cato and then adds "and others of the
same sort whom we collected in the *Consolation*" (*quales reliqui, quos in
Consolatione collegimus*). Jerome, in a passage that names as his authority
the *Consolatio* (*Ep.* 60.5), begins his series of bereaved fathers with a
brief description of Horatius Pulvillus; second is a brief description of
L. Paulus and last, in a *praeteritio*, the names of several others, including
Maximus, Cato, and Marcius.[14] This is the clear and direct evidence
that Cicero wrote of Horatius in the *Consolatio*.

13. Helm 1939, 132.
14. Jerome, *Ep.* 60.5: *Pulvillus Capitolium dedicans mortuum, ut nuntiabatur,*

What Helm has failed to note is that the notice in Jerome, admittedly very condensed, is in direct contradiction to the version of Valerius and Seneca. These two authors, like Livy, do not dwell on the son's burial with father absent. Indeed, Seneca implies the opposite: Horatius returned home, grieved, and performed the customary rites for the dead. From the slender evidence of Jerome (*Pulvillus . . . filium . . . iussit . . . sepeliri, L. Paulus . . . inter duorum exequias filiorum*) and Cicero (who in the *Tusculans* reports the series, beginning *qualis fuit Q. Maximus efferens filium consularem*), the *Consolatio* seems to have emphasized the moment of the funeral. Perhaps Cicero wrote as if bracing himself for Tullia's ceremony.

Elsewhere, Seneca, like Jerome, refers to the long string of such consolatory exempla (*Ep.* 99.6). Here Seneca too sees father and funeral as the important elements; in a *praeteritio* he classifies these exempla thus: "There are countless cases of fathers who endured the deaths of their grown children without shedding a tear and who returned from the funeral to the senate's or some other public or private business."[15] Valerius' and Seneca's stories have no mention of the order for burial, although Livy does relate the father's command. Seneca's departure from this is, as we shall see, a response to Valerius' rhetorical closure and is, in its emphasis on the tears and wailing of the bereaved, quite contrary to Cicero's purposes.

To posit Cicero's *Consolatio* as Valerius' model raises additional difficulties. The discrepancies of Valerius' and Livy's accounts, which I have argued are a consequence (in part) of the streamlining of plot for a declamatory illustration, would by Helm's thesis (as well as by Klotz's and Bosch's) be the result of a different source. Could Valerius, however, have taken the essentials of the story from Cicero and modified these to produce the present exemplum? Possibly, but the strongest ar-

---

subito filium se iussit absente sepeliri; L. Paulus septem diebus inter duorum exequias filiorum triumphans urbem ingressus est. praetermitto Maximos Catones Gallos Pisones Brutos Scaevolas Metellos Scauros Marcios Crassos Marcellos atque Aufidios, quorum non minor in luctu quam in bellis virtus fuit et quorum orbitates in Consolationis libro Tullius explicavit.

15. *innumerabilia sunt exempla eorum qui liberos iuvenes sine lacrimis extulerint, qui in senatum aut in aliquod publicum officium a rogo redierint aut statim aliud egerint.*

gument remains that Valerius has followed Livy, for Valerius' account parallels Livy's in ways more revealing than an occasional correspondence of diction. Livy's sequence of narrative events (the successive elements of the story) has been followed but with telling omissions, and his phrasing and diction (the verbal structure or sequence) have been followed but with characteristic transformations.

This positive evidence should not be set aside on the hope of rediscovery of a fragment of the *Consolatio*. One can only speculate about this lost version, but Helm's contention that it was responsible for Valerius' exemplum seems unlikely. The absence of the factional partisans, the *necessarii* as Livy calls them, is hardly credible in Cicero, who at the time of composition was much in need of Horatius' philosophical equanimity in the face of personal bereavement and political attack. Horatius, victim of private loss and of the partisans of his political rival, was an appealing and consoling precedent for Cicero. Cicero's treatment of Horatius in the *Consolatio* may well not have fit Valerius' purposes. If it was one in a string of exempla, it may have been too short, and the (reconstructed) emphasis on the private occasion of burial did not accord with the aims of the declamatory author who wanted above all the antithesis of private and public behavior. Only with this emphasis would the reversal of expectation be set in a novel sphere: Horatius is no longer simply an exemplary sufferer (preferring fortitude to grief) but an exemplary patriot (the priest who prefers *patria* to *familia*). Livy's history provided the inspiration for this transformation.

Apparently, then, Valerius found a sequence of exempla in Cicero but has followed only the sequence and not the version. This sort of *contaminatio* he practices elsewhere as well; the direct influence of the *Consolatio* has, therefore, been overstated. From its supposed use by both Valerius and Seneca, the relationship of these two authors has been misrepresented, and as a consequence a paradigm was established by which it was possible to treat Seneca's material as independent evidence for lost sources. Horatius Pulvillus provided a case study with an extant parallel (Livy). The thicket of difficulties grows denser when no parallel passage survives. Surprisingly, this has often emboldened the suggestions and reconstructions of scholars. The case of Aemilius Paullus, publicly unmoved by the death of his sons, offered just such a freedom to the source reconstructors. The speech of Aemilius Paullus in

Valerius Maximus is important for our study as a test of such methodologies and more essentially as an index to the hazards of alleging Valerius' differences as evidence of a lost source. Münzer's arguments, for it is this scholar's authority that emboldened Helm to make his claims, must be reconsidered.

In an appendix to his magnum opus, *Römische Adelsparteien und Adelsfamilien,* Münzer had reconstructed the historical allusions in Cicero's *Consolatio.* His identification of the "historiographical version" of the careers of various characters and consequently the particular written source followed by Valerius is of fundamental importance for the present question. As has already been mentioned, evidence culled from Cicero, Valerius, Seneca, and Jerome establishes the presence and implies the sequence of Horatius Pulvillus, Aemilius Paullus, and Marcius Rex in the *Consolatio.* This same evidence suggests, however, something further: this is all very familiar material; in short, it has become commonplace illustration. Thus it is no accident that *praeteritio* is the recurrent figure that presents these names.[16] Seneca calls such exempla "innumerable" both in the *Consolatio ad Marciam* (6.14.1) and at *Epistles* 99.6. Similarly, Cicero himself had abridged his list of bereaved fathers in the *Tusculans* (3.70) by allusion to the *Consolatio.* Innumerable examples, examples that can be known by allusion, are those held in common memory. In writing the *Tusculans* Cicero clearly did not need to check his *Consolatio,* nor did his reader. This means that—unlike what has been implied by this discussion of scholarly issues, at least so far— the choices for Valerius' source should not be formulated as a clear-cut alternative, Cicero or Livy. Indeed, the very abundance and familiarity of famous fathers bereaved require, if one wished to write at any length, a certain injection of novelty. The commonplace could not simply be retailed, especially to an audience educated and experienced in declamation; it demanded either an apology for its inclusion, an obliqueness of reference or a full-scale figure such as *praeteritio,* or embellishment, some novel treatment. The lost version of Cicero's *Consolatio* would not have held the same fascination for Valerius as it does for the scholar. Valerius had heard Horatius inserted into many speeches.

16. For example, Jerome: *praetermitto* (*Ep.* 60.5).

The identification of a source for Valerius should not be seen as the solution to a problem but as an aid to the understanding of his composition. Undeniably Valerius has read Cicero and indeed the *Consolatio,* but in the case of a lost source more exact conclusions resist investigation. Aemilius Paullus, for example, gives in Valerius' next exemplum a speech that Seneca (*Dial.* 6.13) has not followed, but caution is needed here. One cannot conclude from this that Seneca has or has not read Valerius. Without dilating on ancient authors' freedom in reporting historical speeches, it is clear that in this particular instance the schools are again an essential influence. For Seneca has just reported (6.13) the case of an anonymous Greek father who finished his sacrifice, though his son's death was announced to him. This is a clear foil for Horatius Pulvillus and the patriotic transition from Greece to Rome. Just as clearly, such anonymous fathers are not matters of historical record but the creations of rhetorical exercises. So Valerius at 5.9.4, immediately preceding Horatius, had spoken of an anonymous father's moderation toward a suspected son. This exemplum is foreign to Cicero's purpose in the *Consolatio,* but the juncture of anonymous father and a most famous Roman seems to have influenced Seneca. Seneca has used Valerius. And Valerius? He has used or remembered a series of fathers employed by Cicero in his *Consolatio.* His more immediate model, where this is capable of demonstration (the case of Horatius Pulvillus), was Livy. And the commonplace quality of these famous stories should make the scholar reticent to declare the particular lost source known to him "the source."

The Roman historian may have to be even more wary when comparing Seneca and Valerius. Their "versions" of historical figures, once we realize they do not represent uncontaminated traditions, can only be compared with justifiable suspicion—if the aim is to reconstruct prosopography. As with Horatius Pulvillus, the figure of Aemilius Paullus is complicated by the loss of an original source, Polybius, whose account of the triumph of the victor at Pydna is missing, a lacuna in book 30. Polybius may have been Cicero's source; he was not Valerius'. About the time of his triumph Paullus had lost two of his sons. Quite possibly, Valerius took this material from Cicero's *Consolatio,* for he is fond of adapting direct speech from Livy and Cicero; he does not seem to invent *dicta* altogether. The differences in Valerius' and Seneca's treatments of Aemilius Paullus are instructive. Seneca's is by far the fuller account; he names Paullus' opponent Perses and is more concerned, in general, in describing the historical setting. In contrast, Valerius has only the barest essentials of the story; he has focused his attention on those elements most suited for generalizing, rhetorical embellishment. So, unlike Seneca, he does not identify the adopted sons; the dead, the pathetic need only be generic, and as a consequence historical context is restricted to a brief introduction to the speech itself. Valerius seems in a certain haste to reach this speech. The final, pointed antithesis—the rhetorical flourish, where Paullus voices thanks that calamity has come to his family and not to the Roman people—is what this incident has to offer to Valerius: "that you might grieve for my misfortune rather than I groan for yours."

Comparison of this speech with Seneca's or Livy's reporting will not reveal an archetype, since Valerius is relating a different portion of the speech. Aside from the common *sententia*—Aemilius preferring private to public loss—Valerius presents an entirely different passage, apparently Paullus' recollection, in the speech that followed his triumph, of his prayer upon taking up his office. A number of possibilities suggest themselves: Valerius is conflating two speeches; or, perhaps, accurately representing the reminiscence of one speech in another as related by Cicero; or even following an embellishment of the schools whose exercises often focus on a *suasoria* to a general at the outset of a grand campaign. Of the *Consolatio* again one cannot say much more than that it offered a certain sequence of exempla. This series may have become enshrined through the practices of the schools. Valerius may well have read or remembered the *Consolatio,* but this reading does not exclude the influence of other versions.

The remaining evidence for the influence of the *Consolatio* is the title *pontifex* that Valerius gives Horatius. (The case of Marcius Rex affords little inquiry as the parallel passages are so slight: besides his appearance in Valerius, a brief notice in Seneca's *Epistles* 99.6 describes his situation—the bereaved father who nonetheless conducts business in the senate—but does not name him.) Münzer understood a passage from the *De domo sua* (139) to indicate that Cicero called Horatius *pontifex.*[17] In his *Pauly Wissowa* article on Horatius, Münzer distinguished

17. Cicero's *De domo sua* is addressed to *pontifices,* but in this passage, which

this Ciceronian version, and what he deemed the dependent accounts of Valerius and Seneca, from the version of the historians that identified Horatius as consul. Münzer's ingenious and economical solution to the alternate titles was to posit a lost source, an inscribed Capitoline dedication. This inscription could have served as source for both only if it had had no indication of Horatius' office. The annalists then reported Horatius completed his allotted dedication during his consulship (since they believed only consuls could dedicate temples). An originally separate anecdote about the steadfast *pontifex* was later connected to Rome's most famous temple.[18] Münzer proceeds to doubt that Horatius was consul in 509: an association of the dedication of the Capitoline Temple with the expulsion of the Tarquins caused Horatius to be listed as consul. The suggestions of an inscription and the confusions of the annalists are ingenious, but the web of traditional history is surely more complex than this solution allows. The tendency to attribute anecdotes to the most familiar or famous time or office of a historical figure should not be discounted. So not only do apocrypha cluster about a famous figure, but individual events from an individual's life may be transposed to a famous office or stage in the subject's

---

has led to such speculative reconstruction, Cicero does not call Pulvillus *pontifex*. A reader might be misled because the immediately preceding historical figure is named a *pontifex*. Cicero is acknowledging his judges' religious expertise and maintains that he will not trespass on their subject or authority: his omission of any title for Pulvillus may then be scrupulous since the *pontifices* would have known Pulvillus had not been a *pontifex*. Cicero's words on which all this depends are, *Quae si omnia e Ti. Coruncani scientia, qui peritissimus pontifex fuisse dicitur, acta esse constaret, aut si M. Horatius ille Pulvillus, qui, cum eum multi propter invidiam fictis religionibus inpedirent, restitit et constantissima mente Capitolium dedicavit, huius modi alicui dedicationi praefuisset, tamen in scelere religio non valeret* ("But if it were the case that everything had been performed in accord with the expertise of Ti. Coruncanus who is said to have been the most knowledgeable *pontifex* or if the famous M. Horatius Pulvillus, who stood steadfast and with unflinching attention dedicated the Capitoline Temple when many, out of hatred and under the pretext of religion, were trying to block him, had been leading a dedication of this sort, still religion would not be valid in the pursuit of crime").

18. Münzer, "Horatius Pulvillus," *RE* 8.2, 2402 (no. 13).

life. In the end Münzer has accepted the version of two lost sources while positing a third to explain them. The lost sources are the *Consolatio* of Cicero, the authority for the *pontifex* version, and the old authors who, Livy says, mentioned only one consulship for Horatius. We need not attempt to resolve the question of his consulships; it is more than sufficient that Livy was in some doubt. Where authority wavered, Valerius may simply have repeated the title from Cicero.

Klotz's dismissal of Seneca's dependence on Valerius was even briefer than his denial of Valerius' use of Livy: after denying Seneca's use of Livy or an epitome of Livy, he conjures up the lost source: "Aber ebenso ist aus geschlossen, daß Seneca aus Valerius Maximus schöpft. Wir müssen uns nach einer anderen Quelle umsehen."[19] The stemmatics of literary imitation are more difficult of proof than those of paleography. Indeed, the very comparison of scribal and authorial composition is misguided. But some methodology—short of Klotz's mechanical criteria of similarity—may yet illumine the subjective judgment that one author has or has not used another. Klotz has here concluded without argument that Valerius was not a source for Seneca. This he concludes is as self-evident as the fact that Valerius and Seneca are closer than Seneca and Livy. Before we conclude that he is right, that Valerius and Seneca are closer—because Seneca has used Valerius—let us consider the similarity of these two accounts of Horatius Pulvillus and, in particular, the indications of allegiance first between Seneca and Livy and then Seneca and Valerius. First and most clearly, all are telling the same story with only minor differences of detail. Klotz has of course relied on a comparison of diction, a technique that demonstrates well the affinity of Valerius and Seneca. Valerius and Seneca do share against Livy the following distinctive words: *Pulvillus, pontifex, sollemni(a) verb(a), vultum, interrumpere, audisset/exaudisse.* These forms may be declined differently by Seneca and Valerius Maximus, but they are altogether absent in the parallel passage from Livy.[20] Choices of

19. Klotz 1909, 199.

20. Livy has given the full name of the consul, "M. Horatius Pulvillus," two sentences before the "parallel passage" as Klotz has quoted it. Clearly, Valerius took the full name from the earlier sentence. Valerius' reading of Livy (and not just of Cicero) may also be responsible for the supposed mistake of pontifex

diction, however, cannot simply be compared as if these were significant variants in three manuscripts. Livy has *postem iam tenenti,* Seneca *postem tenenti,* Valerius *postem tenens.* (Livy does have *tenens postem* at the passage's end, but the position within the story of the first three phrases is the same: the announcement of the son's death while the father is touching the temple column.) These three variants prove no cleavage. Valerius, as so often, makes the historical subject of his exemplum the grammatical subject. Changes of cases and even the variation of simple for compound verbs and vice versa, as Bliss has shown, indicate no additional source; they constitute the essentials of Valerius' transformation of his model's style.

The one principle borrowed from paleography that should apply, the "common error" in Valerius and Seneca of pontifex for consul, Klotz has discarded or rather relegated to the lost source. Perhaps the one sure conclusion this much-discussed title points to is that Seneca has not here checked Livy. Finally, Seneca has not introduced any new material that might point to any lost source. The one departure from Valerius comes at the end of Seneca's exemplum: he notes that the father did indeed weep for his son, at home, and did perform the usual rites. No source need be sought. Seneca has departed from Valerius in this rhetorical closure. In fact he has extended and amplified Valerius' final *sententia* and so constructed an event from a rhetorical trope. Seneca's

---

for consul. Livy has just explained (2.8.4) that upon Sp. Lucretius' death Horatius was consul suffectus and that not all authors include Sp. Lucretius in the list of consuls but instead skip to Horatius. Valerius may, in the face of antiquarian controversy, be confused or simply be avoiding the issue and substituting what seemed, to him, well supported. It should be noted that no one now believes that Horatius was pontifex or even consul in 509 B.C. Alföldi (1963, 327–28) explains the ancient confusion thus: "Cn. Flavius, who in 304 B.C. counted the 204 nails in the *cella* of Jupiter, and his followers believed that the M. Horatius whose name they read on the architrave of the temple was the magistrate who had dedicated it in 509 B.C." The M. Horatius who restored the temple and whose name adorned it "was the *tribunus militum consulari potestate* of 378 B.C." Szemler (1972, 48) concludes, "It is impossible without question to accept the identity of the earliest Roman priests." Horatius heads his list of the hopelessly unidentifiable. Szelmer too objects to the title *pontifex,* since Horatius is portrayed as a dedicator (54 n. 9).

habit of variation is clear from the juncture he continues to make: he compares Horatius to an anonymous Greek father—a figure no doubt suggested by the anonymous father who precedes Horatius in Valerius (5.9.4). Valerius had closed by saying that Horatius "turned not his face from the public ceremony to private grief lest he seem to play the father more than the priest." Seneca is not content with this antithesis of public and private demeanor; he makes his audience see first the part of father and then the role reversal, again, to public priest. Seneca is, therefore, not so much humanizing the figure of Horatius as expanding Valerius' final rhetorical figure. He is more graphic—perhaps needlessly so—in fleshing out this implied antithesis of Valerius.

As with a series of related manuscripts, the scholar cannot unequivocally deny the possibility of contamination: we may demonstrate that the last has used the middle and needed no other, but it is always possible that the last has seen the first as well. We can, however, reasonably credit independent material to the scribe's correction or author's invention and not to a hypothetical, lost version. At the very least, the source intermediate between Livy and Valerius can be eliminated. In this particular case, Livy alone cannot have provided Seneca with the story; the last of our three authors needed and has used no source but Valerius. Klotz's and Bosch's collection books are not at work here. A lost work of Cicero may well have been read by Valerius, but enthusiasm for rediscovery and the supposition that Valerius is but parroting his source should not mislead. Cicero's work may have provided the series, to some declaimer, school rhetorician, or even Valerius, but it is not the model here. Livy's treatment of Horatius has been mined for diction, phrasing, even the sequence of events. We have, therefore, reestablished as crucial the examination of differences between known sources and Valerius Maximus. Comparison of these is meant not to reconstruct lost sources but to see Valerius' originality, his peculiar interests in and contributions to these inherited stories.

Margins of Reading: The Individual Sources

Once the direct reading and use of sources are restored to Valerius, the hypothetical sources, for the most part, vanish of necessity. Before consideration of his use of Livy and Cicero, his primary sources, and of the influence of declamation, both source and context for this author, a delineation of the margins of his reading and knowledge will reveal much about his composition. One sure consequence is a wholesale revision of the list of authors proposed as sources by critics and even those cited as such by Valerius; in their place more concrete data will emerge. The first issue remains to determine whom he read. Only then can we begin to understand the pattern and consequences of his reading. The use of certain authors does seem to have precluded the use of others. In turn, a finite or shrinking corpus of sources used presages the creation of a canon.

Greek Sources

The most fundamental division of potential sources is one of language. At first it seems inconceivable that an author of Tiberian times could have ignored Greek intellectual culture. The Augustan age is celebrated by Latinists for its poets, but its intellectual culture is defined as much by Hellenistic encyclopedic scholars. One need mention only Diodorus Siculus, Dionysius of Halicarnassus, or Strabo. Valerius' more exact contemporaries—Celsus, Phaedrus, and Manilius—have as a chief characteristic the translation and emulation of Greek models. Similarly, Valerius was engaged in an encyclopedic effort, though he quite consciously strove to promote the Roman at the expense of the Greek. However, in Valerius' case, both the tradition of Roman historiography, which provided him with ample Latin sources, and a contemporary stylistic program—the declamatory emulation of classical Latin authors—offered reason enough to eschew Greek literature.

Scholars have taken seriously Valerius' repeated, almost insistent disparagement of Greece and the Greeks. So Krieger and Comes have denied altogether Valerius' use of Greek sources, and others have argued against the use of particular authors.[21] Siegfried Maire is the ex-

21. Krieger 1888, 79–80. Comes (1950, 37) maintains that all of Valerius' Greek citations are secondhand; he follows Rabenhorst's thesis (*Der ältere Plinius als Epitomator des Verrius Flaccus* [Berlin 1907], 2 ff.) that the correspondences in Valerius 8.13 and Pliny, *NH* 7.152–54 are due to common use of Verrius Flaccus. Caltabiano (1975, 77–80) argues against the use of Polybius.

ception, and his case for Diodorus Siculus has been generally accepted[22] but for the most part ignored. The various strands of argument about Valerius' knowledge and use of Greek authors need to be separated. He does cite Greek authors and even quotes Greek words and a hexameter. However, neither his citation nor noncitation is any indication of his actual reading. The disparagement of the Greeks is likewise ambiguous evidence. Once the pedigree of this polemic is recognized, the invective is all the more suspect: behind it lies Cicero's stated, prescriptive preference for Roman exempla. Cicero's injunction involves more than a traditional cultural bias, although it does have considerable share in what the elder Cato had long since made a historiographical and oratorical commonplace. Cicero's practical motive in preferring a Roman subject for his Roman audience directs both his practice and theory. Like his citations of authority, Valerius' assertions of Roman superiority are no sure guide to his pattern of reading.

Diodorus Siculus

The solid evidence for Valerius' use of Greek in composing his work—for that he knew and read Greek and had traveled through Greece is beyond doubt—is a number of anecdotes that have striking parallels in the work of the Augustan encyclopedic historian Diodorus Siculus. Despite the peculiarities in Maire's argumentation, an analysis of his methods and results is still worthwhile, for Diodorus remains the likeliest candidate as a Greek source. In addition, the use of Diodorus would reveal a reliance on an author outside the Roman mainstream for subjects where Livy might well have served. The case of Diodorus offers a further methodological interest. Bliss's criteria of stylistic inversion and variation may not apply or apply only with difficulty to a work of translation. Finally, demonstration of Valerius' use of Diodorus remains elusive since one must often rely on a Byzantine excerptor to reconstruct the original.

The arguments of Maire's thesis are indeed peculiar at times. He asserts similarities of purpose and style as if these were proofs of de-

22. Maire 1899. Bosch (1929, 1) labels belief in the use of Diodorus, among others, as the *communis opinio* of scholars.

pendence; further, what he deems the likeliest candidates of imitation are not. Maire proposed to prove dependence by arguments from Valerius' arrangement, his general plan of relating things worthy of record, from his style (*ex inani loquacitate*), and from verbal and substantial agreement.[23] Only the first and the last methods have much merit; the others could link any number of historians. In practice Maire does not rely on the arguments from style and general purpose (what Maire calls the two authors' *consilium,* their moral program in writing history); and unlike many critics he is keenly aware of the difficulties of verbal comparison, especially since he recognizes Valerius' habit of combining sources. Maire begins his arguments from the text with a notorious anecdote of the young Alcibiades; this exemplum (3.1.ext.1) heads Maire's list of those certainly drawn from Diodorus.[24]

The core to all versions of this anecdote, as with so many historically suspect stories, is a witticism. Here Alcibiades has told Pericles, worried about inquiry into the Parthenon's expenses, to consider not how to give an accounting to the Athenians but how not to render an accounting. This whole episode is much more murky to the modern historian than it was to either Diodorus or Valerius.[25] Maire can hardly be faulted for not anticipating the skepticism of contemporary historians, but he has glossed over significant differences in Diodorus' and Valerius' versions of the anecdote. Diodorus suggests Pericles embezzled the money for private use; Valerius, that he had overspent on the Propylaea to the Parthenon. Maire believed Valerius rejected those elements of Diodorus' account that he found unbecoming to Pericles' dignity and then added the detail of the Propylaea from what Diodorus continues to say. To this discrepancy the following differences should be added (I have not listed what could arise from omission but only what are clearly inventions or additions): Diodorus has no mention of Alcibiades coming

23. Maire 1899, 3.

24. Maire 1899, 7: combining sources; 8: 3.1.ext.1.

25. Kagan (1969, 195) considers the tale slander—like the rumor that Pericles passed the Megarian Decree and so began the war to avert his own trial. Nepos, *Alc.* 11, notes the variety of opinion among ancient historians on the veracity of Alcibiades' remark.

to Pericles, nothing to parallel *eumque secreto tristem sedentem vidisset,*[26] nothing in particular of Pericles' expression (only λυπούμενον, "grieving"). These may well be the dramatic invention of situation and setting with which the declaimer must invest the reported *dicta* and the addition of emotion—palpably discernible—that he supplies his audience. The crucial difference, which points to a different source, is that in Diodorus the money is from the Delian League; in Valerius from the funds for the construction of the Propylaea. The story of Pericles' supposed embezzlement (with Phidias' connivance) does occur in Diodorus at 12.39, immediately after the passage parallel to Valerius. Diodorus, however, designates the funds as intended for the statue of Athena. Happily, a Roman source connects this embezzlement with the Propylaea—one need not call in Ephorus, Diodorus' source for this anti-Periclean matter. In the *De officiis* (2.60) Cicero writes, "Demetrius of Phalerum censured Pericles, the leading man of Greece, for squandering so much money in the famous Propylaea." Like Valerius Cicero has not mentioned embezzlement, only lavish expense. This passage is too brief to be Valerius' model, but Cicero immediately continues, "There is a thorough discussion of this kind of public building project in my *Republic.*"[27] This Ciceronian full-scale treatment of Pericles' alleged overspending on the Propylaea is a far more likely source for Valerius' anecdote.

The conjunction or proximity of the same material in both Valerius and an alleged source is a compelling indication of a relationship between the two. We can readily imagine the author excerpting a particular illustration from a book and being led on by the adjacent stories to include these too as instances of the same chapter heading. This is the implication of the second of Maire's parallels for Diodorus and Va-

---

26. Plutarch, it is true, also has no mention of Pericles sitting in secret, but he is clearly alone. Alcibiades, paying a call on Pericles, learns his guardian is not receiving visitors: [Alcibiades] πυθόμενος δὲ μὴ σχολάζειν (*Alc.* 7).

27. *Phalereus Demetrias qui Periclem, principem Graeciae, vituperat, quod tantam pecuniam in praeclara illa Propylaea coniecerit. sed de hoc genere toto in eis libris, quos de re publica scripsi, diligenter est disputatum.* Probably in book 5 of the *De re publica* as H. A. Holden suggests, *M. T. Ciceronis De Officiis* (Amsterdam: Hakkert, 1966).

lerius: two chapters after Alcibiades' quip in Valerius comes the rather vivid, even bizarre tale of a philosopher biting off a tyrant's ear (3.3.ext.3). Diodorus had also told of Zeno of Elea exacting his revenge on Nearchus; the excerpted version of Constantine Porphyrogenitus preserves the story (Diodorus 10.18). Before concluding that Maire has detected a transplanted series, one must remember that, in addition to the probability that Valerius has the first story from Cicero's *Republic* and not Diodorus' *History*, these two stories are not adjacent or even proximate in Diodorus (12.38 and 10.18). It would be peculiar indeed to imagine Valerius reading books 10 through 12 and excerpting only these two stories. Further, in the case of this second story supposedly taken from Diodorus, both Valerius' version and its surrounding exempla suggest Diodorus is not the source. Maire found the inclusion of this story in the chapter on "Patience" so incongruous that he concluded Valerius had neglected the point of Diodorus' story, which he took to be vengeance.[28]

This rather unlikely philosophical tale has become, in Valerius, the second of three exempla of philosophers' endurance. Indeed, the foreign examples of this chapter have a second proem (3.3.ext.1), which announces the series of philosophers. The transition from the first to the second philosophical exempla is particularly important, and not simply as a characteristically Valerian metonymic juncture. The passage 3.3.ext.3 begins "A like-named philosopher"—Valerius believes he is telling, in the second and the third foreign exempla, anecdotes of separate Zenos. Here, as Diogenes Laertius attests, Valerius has blundered.[29] Zeno of Elea is responsible for both the stoning of Phalaris and the maiming of Nearchus. Perhaps Valerius' notes are to blame: he may have omitted the identifying place name in making an excerpt and then not bothered to check the original.

Where has Valerius found his series of tortured, tyrant-punishing philosophers? Or has he assembled these from different sources? Cicero (*De nat. deor.* 3.82) juxtaposes the deaths, at tyrants' hands, of Zeno of Elea and Anaxarchus. The death of Anaxarchus follows that of Zeno in Valerius also. Better yet, in the second book of the *Tusculans* (2.52)

28. Maire 1899, 10.
29. Diogenes, *Lives of the Philosophers*, 9.5.26.

Cicero has as a series the deaths of Zeno of Elea, Anaxarchus, and the self-cremated Indian Calanus. This must be the remarkable conjunction that has directed Valerius, for the penultimate example of his chapter on "Patience," immediately following the demise of Anaxarchus, is the case of the Indians who expose themselves to flame and to Caucasian cold. To the objection that Cicero's suicidal Calanus has become nameless Indian fakirs, the answer is that the *Tusculans'* abbreviated reference and general theme of suicide do not fit Valerius' category and were therefore altered.

Examination of the second supposed instance of Valerius' borrowing from Diodorus like the first restores Cicero as the source. A series of philosophers has been inserted in the foreign examples, framed by the Scaevola-like tale of a young Macedonian sacrificant and the final example of the slave who killed Hasdrubal. There is even evidence of Valerius' reading of this particular section of the *Tusculans*, for the transition from the philosophical trio to the final exemplum ("These were the products of profound and learned souls; the following is no less worthy of regard despite its servile origin. A barbarian slave . . .") with its contrast of philosopher and barbarian shows the displaced influence of Cicero's introduction to his third example, "The Indian Calanus, uneducated and a barbarian . . ."[30] The composition of the foreign examples of patience has, then, begun with the Greek counterpart to Mucius Scaevola (the subject of the first exemplum of this chapter); on this Valerius has grafted a series of three philosophers suggested by Cicero's *Tusculans*. He has added another story of Zeno and is either confused about that man's identity or, since he did not find this somewhat undignified (and perhaps declamatory) episode in Cicero, credited it to a different (i.e., unknown to him) philosopher of the same name. Finally, the suicide of the unlearned Indian has become the patience of unlearned Indians while Cicero's transitional antithesis provided the rhetorical germ for his own introduction to the barbarian assassin of Hasdrubal.

This particular case reveals far more about Valerius' composition,

---

30. Valerius 3.3.ext.7: *Haec e pectoribus altis et eruditis orta sunt: illud tamen non minus admirabile, quod servilis animus cepit. servus barbarus . . .* ; Cicero, *Tusc.* 2.52: *Calanus Indus, indoctus ac barbarus . . .*

the stringing together of his material, than about the use of Greek authors. Cicero in the *Tusculans* has given a series of three philosophers and has said only that Zeno of Elea suffered all rather than betray his friends and fellow conspirators. Valerius has found fuller information elsewhere. This detail may come from a lost work of Cicero—brief strings of exempla are often found in more than one work of Cicero.[31] But it is certainly clear that the tracing of a series of exempla in Valerius, be they bereaved fathers or patient philosophers, to a series of exempla in another source such as Cicero can be only the beginning of the source critic's hunt and that multiple sources are very possible.

The remaining "Diodoran" material can be divided into Maire's categories of more and less certain imitations, although with the second grouping even Maire was forced to recognize these are of combined sources—that is, Diodorus can be at best a partial source, since Valerius' versions are richer in detail or significantly different. Maire consigned these differences either to an additional source or to the omission of Diodorus' Byzantine excerptor. In these examples Maire's argument is at its worst, although to his credit it should be noted that the exempla of Masinissa and of Regulus have also plagued subsequent Valerian scholars. First, however, Maire should be judged on his strongest cases. The examples he deemed of certain dependence prove rather familiar fare: a fish story taken up ultimately by the Roman jurists, the famous, philosophical friendship of Damon and Phintias, and the story of Charondas, the lawgiver of Thurii.

Diodorus and Valerius provide the earliest accounts of the Milesian fishermen who raised in their net a tripod, which ultimately made its way to Delphi. Maire treats this story, which is both the instigation and

31. A brief exemplum in Cicero and especially an abbreviated series may well frustrate those intent on a single source. After all, repeated exempla in Cicero have nothing to do with intertextual allusion or dependence but are the consequence of his memory technique. In composing, Cicero no doubt pulled from a mental stock of familiar stories and figures, which could be embellished or passed over with a *praeteritio* as he saw fit. Here for a series on "Patience" Valerius has probably used a book he uses elsewhere in his collection, Cicero's *Tusculans*. But we will never determine just where else Cicero or his early imitators used a similar series.

the solution to a Delphic hexameter and which was connected to the Seven Sages, no differently from any other historical information transmitted by Diodorus and Valerius. Maire is determined, even when he cannot trace Valerius to an extant source, at least to seek a written source, but here he has failed to take into account the sort of tale being told. This is not an issue of historical veracity, of what did or did not befall certain Aegean fishermen, but a question of anecdotal transmission, embellishment, and variation. A tall tale does not enjoy the same authority as a historical episode; its various elements do not retain the same permanence. Clearly, such a story is ripe for embellishment. Individual variation cannot, as Maire has done, simply be laid to the first written source extant. Furthermore, Diodorus' excerptor actually offers three different versions of this story. Maire's conclusion that Valerius is a more faithful recorder of Diodorus than the excerptor,[32] besides being an indeterminable conclusion, is nothing more than the observation that Valerius simply tells one version of the story.

Diodorus' three versions are, in essence, the following. At 9.3 he records the Pythia's two-hexameter response with no mention of the origin of the tripod. Immediately following is a version that adds a different context: the Pythia was asked about the solution to a local war; her four-verse response directs that a tripod, newly raised by some fishermen, be given to the wisest of all; the tripod is given in turn to each of the Seven Sages and ends up with Apollo. Last, at 9.3.2 the scene is set at Messenia, not Milesia, and the excerptor states only that fishermen found in their net nothing but a tripod with the inscription "to the wisest," which they gave to Bias. The three variants cannot be blamed on a careless excerptor. Given the nature of the story, they undoubtedly were genuinely in existence. Failure to resolve variants is a characteristic of the eclectic, even indiscriminate Diodorus. In the search for borrowings, the most one can say is that Valerius 4.1.ext.7 has the scene in Milesia, the second hexameter of the first response as reported by Diodorus, and the progress of the tripod from Thales through the Sages to Solon and on to Apollo.

Valerius does, however, offer something completely novel, which has

32. Maire 1899, 10.

a parallel in the Digest (19.1.11.18 and 19.1.12).[33] The Greek versions make no mention of a contractual dispute between the hirers of the fishermen and the fishermen themselves. This legal issue—does the hiring of a haul refer to fish alone or to anything raised in the net?— has been fused with a story that centered about a search for the true superlative, the wisest of all. Diogenes Laertius tells the same story, although he notes Callimachus' different version.[34] Maire maintained that the only discrepancy in Valerius' and Diodorus' accounts was the translation of *mensa* for tripod. In fact, Valerius presents a different version of a story that by no means has or could keep a canonical form. The rudiments of the story that concur with the earlier written versions are the locale and the Pythia's response. These are exactly the minimum needed to memorize the anecdote. That Diodorus and Valerius are the earliest to transmit the story is no argument for postulating that Diodorus is the source. Both Diodorus and Valerius are commonplace authors working in what can be most grandly described as the cultural mainstream, the traffic of schoolmen, not the research of scholars. In Roman hands, if not in earlier, this particular story has become an instance of a legal controversy as well.

Without dragging the reader through every one of Maire's alleged parallels it is abundantly clear that Diodorus has not proved to be a source for Valerius. Again and again tyrants and philosophers, those friends of the schools' declamations, are the points of overlap. These anecdotes would have been familiar from Roman education and, in fact, are often found in Cicero's philosophical works. Indeed, the *De officiis* is the actual source for the last two cases of "certain Diodoran influence" to be considered here.

The case of the friendship unto death of Damon and Phintias reveals the perils of the presentation of the source critics. Considered in iso-

33. The plot of Plautus' *Rudens*, of course, turns on this same issue: the tokens of identity—necessary to free the young heroine—are in a shipwrecked trunk netted by a fisherman in the employ of another (her unrecognized father).

34. *Thales* 1.27. Various accounts report various gifts given Thales who always sends them on to Apollo. For the different forms of the fish tale, cf. Callimachus (Pf.) 191.32 and Schol. ad Aristoph. *Plut.* 9.

lation, Diodorus and Valerius do display such a similarity of plot that the reader is borne away, convinced the latter derives from the former. Maire assures that such discrepancies as do exist are of little importance, the fruit of Valerius' invention.[35] The passages deserve direct inspection:

> For instance, during the tyranny of Dionysius a certain Pythagorean philosopher Phintias had conspired against the tyrant, and when about to pay the penalty asked Dionysius for time to set his domestic affairs in order. He said he would give one of his friends as surety. Dionysius was amazed that there would be found a friend to take the place of the prisoner. Phintias summoned one of his intimates, Damon, a Pythagorean philosopher who without hesitation became surety for the condemned. Some praised this extreme devotion of the friends; some judged the pledge recklessness and insanity. At the set hour all the people assembled waiting to see if the one who had made the pledge would keep it. With time running out everybody gave up hope, when Phintias, quite contrary to expectation and at the last moment, came running up, while Damon was being led off to execution. There was universal amazement at the friendship. Dionysius freed the accused and asked that these two add him as the third to their friendship. (Diodorus 10.4.3–6)[36]

35. Maire 1899, 12.
36. καὶ γὰρ Διονυσίου τυραννοῦντος Φιντίας τις Πυθαγόρειος ἐπιβεβουλευκὼς τῷ τυράννῳ, μέλλων δὲ τῆς τιμωρίας τυγχάνειν, ᾐτήσατο παρὰ τοῦ Διονυσίου χρόνον εἰς τὸ περὶ τῶν ἰδίων πρότερον ἃ βούλεται διοικῆσαι· δώσειν δ' ἔφησεν ἐγγυητὴν τοῦ θανάτου τῶν φίλων ἕνα. τοῦ δὲ δυνάστου θαυμάσαντος, εἰ τοιοῦτός ἐστι φίλος ὃς ἑαυτὸν εἰς τὴν εἱρκτὴν ἀντ' ἐκείνου παραδώσει, προεκαλέσατό τινα τῶν γνωρίμων ὁ Φιντίας, Δάμωνα ὄνομα, Πυθαγόρειον φιλόσοφον, ὃς οὐδὲ διστάσας ἔγγυος εὐθὺς ἐγενήθη τοῦ θανάτου. τινὲς μὲν οὖν ἐπῄνουν τὴν ὑπερβολὴν τῆς πρὸς τοὺς φίλους εὐνοίας, τινὲς δὲ τοῦ ἐγγύου προπέτειαν καὶ μανίαν κατεγίνωσκον. πρὸς δὲ τὴν τεταγμένην ὥραν ἅπας ὁ δῆμος συνέδραμεν, καραδοκῶν εἰ φυλάξει τὴν πίστιν ὁ καταστήσας. ἤδη δὲ τῆς ὥρας συγκλειούσης πάντες μὲν ἀπεγίνωσκον, ὁ δὲ Φιντίας ἀνελπίστως ἐπὶ τῆς ἐσχάτης τοῦ χρόνου ῥοπῆς δρομαῖος ἦλθε, τοῦ Δάμωνος ἀπαγομένου πρὸς τὴν ἀνάγκην. θαυμαστῆς δὲ τῆς φιλίας φανείσης ἅπασιν,

Damon and Phintias, initiates of the sacred wisdom of Pythagoras, were so closely united in friendship that when Dionysius of Syracuse wished to kill the latter the former did not hesitate to give himself to the tyrant as guarantor for the other's return (who had obtained leave from Dionysius to set out for home and put his domestic affairs in order before his death). The one with the knife at his throat had been delivered from mortal peril; the one free to live had put his throat beneath the knife. And so everybody and especially Dionysius were wondering at the outcome of this novel and perilous situation. On the arrival of the set date without Phintias' return, everyone deemed folly the reckless pledge. But Damon declared he had no doubt about the reliability of his friend. At the very same instant arrived the hour set by Dionysius and the one who had agreed to it. In wonder at the spirit of both, the tyrant canceled the sentence for reason of their fidelity and in addition asked that they receive him into their friendship as a third order of comradeship to be cherished with joint goodwill. (Valerius 4.7.ext.1)[37]

While conceding that Diodorus offers no parallel for two of Valerius' sentences (*solutus . . . licebat* and *at is . . . praedicabat*), Maire explains these as rhetorical color. Valerius, however, has the situation so differently presented that his treatment cannot be summarily dismissed as

---

ἀπέλυσεν ὁ Διονύσιος τῆς τιμωρίας τὸν ἐγκαλούμενον, καὶ παρεκάλεσε τοὺς ἄνδρας τρίτον ἑαυτὸν εἰς τὴν φιλίαν προσλαβέσθαι.

37. *Damon et Phintias Pythagoricae prudentiae sacris initiati tam fidelem inter se amicitiam iunxerant, ut, cum alterum ex his Dionysius Syracusanus interficere vellet, atque is tempus ab eo, quo prius quam periret domum profectus res suas ordinaret, impetravisset, alter vadem se pro reditu eius tyranno dare non dubitaret. Solutus erat periculo mortis qui modo gladio cervices subiectas habuerat: eidem caput suum subiecerat cui securo vivere licebat. igitur omnes et in primis Dionysius novae atque ancipitis rei exitum speculabantur. adpropinquante deinde finita die nec illo redeunte unus quisque stultitiae tam temerarium sponsorem damnabat. at is nihil se de amici constantia metuere praedicabat. eodem autem momento et hora a Dionysio constituta et eam qui acceperat supervenit. admiratus amborum animum tyrannus supplicium fidei remisit insuperque eos rogavit ut se in societatem amicitiae tertium sodalicii gradum mutua culturum benivolentia reciperent. . . .*

the addition of several rhetorical cola to a translation of a Greek original. Diodorus had Phintias plotting against Dionysius. Conceivably, in omitting this Valerius has merely simplified; all he relates is that the tyrant wished to kill Phintias. The contrasting sentiments of public opinion, a recurring element in Diodorus, have become the unequivocal reaction of all (cf. τινὲς . . . τινὲς and *omnes*). Perhaps Valerius has deliberately written out these elements, thus making the tyrant's actions more arbitrary and unjust by removing ambiguity of motive or variance of judgment. Certainly these aspects are not to be found in Cicero's versions (*De off.* 3.45 and *Tusc.* 5.63). Maire has pointed out that the tyrant's hesitation, the people's expectation, and the late arrival of Phintias are absent from Cicero's two versions. Valerius too does not narrate them. Indeed, the dramatic conclusion and the opportune arrival must be surmised from Valerius' compressed conclusion of the action (*eodem autem momento et hora a Dionysio constituta et eam qui acceperat supervenit*). Valerius has been reading Cicero and not Diodorus here.

That Valerius did read Cicero and not Diodorus is clear from the next example that Maire proposed. The suicide of the scrupulous lawgiver Charondas (who had appeared armed in the assembly, accidently but in contravention to his own law) told by Diodorus, Cicero, and Valerius (6.5.4) is strikingly similar to the problem of Damon and Phintias. These latter two were narrated at *De officiis* 3.45; a story of Themistocles follows at 3.49, which Valerius has put at 6.5.ext.2 (just before Damon and Phintias). Maire chose Diodorus (12.19) as the source of the story of Charondas presumably because this offers a full account. Discrepancies in this case are of the same order as in the last case: Valerius has no verbal parallel for ταραχῆς ἐν τοῖς πλήθεσι; the lawmaker's personal enemy (who points out Charondas' violation of his own law) has been removed (*dignitatis causa* Maire concludes);[38] but Cicero has a similar dignity of omission. Finally, Diodorus mentions a variant tradition that Valerius completely bypasses. The conjunction of stories provides a final clue. A story of Zaleucus follows that of Charondas in Diodorus; in Valerius, Zaleucus comes just before, although the story is a different one. Cicero, however, has these same characters and stories joined at *De legibus* 1.57 and 2.14.

38. Maire 1899, 13.

Thus in four out of five of Maire's major examples, Cicero and not Diodorus is almost certainly Valerius' source. Cicero cannot be ascribed as the probable source in the next cases. These final three examples of Valerius' certain imitation are the most compelling instances of Valerius' modeling of Diodorus. The elder Hannibal's report to the Carthaginian senate after the disaster of the Aegates Islands has Diodorus and Valerius as its earliest testimonia. In the case of Zisemis, king of the Thracians (9.2.ext.4), Valerius and Diodorus are the only sources. In both these exempla the compelling indication of dependence is not the accident of transmission but for the first a striking similarity of form, which is not merely verbal but syntactic, and in the second a demonstrably repeated conjunction of stories. The descriptions of the elder Hannibal's scheme to forestall criticism are these:

> When the Carthaginian commander Hannibal had been defeated in a naval battle and feared that the senate would punish him for the defeat, he contrived the following. He dispatched a friend to Carthage with orders which he deemed advantageous. The friend sailed to the city, appeared before the senate, and said that Hannibal charged him to ask the council whether he should order his 200 ships to engage the Romans' 120. When they shouted out that they did order it, he said, "Well then, the battle has taken place, and we have been defeated. Since you so ordered, Hannibal is freed from responsibility." Hannibal knew from experience that the citizens trump up charges against commanders and in this fashion evaded the coming accusations. (Diodorus 23.10.1)[39]

39. Ὅτι ὁ τῶν Καρχηδονίων στρατηγὸς Ἀννίβας ἡττηθεὶς ναυμαχίᾳ καὶ φοβούμενος μὴ διὰ τὴν ἧτταν ἀπὸ τῆς γερουσίας τύχῃ τιμωρίας τεχνάζεταί τι τοιοῦτον. ἀπέστειλέ τινα τῶν φίλων εἰς Καρχηδόνα δοὺς ἐντολὰς ἅς ποτε ἔδοξεν αὐτῷ συμφέρειν. ὁ δὲ καταπλεύσας εἰς τὴν πόλιν καὶ πρὸς τὴν γερουσίαν εἰσαχθεὶς εἶπεν ὅτι προσέταξεν Ἀννίβας ἐρωτῆσαι τὴν βουλὴν εἰ κελεύει ναυμαχῆσαι διακοσίαις ναυσὶ πρὸς Ῥωμαίων ἑκατὸν εἴκοσι. τῶν δὲ ἀναβοησάντων καὶ κελευσάντων, Τοιγαροῦν, ἔφη, νεναυμάχηκε καὶ ἡττήμεθα. ἐκεῖνος δὲ ὑμῶν προσταξάντων ἀπολέλυται τῆς αἰτίας. ὁ μὲν οὖν Ἀννίβας εἰδὼς τοὺς πολίτας ἐκ τῶν ἀποτελεσμάτων συκοφαντοῦντας τοὺς στρατηγούς, τοιούτῳ τρόπῳ τὰς ἐσομένας κατηγορίας ὑπεξείλατο.

Hannibal, having been defeated by the consul Duilius in a naval battle and fearing punishment for the loss of the fleet, avoided injury by a brilliant stratagem. Before the messenger of the disaster could return home from the unfortunate battle, he sent one of his friends, trained and rehearsed. After he entered the senate chamber of this city, he said, "Hannibal asks you whether he ought to engage the Roman commander who has arrived with a large naval force." The senate in a body shouted out that undoubtedly he should. Then he said, "He has engaged and been defeated." Thus he did not leave them free to condemn the event because they had ordered that it should occur. (Valerius 7.3.ext.7)[40]

Maire had pointed out the striking verbal correspondences of the two passages. More significant than the parallelism of individual words and phrases are the order and syntax of the parallel phrases. These latter demonstrate more convincingly that one author had another before him. There can be no question of a coincidence of phrasing, of the interjection of some intermediate source, or the hazy recollection of something read long ago. Hannibal is the grammatical subject of each passage. Valerius identifies him from a Roman point of view, a natural addition for a Roman author. The translation of participles and the tenses of translated verbs concur to indicate a translation of the entire passage and not, as one suspects with other stories, simply the commonly known *dicta* of a story. Further, the discrepancies of Valerius' passage do not betray another source or version but are the sort of detail likely to be omitted by the excerptor who preserves Diodorus (e.g., mention of the first messenger whom Hannibal's friend is to anticipate). This passage constitutes the only good, direct evidence of the correspondence of a passage in Valerius with the text of Diodorus.

40. *Hannibal a Duilio consule navali proelio victus timensque classis amissae poenas dare, offensam astutia mire avertit: nam ex illa infelici pugna prius quam cladis nuntius domum perveniret quendam ex amicis conpositum et formatum Karthaginem misit. qui, postquam civitatis eius curiam intravit, "consulit vos" inquit "Hannibal, cum dux Romanorum magnas secum maritimas trahens copias advenerit, an cum eo confligere debeat." adclamavit universus senatus non esse dubium quin oporteret. tum ille "conflixit" inquit "et superatus est." ita liberum his non reliquit id factum damnare, quod ipsi fieri debuisse iudicaverunt.*

Nonetheless, this single example on the subject of Rome's favorite villain hardly constitutes reading of Diodorus. Our task is not to multiply possible sources (Diodorus himself is notorious as a copier of sources) but to try to ascertain whom Valerius read. A single correspondence especially on a famous subject does not counterbalance the positive evidence of Valerius' preference for Cicero. The general pattern of Valerius' reading is clear, but there is more, if still slight, evidence of his use of Diodorus.

Two of Valerius' foreign examples of "Cruelty," those of Zisemis (Zibelmios in Greek) and Ptolemaeus Physcon, are so abbreviated that they cannot offer the same sort of verbal and syntactic parallels. Here, however, the sequence and the proximity of the examples indicate probable reading of Diodorus (9.2.ext.4 and 5 correspond to Diodorus 34.12 and 34.14). Zisemis' cruelty is known only from these passages; and while this is no proof in itself, Valerius' example can be construed as merely an abridgment of Diodorus. The succeeding example also abridges Diodorus, although the passage is lengthened by Valerius' introduction and the final connection to a separate outrage. Valerius' additions, as Maire pointed out, are those an epitomator might omit. And an omission such as the location of Ptolemy's parricide does not affect the point of the story and is in keeping with Valerius' tendency to simplify or even eliminate historical context. Valerius, as he himself notes (9.2.ext.5 referring to 9.1.ext.5), had just written of Ptolemy's lust, but the stories are so brief that an examination of the individual exempla in Valerius will not resolve whether Valerius read Diodorus and then used his material on Ptolemy in these two places.

The foreign examples of the first two chapters of the ninth book are predominantly the highly abbreviated outrages of foreign despots. The pair of stories of Zisemis and Ptolemy should be compared with another pair in the twelfth chapter of the same book, the deaths of the athletes Milo and Polydamnus, which are also adjacent in both Valerius and Diodorus.[41] The conventionality of these stories and of the moral Valerius draws prevents any division into variant traditions. Indeed, Strabo and Pausanias tell the same story of Milo, and if it were not for the slightly absurd detail of Milo inserting his hands and feet into the

41. Valerius 9.12.ext.9 and 10. Diodorus 9.24. See Maire 1899, 16.

cracks of the tree stump, as the geographer relates, Strabo could be advanced as Valerius' source. The story, in short, is briefly presented and commonplace, and the abbreviated form of one authority precludes conclusion by verbal agreement. Despite the triumphant declarations of the source critics, it is of fundamental importance to understand that these deductions from parallels usually must remain potentialities. Similarities of diction, syntax, and plot are lacking by which to judge between the possibilities. One can say that the conjunction of Zisemis and Ptolemaeus Physcon is more striking than the hackneyed theme of the unavailing strength of the two Greek athletes— that is, the relative novelty of the tyrants' cruelty can be an argument for Valerius' source.

Moreover, adjacent material allows more concrete inquiry into the use of Diodorus. The torture of Atilius Regulus (9.2.1) provides a more substantial clue to Valerius' reading of Diodorus. Of all the remaining cases of the imitation of Diodorus that Maire classified as less certain, only Regulus and Masinissa (8.13.ext.1) have sufficient parallel passages to afford comparison. (This did not prevent Maire from positing several others, but the grounds of his argument are slight.) The location of these exempla in this general section of Valerius' work constitutes the major reason Maire advances them. Here too arguments about source and model are not simple; Maire maintains that these exempla have at least one source other than Diodorus.

> Scipio, I believe you know the daily routine of your grandfather's ninety-year-old guest friend Masinissa. Once he set off by foot, he would never ride. Once he was riding, he would never dismount. No snow or rain compelled him to cover his head. Such was his physical hardiness. And so he performed all the royal duties and functions. (Cicero, *De sen.* 34)[42]

> Masinissa, king of Numidia, surpassed this record, ruling sixty years, the most remarkable man in terms of the vitality of old age.

42. *audire te arbitror, Scipio, hospes tuus avitus Masinissa quae faciat hodie nonaginta natus annos; cum ingressus iter pedibus sit, in equum omnino non ascendere, cum autem equo, ex equo non descendere, nullo imbri, nullo frigore adduci, ut capite operto sit, summam esse in eo siccitatem corporis, itaque omnia exsequi regis officia et munera.*

It is sure, as Cicero reports in the book that he wrote about old age, that no snow or rain could compel Masinissa to cover his head. They say he used to stand motionless in the same place for several hours and would not stir his foot before young men employed in the same exercise grew tired; and if he had to sit to do anything, quite often he remained the whole day upon the ground without stretching a limb. In fact for a night and the greater part of a day he led his army from horseback, and he never relaxed the harsh discipline he had learned to endure from youth, so as to soften his old age. He was potent as long as he lived and sired a son, Methymnus, after his eighty-sixth year. His constant concern for agriculture left fertile the barren, desert land he had inherited. (Valerius 8.13.ext.1)[43]

Masinissa, who was king of the Libyans and the constant friend of Rome, lived ninety years in full health. On his death he left ten sons whose upbringing he entrusted to the Romans. His physical condition was exceptional, schooled from childhood in endurance and toil: for instance, he used to remain motionless, fixed in his tracks for the entire day. Once seated he spent the day conducting affairs and did not rise until nightfall. Once mounted, he did not grow faint, riding the entire day and night. The following is the clearest indication of his strength of constitution: at nearly ninety years of age he had a four-year-old son of remarkable health. He so diligently cared for his property that he left to each son a fully

43. *Masinissa Numidiae rex hunc modum excessit, regni spatium LX annis emensus, vel ante omnes homines robore senectae admirabilis. constat eum, quem ad modum Cicero refert libro, quem de senectute scripsit, nullo umquam imbri, nullo frigore ut caput suum veste tegeret adduci potuisse. eundem ferunt aliquot horis in eodem vestigio perstare solitum, non ante moto pede quam consimili labore iuvenes fatigasset, ac si quid agi ab sedente oporteret, toto die saepe numero nullam in partem converso corpore in solio durasse. ille vero etiam exercitus equo insidens noctem diei plerumque iungendo duxit nihilque omnino ex his operibus, quae adulescens sustinere adsueverat, quo mollius senectutem ageret, omisit. veneris etiam usu ita semper viguit, ut post sextum et octogesimum annum filium generaret, cui Methymno nomen fuit. terram quoque, quam vastam ac desertam acceperat, perpetuo culturae studio frugiferam reliquit.*

equipped estate of ten thousand plethra. He ruled with distinction for seventy years. (Diodorus 32.16.1)[44]

The relation of Cicero and Valerius seems clear. Not only are there verbal parallels, but Valerius names his source. Why is Diodorus necessary or relevant? Maire contended that Valerius' notice of the length of Masinissa's rule and the second half of this exemplum derive from Diodorus. Indeed, it is true that Valerius indicates his change of source with *ferunt*. Maire has preferred Diodorus to the lost section of Livy since Polybius, Livy's source, named the late-born son as Stembanos and not, as Valerius and presumably Diodorus, Methymnus. The epitome of Livy book 50, however, offers stronger direct evidence than this extrapolation of what Livy may have called the king's last-born son. The epitome writes of these events: "Masinissa, the king of Numidia, died at over ninety years of age, an exceptional man. Among his other youthful exploits, performed up to his death, his potency in his old age was such that he fathered a son after his eighty-sixth birthday."[45] The abbreviator's "among other youthful exploits" betrays the subject of the first part of the second half of the exemplum, that which Maire assigned to Diodorus. Valerius' penultimate sentence then corresponds to the final result clause of the epitomator. Both a verbatim repetition and the syntax, the result clause itself, have been preserved. The

---

44. Ὅτι Μασανάσσης ὁ Λιβύων βεβασιλευκὼς καὶ τὴν πρὸς Ῥωμαίους φιλίαν τετηρηκὼς ἐνενήκοντα μὲν ἐβίω ἔτη ἐν δυνάμει, παῖδας δέκα ἐν τῷ ἀπαλλάττεσθαι καταλιπών, οὓς καὶ Ῥωμαίοις ἐπιτροπεύεσθαι παρεκατέθετο. ἦν δὲ καὶ κατὰ τὴν τοῦ σώματος εὐτονίαν διαφέρων καὶ καρτερίᾳ καὶ πόνοις συνήθης ἐκ παιδός· ὅς γε στὰς ἐν τοῖς ἴχνεσιν ὅλην τὴν ἡμέραν ἀκίνητος ἔμενε, καθεζόμενος δὲ οὐκ ἠγείρετο, μέχρι νυκτὸς ἐνημερεύων ταῖς τῶν πόνων μελέταις, ἐπὶ δὲ τὸν ἵππον ἐπιβαίνων συνεχῶς ἡμέραν καὶ νύκτα καὶ ταῖς ἱππασίαις χρώμενος οὐκ ἐξελύετο. σημεῖον δὲ τῆς περὶ αὐτὸν εὐεξίας τε καὶ δυνάμεως μέγιστον· ἐνενήκοντα γὰρ σχεδὸν ἔχων ἔτη υἱὸν εἶχε τετραετῆ διαφέροντα τῇ τοῦ σώματος ῥώμῃ. ἐν δὲ ταῖς τῶν ἀγρῶν ἐπιμελείαις τοσοῦτον διήνεγκεν ὡς ἑκάστῳ τῶν υἱῶν ἀπολιπεῖν ἀγρὸν μυριόπλεθρον, κεκοσμημένον πάσαις ταῖς κατασκευαῖς. ἐβασίλευσε δ' ἐπιφανῶς ἔτη ἑξήκοντα.

45. *Masinissa Numidiae rex maior nonaginta annis decessit, vir insignis. inter cetera iuvenalia opera, quae ad ultimum edidit, adeo etiam veneris usu in senecta viguit, ut post sextum et octogesimum annum filium genuerit.*

epitomator has glossed over the king's display of youthful energy that Valerius took from Livy in full.

This exemplum provides an object lesson in the deduction of sources. Without the epitome (and Maire does not quote it), the coincidence of events, the series of the narrative, does correspond to Diodorus. Thereupon, a lost source is reconstructed (Livy's source's name for the son) to demonstrate the lineage of Valerius' version. The first caveat for the critic must be to remember that these stories were familiar and that all extant versions need not depend upon each other. A second temptation is to refer such troublesome cases to lost sources. Indeed, this chapter (8.13) with its many Greek references has been attributed to Verrius Flaccus. This may be true for those foreign exempla that cite Greek sources, but Valerius can combine sources, as he has here Cicero and Livy. From such concrete, if at one time controversial, cases as Masinissa, the reader should be skeptical of attributions of famous Roman anecdotes, especially when treated by Cicero and Livy, to lost, epitomized, or Greek sources. An exemplum is a very short story, and a rhetorical exemplum is a stock story with inherited elements. In discriminating between possible sources, a parallelism of syntax and not just coincidence of diction or event reveal more surely from what author Valerius is working.

The bizarre case of the painful end of Atilius Regulus reveals in similar fashion the failings of Maire's methodology. Cicero, Valerius, and John Tzetzes, versifying Diodorus in the twelfth century, all relate the death of the captured general. Krieger had argued that the first part of this exemplum (9.2.ext.1a) derived from Cicero's speech *In Pisonem* 43. Maire proposed instead Diodorus on two grounds: first, the proximate positions of Regulus and Xanthippus (9.2.ext.1 and 9.6.ext.1 and Diodorus 23.16) indicate a pair taken from Diodorus; and second, Maire finds Appian's version (*Lib.* 15–17) similar to Valerius and believes Diodorus to be Appian's source.[46] But if one relies on the concrete evidence of Tzetzes, who declares he is taking the stories of

46. Krieger 1888, 4, 5, 37. Maire (1899, 24–25) uses the concurrence of subject matter in Appian with two other exempla from this general section of Valerius (9.6.ext.1 and 2) to argue for a widespread use of Diodorus in these chapters.

Regulus and Xanthippus from Diodorus (23.16), and on Cicero's phrasing, Diodorus becomes a most unlikely source.

Tzetzes' verses concur with Cicero and Valerius in having the Carthaginians excise Regulus' eyelids, but Diodorus' versifier continues:

> Forcing him into a small, narrow enclosure,
> Goading a wild elephant to frenzy,
> They drove the elephant to drag him under and grind him up.[47]

No rampaging elephant enlivens Valerius' and Cicero's pages. Instead, Cicero relates, "The Carthaginians cut out M. Regulus' eyelids, tied him into a device, and killed him with sleeplessness."[48] Valerius' single addition to this is a gloss on the instrument of torture and on the reason for death, "The Carthaginians cut out Atilius Regulus' eyelids, shut him up in a device lined with very sharp spikes, and killed him by lack of sleep as well as by unremitting pain—a method of torture not fit for the victim, most fit for the perpetrators."[49] *Machina* and *vigilando* have been explained, and a rhetorical antithesis has been added to close the example. Valerius' chapter heading is cruelty, and, of course, the Carthaginians lead the way, providing the first three illustrations. Cicero's theme was the philosophical commonplace that the virtuous man cannot suffer, and so he told the story of Regulus in order to maintain the paradox that he suffered no punishment (*supplicium*). Immediately before, Cicero had written of the wise man ever happy even if roasted in the bull of Phalaris. This story Valerius narrates as the ninth of the foreign examples, though with a change of theme. Valerius emphasizes the tyrant's cruelty; still, his words echo Cicero even as he again dilates on the length of the torture—compare "Cruel was the inventor of that

---

47. Diodorus 23.16.5–7 (Tzetzes 3.359–62):

> μικρᾷ δὲ τοῦτον εἴρξαντες καλύβῃ στενωτάτῃ,
> ἄγριον ἐξοιστρήσαντες ἐλέφαντα θηρίον,
> ἐκίνουν τοῦτον καθ᾽ αὑτοῦ συγκατασπᾶν καὶ ξέειν.

48. *In Pison.* 43: *M. Regulus, quem Karthagienses Atilium Regulum resectis palpebris inligatum in machina vigilando necaverunt.*

49. *Karthaginienses Atilium Regulum palpebris resectis machinae, in qua undique praeacuti stimuli eminebant, inclusum vigilantia pariter et continuo tractu doloris necaverunt, tormenti genus haud dignum passo, auctoribus dignissimum.*

bull inside which the victims, once the fire was kindled from below, in a long, confined torture . . ." and "the victim was roasted inside the bull of Phalaris once the fire was lit from below."[50]

Comparison of Valerius with Cicero and Diodorus repeatedly and unsurprisingly restores Cicero as the source, for the majority of the stories for which Maire sought parallels in Diodorus is the common fare of rhetorical illustration. Regulus and Hannibal and not Zisemis—Roman and not Greek exempla—are the rule. That Valerius used any traceable written source for the first two men is remarkable. His repeated recourse to Cicero demonstrates both the canonicity of that orator and the nature of Valerius' use of a source. Rhetorical introduction, comment, and closure are often his own embellishments of a word, phrase, or figure from Cicero; the narrative of the anecdote is frequently taken from the source but with variation of diction and phrasing. The present discussion of Valerius' use of Diodorus will conclude with an examination of three famous Greek biographical anecdotes where the slightness of verbal correspondences to other sources leads Maire to assert Diodorus. The nature of the correspondences and the particular case of the subject of the latter two, Alexander the Great, will, however, imply otherwise.

In the death of Epaminondas (3.2.ext.5) and in two stories of Alexander (4.7.ext.2 and 6.4.ext.3), Maire's arguments are more involved than they need be in part because any story of Alexander raises the specter of his biographers (especially Curtius Rufus and Justin the epitomator of Pompeius Trogus), and in part because Maire again overlooks the nature of what Valerius has transmitted. Epaminondas reflects the latter problem distinctly. Maire granted some verbal agreement at 3.2.ext.5 with *De finibus* 2.97, but postulated an additional source. The correspondence of Cicero (quoted first) and Valerius is here limited to the *dicta* of the dying hero.

> He asked if his shield was safe. . . . He inquired if the enemy was routed. . . . He ordered the spear that had transfixed him be pulled out.

50. Valerius 9.2.ext.9: *Saevus etiam ille aenei tauri inventor, quo inclusi subditis ignibus longo et abdito cruciatu.* Cicero, *In Pison.* 42: *in Phalaridis tauro inclusus succensis ignibus torreatur.*

> First he inquired whether his shield was safe, then whether the
> enemy would be completely routed. . . . Finally he ordered the
> spear be drawn out.[51]

Maire admits that much of the non-Ciceronian material may be Valerius' own addition, especially since this matter is couched in rhetorical,
antithetical form.[52] Indeed, the final contrast of the hero's features with
his fate is typically Valerian (cf. the final antithesis of Horatius Pulvillus'
vultus). What Valerius has remembered or taken from Cicero is the
essential kernel of the story, those noble and surprising last words. Valerius' only additions are the temporal particles that delineate the order
of the *dicta*. Diodorus, on the other hand, is an unlikely additional
source. Against Cicero and Valerius he mentions physicians and an ar-
mor bearer, Epaminondas' interlocutors, and his version of the con-
versation is different: Epaminondas has to ask, in Diodorus, which side
won. Like any practitioner of declamation, Valerius would have memorized scores of exempla, and the *dicta* of famous men. Here the *dicta*,
perhaps the only words he would memorize verbatim, are drawn from
Cicero.

Pompeius Trogus

A similar mnemonic and compositional technique shaped the two
stories of Alexander. Led on by his faith in the dependence of the prior
exemplum (Damon and Phintias), Maire contended that 4.7.ext.2, in
which Darius' mother mistakes Hephaestion for Alexander, also derived from Diodorus. Crohn had suggested Pompeius Trogus (Curtius
Rufus 3.12.16–17).[53] Curtius Rufus has all the royal women (*reginae*)
and not simply Sisigambis venerating the wrong man and further peo-
ples his scene with eunuchs who inform the queen of her mistake. Dio-

51. *De finibus* 2.97: *quaesivit, salvusne esset clipeus. . . . rogavit, essentne fusi hostes. . . . evelli iussit eam, qua erat transfixus, hastam.* Valerius 3.2.ext.5: *primum an clipeus suus salvus esset deinde an penitus fusi hostes forent interrogavit. . . . e corpore deinde suo hastam educi iussit.*

52. Maire 1899, 20.

53. H. Crohn, "De Trogi Pompeii apud antiquos auctoritate" (dissertation, Strassburg, 1882), 7, 31, 32, cited by Maire 1899, 20 n. 2.

dorus refers to "bystanders" who corrected the queen. Valerius has eliminated the princesses and attendants as extras with no speaking parts. Maire had argued that no verbal parallels, however, substantiate any alleged dependence of Valerius on Curtius Rufus (Valerius' *excusationis verba quaerebat* Crohn had asserted was an echo of *ignorantiam . . . excusans*). Valerius, as Maire pointed out, is much closer to Diodorus, which is to say that there is one more verbal similarity. On the one hand, the final *dicta* of all three are predictably similar: Diodorus, "Don't worry, mother, he too is an Alexander"; Valerius, "He said, 'No matter your confusion of the name, he too is an Alexander'"; and Curtius Rufus, "He said, 'You made no mistake, mother; he too is an Alexander.'"[54] On the other hand, Maire rested his case on a similarity at another point in the anecdote. Diodorus' τῷ μεγέθει δὲ καὶ κάλλει προέχοντος τοῦ Ἡφαιστιῶνος (17.37.5) seems translated by Valerius as *Hephaestionemque, quia et statura et forma praestabat*. On the basis of the general similarity of the final *dicta* and the striking similarity of this one phrase, Maire identified Diodorus as Valerius' source. This, he thought, was the best solution from the extant sources, but of course the task at hand is not to rank the similarity of surviving candidates. Maire's conclusion is untenable for two reasons. First, the echoing of a single phrase is not in Valerius' manner. Second, the sequence and quality of the other parallels, both *praestabat* and the final words, suggest that Valerius has used Trogus and not Diodorus for this foreign story.[55] Famous *dicta*, especially a famous joke or retort, may well retain their form in many tellings, and this similarity does not indicate the linear dependence of written sources. Oral versions and even variant written traditions would have this essential element of the story the same while scene and characters could be varied.

Despite these general considerations, the evidence, specifically the

---

54. Diodorus 17.37.5: μηδὲν φροντίσῃς, ὦ μῆτερ· καὶ γὰρ καὶ οὗτος Ἀλέξανδρός ἐστιν. Valerius 4.7.ext.2: *"nihil est,"* inquit, *"quod hoc nomine confundaris: nam et hic Alexander est."* Curtius Rufus 13.12.7: *"non erravisti,"* inquit, *"mater, nam et hic Alexander est."*

55. This conclusion rests on comparison not with Justin, the third-century epitomator of the Augustan Pompeius Trogus, but on the Claudian Curtius Rufus, who often borrowed the diction and phrasing of Trogus.

closest verbal alignment, which Maire ignored, does point to a different conclusion. The final words of Valerius and Curtius are more similar than Maire concedes and, once Valerius' habit of composition is recalled, more similar than first inspection reveals. Curtius ends his story thus: ". . . [the queen] trying to excuse her failure to recognize the king she had never seen before. Lifting her by the hand the king said, 'You made no mistake, mother; he too is an Alexander.'" Valerius wrote, "Once corrected, in abject terror she tried to express her excuse. Alexander replied, 'No matter your confusion of the name, he too is an Alexander.'"[56] Not only are the final words the same, as one expects in such a story, but the sentence structure is parallel. In addition, note that the parallels of these authors are not limited to the final words; both have *praestabat* earlier. Valerius has removed some of the unseemly groveling: for Curtius' *Sisigambis advoluta est pedibus eius* Valerius has *admonita*. Both participles are at the beginning of the cola. The next colon in Curtius (*ignorantiam . . . excusans*) is the model for Valerius' next colon. This dependence is at first not obvious because Valerius has engaged in his customary transformation of diction: *erroris* was suggested by *errasti* in Curtius' final *dicta,* and consequently Valerius uses a different stem altogether when he comes to this, *confundaris.* Valerius is working colon by colon. The next colon, the first of the final sentence in each author, begins with a relative pronoun referring to the queen. The syntactic similarity continues in the division of the cola of the direct speech: two words, *inquit,* another separate unit—the vocative in Curtius, an explanatory relative clause in Valerius (made necessary by the avoidance of *errasti* whose stem Valerius had already used). The final words are the same. This similarity of structure, of phrasing, and of syntax, and the indications of the transformation of diction reveal dependence on a particular passage and not simply on the commonly known and remembered witticism of a famous historical character.

Maire sought to attribute a second story of Alexander to Diodorus, but this too should be restored to Pompeius Trogus. In counsel Par-

---

56. Curtius: . . . *ignorantiam numquam antea visi regis excusans. quam manu adlevans rex, "non errasti," inquit, "mater, nam et hic Alexander est."* Valerius: *admonita deinde erroris per summam trepidationem excusationis verba quaerebat. cui Alexander, "nihil est," inquit, "quod hoc nomine confundaris: nam et hic Alexander est."*

menion told Alexander to accept Darius' terms. Valerius tells the story of Alexander's reply in the chapter on "Dignified Words and Deeds" (6.4.ext.3). This chapter is a series of short notices that, with the barest sketch of context and protagonists, quotes famous replies. The epitomator of Trogus does not relate this story; for though he mentions the third embassy Darius sent Alexander, the point at which this anecdote occurs, he characteristically omits councils and debates. Curtius Rufus, however, does have a version that suggests Valerius' source is again Trogus. The direct parallel is a version of Alexander's reply to Parmenion's rather long speech of advice urging Alexander to accept Darius' generous peace proposal: "He said, 'I too would prefer riches to glory, if I were Parmenion.'" Valerius has, "When Parmenion said that if he were Alexander, he would accept the offer, Alexander replied, 'I too would accept, if I were Parmenion.'"[57] Maire, of course, advanced Diodorus because he felt this parallel too slim, but here Valerius' diction does provide another clue. Curtius', and probably the original's, antithesis of money and glory has been replaced in Valerius with the rather abstract "condition." This word is to be found in Curtius at the end of the paragraph that precedes Alexander's words. Parmenion summarizes his advice: "he could gain through treaty, not war, a prosperous kingdom and that no other man had possessed the country between the Hister and the Euphrates, a territory far flung and vast" (4.11.13).[58] This final sentence of Parmenion's advice has also supplied Valerius with the terms of Darius' offer, though here an error has crept in. Valerius does not follow Trogus' diction as preserved by Rufus: he has identified the territory from a Roman perspective and thus does not refer to the two rivers but instead writes "the portion of the kingdom this side of Mount Taurus" (*partem regni Tauro tenus monte*).

The next discrepancy allowed Maire to posit that Valerius was using a source in addition to Diodorus.[59] The size of Darius' tribute is put at

---

57. Curtius 4.11.14: *"et ego," inquit, "pecuniam quam gloriam mallem, si Parmenion essem."* Valerius 6.4.ext.3: *cum Parmenion dixisset se, si Alexander esset, usurum ea condicione, respondit, "et ego uterer, si Parmenion essem."*

58. *opimum eum regnum occupare posse condicione, non bello, nec quemquam alium inter Histrum et Euphratem possedisse terras ingenti spatio intervalloque discretas.*

59. Maire 1899, 22.

thirty thousand talents by Curtius and Diodorus; Valerius has a million (Curtius Rufus, *XXX milibus talentum*; Valerius, *decies centum milibus talentum*). The source of this error escapes location; one can as easily posit scribal error as the author's lapse of memory. In either case one million talents is clearly wrong; it is not a variant tradition, for no one else writes of this figure. Moreover, the positive evidence of Valerius' and Curtius' similar phrasing classifies this exemplum as another borrowing from Trogus and not Diodorus.

In the last two exempla considered, Valerius has turned to Trogus for material on Alexander and not—despite Maire's arguments—to Diodorus or any of the Hellenistic accounts of the king's campaigns. Valerius seems again to have preferred an Augustan, Latin source. Alexander, a frequent subject in Valerius' foreign examples, and Pompeius Trogus provide significant insight into Valerius' choice of source. In particular, they offer a positive picture of his handling of foreign material, whereas in the case of Diodorus the source hunter is reduced to demonstrating false trails. Trogus is the one source other than Livy and Cicero whose use most critics have granted Valerius. Valerius' borrowings reveal a characteristic variation of word order and of verbal prefix and the substitution of synonyms. Compare Trogus and Valerius on the gory revenge of Tomyris: *Caput Cyri amputatum in utrem humano sanguine repletum coici regina iubet cum hac exprobratione crudelitatis: "satia te," inquit, "sanguine quem sitisti cuiusque insatiabilis semper fuisti"* (Justin 1.8.13) and *Tomyris, quae caput Cyri abscisum in utrem humano sanguine repletum demitti iussit exprobrans illi insatiabilem cruoris sitim* (9.10.ext.1). Cyrus again demonstrates Valerius' dependence: Justin's *Hic [Astyages] per somnum vidit ex naturalibus filiae, quam unicam habebat, vitem enatam, cuius palmite omnis Asia obumbraretur* (1.4.2) is the source for Valerius' *enatam vitem . . . inumbraret* (1.7.ext.5). The tyrant Ptolemy Physcon has the same literary pedigree. Valerius' notice, though brief, of the king's crimes nonetheless reveals a verbal dependence on Trogus: Justin (38.8.5) relates that "after raping his virgin daughter and forcing her to marry him, he divorced his own sister" (*ipsam quoque sororem filia eius virgine per vim stuprata et in matrimonium adscita repudiat*). Valerius' words (9.1.ext.5: *filia eius per vim stuprata ipsam dimisit*) echo these. A less demonstrable case of imitation of Trogus is 4.3.14 where Krieger believed that Pyrrhus' attempted bribery of the Romans showed evidence of combination of Livy and Trogus.[60] Valerius' *nulla cuiusquam dono ianua patuit* is indeed an echo of Trogus (Justin 18.2.7: *neminem, cuius domus muneribus pateret, invenit*). The parallel with Livy is too slight to be convincing: at 34.4.6 the historian reports, as does Valerius, that men and women were resistant to Pyrrhus' bribes. Justin's truncated account certainly implies the same. Further, Justin here writes of *continentia*, which Valerius has taken as his chapter heading.

Maire then was not wrong to seek a universal historian from whose work Valerius took foreign examples. He did, however, choose the wrong individual and, more fundamentally, the wrong language. But did Trogus provide Valerius the majority or even a significant proportion of his foreign material? Was Maire correct to seek a third source ranking just after Cicero and Livy and, like them, providing material on a grand scale? This is difficult to judge in the case of Trogus, in part because his work is preserved in an abbreviated form. But the stories about Alexander at least demonstrate that Valerius used more than just Livy and Cicero and suggest that lack of material did not drive Valerius to fill up his pages from some treatment of foreign history. Valerius has followed Trogus on the subject of Alexander for the stories of Hephaestion's misidentification and Parmenion's advice but also for the story of Alexander' plunge into the river Cydnus, his illness, and subsequent cure at the hands of the suspect physician Philippus.[61] However, for much of the anecdotal material Valerius has to tell of Alexander, no earlier authority survives. Lactantius 2.8, for instance, reports the same story Valerius has at 1.1.ext.5, but no earlier account has survived.[62] The fantastic figures large in such examples, so Alexander dreams of his poisoning in Valerius (1.7.ext.2) but not in Curtius Rufus or Justin. The passage 1.4.ext.1 reports an omen on Alexander's

---

60. Krieger 1888, 78.

61. Cf. Valerius 3.8.ext.6 with Curtius 3.5 and Justin 11.8.5. Atkinson (1980) has taken up the argument that these passages demonstrate Valerius' reading of Trogus.

62. Valerius 1.1.ext.5 (Paris): "When Miletus was captured by Alexander, the soldiers who had broken in to despoil the temple of Milesian Ceres were met with flames and lost their sight" (*Milesia Ceres Mileto ab Alexandro capta milites, qui templum spoliaturi inruperant, flamma obiecta privavit oculis*).

founding of Alexandria; at 7.3.ext.1, to fulfill a prophecy, Alexander executes an ass. Others of Valerius' Alexandrian exempla are also without earlier parallel. At 3.3.ext.1 a young Macedonian silently endures while a coal burns his arm during a sacrifice before Alexander. Athenian resistance to Alexander and the perils of that opposition are summed up in a *sententia* that Valerius alone preserves (7.2.ext.13, "Wise too was the saying of Demades. For when the Athenians refused to decree divine honors to Alexander, he said, 'Consider that while you guard heaven, you may lose land.'"[63] Some of this material could be credited to Trogus—so modern editors include 7.3.ext.4 (Anaximenes delivering his city Lampsacus from Alexander's destruction) in the précis for Curtius' lost first book—but omens, dreams, and prophecies inevitably cluster about Alexander or Scipio or Hannibal, and do not require a historiographical or perhaps even a written source.

At times, however, Valerius is clearly not following what can be reconstructed as Trogus' version, and more frequently Cicero can be demonstrated his source. Alexander warming an old soldier and giving him his seat receives extravagant praise from Valerius. Curtius Rufus' and Trogus' anti-Alexanderism is not felt here, and comparison of Valerius' exemplum (5.1.ext.1) with the corresponding passage in Curtius (8.4.15–17) reveals difference of detail and no verbal borrowing.[64] Instead, Cicero's *Tusculans* has provided Valerius with this and a number of other stories about Alexander. Indeed, Valerius has taken a series of pairs of foreign stories from this work of Cicero. The fifth book of the *Tusculans* (5.91–92) provided Valerius with such a pair, 4.3.ext.3 (Xenocrates not enticed by a "high-born whore at Athens" or by Alexander's money) and 4.3.ext.4 (Diogenes asks Alexander to move out of the sun—Valerius and Cicero both continue with a story of Diogenes and Dionysius). This same work (*Tusc.* 2.52) may have provided the subjects but not the models for 3.3.ext.4 (Anaxarchus spits his bitten-off tongue at a tyrant; Alexander is mentioned as one of his students) and for 8.14.ext.2 (Alexander is distressed at Anaxarchus saying there are infinite worlds). Another Alexandrian pair taken from Cicero is 1.8.ext.9

63. *Demadis quoque dictum sapiens. nolentibus enim Atheniensibus divinos honores Alexandro decernere, "videte," inquit, "ne dum caelum custoditis, terram amittatis."*
64. Atkinson 1980, 40.

and 10. In the latter the Indian self-immolator Calanus tells Alexander, "I'll see you soon" (*"Brevi te," inquit, "videbo"*; cf. *De div.* 1.47). The death of Philip in 1.8.ext.9 is not drawn from, but the subject again paralleled at, *De fato* 5. From the second book of the *De officiis* (2.71) comes 7.2.ext.9 (Themistocles' marriage advice to his daughter); 7.2.ext.10 (Philip advises his son on bought friends) refers to the same letter of paternal advice as *De officiis* 2.48, though here Cicero is not Valerius' model. This Macedonian subject leads to another, 7.2.ext.11 (Aristotle's advice to Callisthenes and Callisthenes' subsequent death on Alexander's order). Valerius strings along his theme, listing two more of Aristotle's *dicta* before passing to the philosopher Anaxagoras' *dictum* (7.2.12) and then Demades' advice to the Athenians. The strain of criticism in these stories of Philip and Alexander is in keeping with Trogus, but Valerius' references are too brief to allow comparison. Curtius (8.5–6) does have a developed account of Callisthenes' opposition to *proskunesis* and Alexander's resulting resentment and cruelty. He narrates Callisthenes' death at 8.8 (cf. Justin 12.7.1 and 15.3.3–5). But the actions and words of philosophers might be known from many sources. Valerius is the first extant source to relate Aristotle's rescue of his native city from the Macedonians' wrath (5.6.ext.5), but this had no doubt served to illustrate many commonplaces on the advantages of philosophy.

In short, even stories to the discredit of Alexander cannot automatically be traced to Trogus. The greatest, most eloquent complaints about Alexander's anger and cruelty are delivered in Hermolaus' speech in Curtius Rufus (8.7, especially 8.7.12–13). Valerius at 9.3.ext.1 lists as victims of the king's anger Lysimachus, Cleitus, and Callisthenes. Justin (15.3) writes of Lysimachus and the lion sent to kill him. The deaths of Cleitus and Callisthenes are told in both Curtius Rufus and Justin, but the three are not strung together. Valerius' compression is the natural reflex of the list maker, the speaker intent on a series of exempla of tyrant's victims.

Similarly, the complaints of 9.5.ext.1 are in accord with the Curtius-Trogus anti-Alexandrian tradition. Hermolaus' speech of protest in Curtius offers some verbal parallel. Here echoes of Trogus' diction may be discerned. Curtius has Hermolaus complain, "Persian dress and lifestyle fascinate you; you hate your fathers' ways and loathe your father

Philip; and if there were any god above Jupiter, you would disdain Jupiter himself " (8.7.12–13).[65] Valerius seems to have from Trogus Alexander's new tastes: "Out of his disdain for Philip he claimed Ammonian Jupiter as father; out of boredom with Macedonian customs and way of life he adopted Persian dress and practices; spurning mortal condition, he imitated the divine."[66] This passage probably does reflect Valerius' reading of Trogus, but stories of Alexander's arrogance like any foreign subject need not be taken from one source. Alexander was a common character in *suasoriae*, and his *dicta* were common possessions. No source can be sought, when verbal parallels fail, for these familiar stories. The biographers of Alexander do relate, for example, that the king would have none but Apelles paint him, none but Lysippus sculpt him. These stories are joined by Valerius, and no doubt by many others before him: Cicero alludes to these artistic preferences in *Ad familiares* 5.12.7, and Horace tells the same at *Epistles* 2.1.237.[67]

Diodorus Siculus was not a source for Valerius Maximus, who took his foreign material—where it is traceable—from Cicero and Pompeius Trogus. We lack the means to compare all of the foreign exempla to alleged sources. But the conclusion remains that, where we can compare Valerius and Diodorus, the Greek author has, with possibly one exception, not been used. Again and again, Valerius has sought the nearer source, the late republican and Augustan Romans whom he used for his domestic examples, and not the Greek. The implications for source reconstruction are clear. Comparison with Diodorus and Cicero has revealed far more about the character of Valerian rewriting: his method is almost agglutinative. The gloss, the addition of lead-in

65. *Persarum te vestis et disciplina delectant, patrios mores exosus es . . . tu Philippum patrem aversaris et, si quis deorum ante Iovem haberetur, fastidires etiam Iovem.*

66. Valerius 9.5.ext.1: *fastidio enim Philippi Iovem Hammonem patrem ascivit, taedio morum et cultus Macedonici vestem et instituta Persica adsumit, spreto mortali habitu divinum aemulatus est. . . .*

67.
    Idem rex ille, poema
 qui tam ridiculum tam care prodigus emit,
 edicto vetuit ne quis se praeter Apellem
 pingeret aut alius Lysippo duceret aera
 fortis Alexandri vultum simulantia.

and final *sententia,* and not variant source are often responsible for Valerius' "discrepancies."

Sallust

Seneca, when asking Cassius Severus—both men were contemporaries of Valerius—why his declamations were so inferior to his actual speeches, received the answer that genius is often limited to one genre, so "the speeches of Sallust are read out of respect for his histories" (*Contr.* 3. pr.8, *orationes Sallustii in honorem historiarum leguntur*). This is actually the second of four examples Cassius offers for his explanation; the others are Cicero's wretched verse, Virgil's poor efforts at prose, and Plato's *Apology* (an unsuccessful speech, after all—a Roman orator's reputation depended on securing an acquittal). Sallust's historical writings were, then, famous and familiar reading for the declaimers. Thus it is odd indeed that Sallust was so long denied as a source for Valerius. Only in 1979 did Roberto Guerrini contend that Valerius had used the historian.[68] His article is distinguished for cogent arguments regarding two specific exempla and, more important, for the realization that Sallust's influence was exercised on more than single exempla: Sallust, Guerrini maintained, provided the theme and even a moral vocabulary for an entire chapter. In addition Guerrini tried to demonstrate the influence upon Valerius' proem of Sallust's statement of methods at the beginning of the *Catilinarian Conspiracy.*

Guerrini's remarks on the imitation of the proem could be strengthened by Bliss's conclusions on Valerius' transfers of diction and the substitution of compound forms for simple and vice versa. Thereby, the relation of Sallust's *statui res gestas populi Romani carptim, ut quaeque memoria digna videbantur, perscribere (Cat. 4)* to Valerius' *Urbis Romae exterarumque gentium facta simul ac dicta memoratu digna, quae apud alios latius diffusa sunt quam ut breviter cognosci possint, ab inlustribus electa auctoribus digerere constitui* becomes clearer. Valerius follows Sallust at the point in the *Catilinarian Conspiracy* where the historian leaves off his autobiographical notice. *Perscribere,* which can hardly apply to his collection book, he then replaced with *digerere.* The relative clause (*quae apud alios*

68. Guerrini 1979, 152–66.

latius diffusa sunt quam ut breviter cognosci possint) that follows in Valerius may have been suggested by Sallust's *carptim,* which Valerius omits. Although Guerrini makes none of these suggestions, he does point to the characteristically Sallustian phrase *cupido incessit* (which Valerius has used as his own autobiographical explanation for writing).

Guerrini departs from the customary work of the source critics in his observation of the use of the same source in different contexts in Valerius and in his observation of the influence of Sallustian themes and moral vocabulary. Even where Valerius has used Sallust as the source for a single exemplum, Guerrini recognizes the possibility of contamination. For example, Cicero, Sallust, and Valerius all report Catiline's retort:

> That if any conflagration had been kindled to threaten his fortunes, he would quench it with destruction not water. (Cicero, *Pro Mur.* 51)

> "Indeed since I have been surrounded and am being thrown down by my enemies, I shall quench my conflagration with destruction." (Sallust, *Cat.* 31.9)

> When M. Cicero said that he had kindled a conflagration, Lucius Catiline said in the senate, "I feel it and indeed if I can't quench it with water I shall with destruction." (Valerius 9.11.3)[69]

Valerius' *quidem* and the ending but not the prefix of *extinguam* seem drawn from Sallust whereas his *incendium excitatum* and *aqua* come from Cicero. Further and most convincingly, he does follow Sallust's syntax (*inquit* and direct speech). So far, however, just conceivably, Valerius might not have read Sallust for these reminiscences. In the *Pro Murena,* on the one hand, Catiline is responding to Cato, not as Valerius imagines, to Cicero. Sallust had represented the scene slightly differently. Cicero speaks; Catiline makes his excuse; the senate shouts him down.

---

69. Cicero: *si quod esset in suas fortunas incendium excitatum, id se non aqua, sed ruina restincturum.* Sallust: *"quoniam quidem circumventus,"* inquit, *"ab inimicis praeceps agor, incendium meum ruina extinguam."* Valerius: *L. vero Catilina in senatu M. Cicerone incendium ab ipso excitatum dicente "sentio," inquit, "et quidem illud, si aqua non potuero, ruina restinguam."*

Valerius' words arise from Cicero's text; his version of the events seems to follow Sallust's. But Catiline and Cicero were favorites of the schools, which may well have changed one protagonist and made the confrontation more dramatic. Famous exchanges could easily have entered the stock of *sententiae* and then have been embellished. The declaimer Fuscus defined the aesthetic of this sort of rivalry in the halls of declamation: "When I struggle against aphorisms of the best sort, I strive carefully not to injure but to overcome them" (Seneca, *Contr.* 9.1.13: *"Do," inquit, "operam, ut cum optimis sententiis certem, nec illas corrumpere conor sed vincere"*). Although the slight verbal echo of a famous proem hardly signifies familiarity with the work, the remaining three cases (2.8.7, 5.8.5, and 9.1) remove any doubts of Valerius' familiarity with the *Catilinarian Conspiracy* and probably the *Histories*.

In the final exemplum (2.8.7) of "Triumphal Practice" (*De iure triumphandi*), Valerius has assembled in chronological order a series of civil war victors who did not celebrate a triumph. The compression required to fit eight victors, from Scipio Nasica to Sulla, into one example should have obscured the sources. Are "sources" even necessary for an educated Roman of the early first century to name the suppressors of Tiberius Gracchus, of Catiline, and of Lepidus? Surprisingly, two clauses of this exemplum echo two different works of Sallust. The identification of the rebel M. Lepidus seems taken from the *Histories*: compare *M. Lepido cum omnibus copiis pulso* (*Hist.* 1.84) with *M. Lepido . . . cum omnibus seditionis copiis † exstincto* (Valerius 2.8.7). Guerrini notes that the end of the exemplum, the apologetic seal Valerius puts on this unhappy series, echoes *Bellum Iugurthinum*: compare *liberius altiusque processi, dum me civitatis morum piget taedetque* (*B.I.* 4.9) with *Piget taedetque per vulnera rei publicae ulterius procedere* (Valerius 2.8.7). The other correspondences that Guerrini alleges are not direct verbal imitation but possible echoes of Sallust's diction. Indeed, seeking a particular passage as *the* source may be vain if Valerius was simply aiming at maintaining a Sallustian style (more exactly, diction) with what he deemed a Sallustian theme. Thus Guerrini suggested a Sallustian background, from such passages as "when the altars and other things sacred to the gods were defiled with suppliants' blood" (*Hist.* 1.47), for Valerius' "L. Cinna and C. Marius were greedy drinkers of citizens' blood but still did not violate the temples of the gods,"[70] although the connection is very loose.

Valerius has distributed the material he found in Sallust into two chapters, 2.8 and 5.8. He borrows Sallust's diction not just for the exemplum that retails the original story but a little later in the chapter in an exemplum of a subject unrelated to the Sallustian original, a practice that demonstrates that Sallust was more than a source for an anecdote. Guerrini has argued that Valerius' chapter, "The Severity of Fathers toward Their Sons" (5.8), is a development and rhetorical amplification of Sallust's theme.[71] For the story of A. Fulvius' execution of his son, a partisan of Catiline, Valerius has borrowed from Sallust's version.[72] Sallust began the story thus: *in iis* [those not of the original conspiracy who had gone to join Catiline] *erat Fulvius, senatoris filius, quem retractum* whereas Valerius begins *A. Fulvius vir senatorii ordinis . . . retraxit.* Valerius has named the father but has taken the phrasing from Sallust.

Both the moral vocabulary throughout these exempla[73] and the transfer of diction from its original context to a thematically related exemplum suggest Valerius composed the chapter as a whole, as a connected series. A direct reading of Sallust provided an individual ex-

---

70. See Guerrini 1979, 154. Sallust: *cum arae et alia diis sacrata supplicum sanguine foedarentur* (the theme of *sanguis civilis* is found at *Histories* 1.55.14, *Cat.* 14.3, *B.I.* 31.8). Valerius: *L. Cinna et C. Marius hauserant quidem avidi civilem sanguinem, sed non protinus ad templa deorum et aras tetenderunt.* At times the argument is forced: Guerrini proposes Valerius' *Gaius etiam Antonius Catilinae victor abstersos gladios in castra retulit* (also from 2.8.7) "could recollect" *Cat.* 61.7, *neque tamen exercitus populi Romani laetam aut incruentam victoriam adeptus erat.*

71. Guerrini 1979, 156.

72. *Cat.* 39.5: *in iis erat Fulvius, senatoris filius, quem retractum ex itinere parens necari iussit*, and Valerius 5.8.5: *A. Fulvius vir senatorii ordinis euntem in aciem filium retraxit . . . inque castra . . . ruentem medio itinere abstractum supplicio mortis adfecit.* Valerius does not use *necari iussit* here, but has put this phrase three exempla earlier in his account of Sp. Cassius' execution of his own son.

73. Guerrini (1979, 155 n. 15) points out that the diction of Valerius' description of Fulvius' morals is also Sallustian.

emplum, a moral theme and tone for the chapter, and diction for another exemplum in this chapter.

At the very beginning of the ninth book Valerius has used Sallust in a similar fashion. One passage from the *Catilinarian Conspiracy* has provided the anecdote and diction for one exemplum and a phrase for another exemplum of the same theme: 15.2 provided Valerius the story of how Catiline's murder of Orestilla's son cleared his way to marry her (at 9.1.9 which, as Guerrini pointed out, displays clear verbal echoes), and also the phrase *vacuam domum scelestis nuptiis fecisse,* which Valerius has rendered (of the tyrant Ptolemaeus Physcon) *ut vacuum locum nuptiis puellae faceret* (9.1.ext.5 is thus a pastiche: the first half of this sentence echoes Trogus—see my earlier discussion of Justin 38.8.5).[74] In addition in the fifth example of this chapter Valerius has taken from *Histories* 2.70 a description of the depraved luxury of Metellus Pius.[75] As with chapter 5.8 the striking features of Valerius' use of Sallust are that these constitute more than the borrowing of phrase and event for his own reworking. For in these two chapters, "The Severity of Fathers toward Their Sons" and "Luxury and Lust," uncharacteristically critical of Rome and Romans, Valerius has used Sallust not only as source for an individual story but for a tone and vocabulary of moral indignation. In the latter chapter, for example, the Sallustian elements range from the chapter heading itself (*luxuria et libido*) to *audacia, abundantia, pudicitia, stupra, edendi et bibendi voluptas,* past banquets, grand private buildings, the squandering of inheritances, and unhealthy interests in youths and women.[76] The moralizing of Sallust seems the germ for the entire chapter; Valerius is then engaged in the rhetorical amplification of a famous Sallustian passage, a piece of righteous condemnation, which had no doubt become a commonplace.

Six borrowings from the *Catilinarian Conspiracy,* two from the *Jugurthine War,* and two from the *Histories* hardly make Sallust a major source for Valerius. As a minor source, however, he is all the more interesting. For other than the alleged imitation in the proem, Valerius used the historian only for lamentable stages in Rome's history: instances of civil

74. Guerrini 1979, 9.1.5: 159; 9.1.ext.5: 165.
75. Guerrini 1979, 158–59.
76. Guerrini 1979, 163–64.

and domestic conflict. In these Sallust's treatment is the point of departure, the famous example that calls to mind other examples of civil war victors, paternal severity, and especially the vice whose introduction the *Catilinarian Conspiracy* had heralded as critical to Rome's fortunes.

Varro

The Augustan scholar—the Roman scholar par excellence—Marcus Terentius Varro seems the perfect source for Valerius, from the point of view of subject. The antiquarian offers the historian or the propagandist a rich trove, material assembled apparently without partisan, factional bias, the very stuff of history awaiting rhetorical embellishment. Such might have been the attitude of Valerius, for ancestral tradition or Cicero's and Sallust's and Augustus' evocation of that *mos maiorum* fills his pages. Especially for the beginning of Valerius' work, Varro's research into Roman religion would have been the best source a modern scholar could reconstruct.

An enthusiasm for this sort of reconstruction guided the doctoral thesis of Bogdan Krieger, though he has the additional refinement of insisting that where he has conjectured use of Varro, the particular source is the *De vita populi Romani*. In the introduction to his edition of this work, Benedetto Riposati is careful both to correct the general ascriptions of some of the Valerian exempla to Varro and to restrict a number of the specific attributions to the *De vita populi Romani*. Krieger had not been the first to see the suitability of Varro's works to Valerius' interests. Cichorius, for instance, had already concluded in passing that Valerius drew all his theatrical material from Varro.[77] To assert probable use of Varro on the grounds of thematic similarity and appropriateness seems now the hallmark of an era of more confident scholarship, or at least the characteristic of scholars who saw the possibilities of source, information, and even inspiration in more finite and hermetic terms. Varro or Nigidius Figulus might be the best to consult on matters of religion and old Roman ways, but their authority may not have informed, much less governed, Valerius Maximus. Again and

77. Cichorius 1888, 429.

again the reader of Valerius, however tantalized by the prospect of uncovering a rich, unnoticed Varronian lode, must remember that community of knowledge and fiction, the oral performances of Roman declamation, which Valerius serves. For us, then, coincidence of theme will not produce the assertion of the direct influence of a particular written source, especially as we realize the probability of borrowing from a nonwritten source or from the numerous perished ancient texts.

Nonetheless, Varro remains a promising source. Once cited by Valerius (3.2.24) and once the subject of an exemplum (8.7.3), Varro might be the authority for much of the first three books of Valerius, which canvass Roman religion and ancient institutions. The archaic flavor of the wife of Egnatius (6.3.9), the divorce of Carvilius (2.1.4), the ideal Roman wife (2.1.3), and an old-fashioned custom of the senate (2.2.6) hints at a researcher skilled in legal and linguistic antiquarianism. In all these cases, the most certain of Valerius' borrowings from Varro, no substantial verbal parallel remains. The evidence that Varro did write of these matters is gleaned from comparison of Valerius with later users of Varro. In the first case Pliny the Elder tells the same story of Egnatius (who killed his wife with a single blow of his fist for drinking wine, *NH* 14.89); two sentences earlier he had cited Varro as his source. The exemplary conduct of the Roman husband is Valerius' theme again at 2.1.4, the first Roman divorce. Here the constellation of existing versions (Dionysius of Halicarnassus 2.25.7; Plutarch, *Rom. & Thes.* 6, *Lyc. & Num.* 3.6–7, *Quaest. Rom.* 14; see too Gellius 4.3, which cites as source Servius Sulpicius, and 17.21.44) makes Varro a likely source; for although there is no direct citation (as in the case of Egnatius), these authors do use Varro elsewhere, and Plutarch cites Varro in the passage of the *Quaestiones Romanae* immediately preceding Carvilius.[78] Further, Dionysius relates at 2.25 that Roman women of old did not drink wine, a notice that Valerius too has immediately following Carvilius at 2.1.5. This entire section of book 2 may be strongly influenced by Varro, but before any examination of Valerius' larger use of Varro, the methodology of this source criticism should be thoroughly plumbed. So far the conjunction of theme—the antiquarian's conclusion about the early family—and the recurrence of this theme in a later author known to

78. Krieger 1888, 46.

have used Varro proffer the probability that Varro is ultimately Valerius' source.

For the most part, Varro's words have not survived, and so direct comparison is precluded. An exception is 2.2.6: Valerius here relates that of old the senate was not assembled by decree: it kept perpetual session in the place, "which even today is called the *senaculum*" (*qui hodieque senaculum appellatur*). Riposati points out the clear parallel from Varro's *De lingua latina* 5.156: *senaculum vocatum ubi senatus aut ubi seniores consisterent, dictum ut γεϱουσία apud Graecos* and criticizes Krieger's rejection of this parallel and substitution, again, of the *De vita populi Romani* as the source.[79] Valerius is in 2.2.6 and 2.2.7 relating obsolete practices of the senate: its constant vigilance and then removal without summons on the rise of any public business to the Curia and, at 2.2.7, the custom of appending a "C" to its decrees to signify the tribunes' approval. Valerius might be combining material from different sources. A simpler explanation is in this case to side with Krieger for the *De vita populi Romani* or at least against Varro's linguistic work as the source for this customary lore from the senate's early days.

The source critics have proceeded to isolate peculiar facts such as these and to refer them to Varro, especially where no earlier source is extant. So the military prowess of L. Siccius Dentatus, enumerated by Valerius at 3.2.24, has long been attributed to the *De bello et pace* of the *Antiquitates rerum humanarum*.[80] Since Livy does not offer these details and since Varro would have treated Dentatus in the *De bello et pace*, Varro is declared the source. This is of course more than argument from Livian silence; the list of Varro's works and reconstruction of their contents direct the critic. For example, at 9.2.ext.1, appended to the story of Regulus (which as I have demonstrated is drawn from Cicero's *In Pisonem* 43) comes as a further instance of Carthaginian cruelty, the keelhauling of Roman captives. The only other ancient authority for this episode is Nonius 163.23. Varro and in particular the third book of the *De vita populi Romani* seem then a likely source.

What sort of source Varro would have been for Valerius at this junc-

---

79. Riposati 1939, 62.

80. Krieger (1888, 28 n. 9), cites Thilo, *De Varrone Plutarchi quaestionum Romanarum auctore praecipuo*, 7.

ture is another question. For it seems an abstruse and labored manner of composition if Valerius is checking Varro to fill out a single exemplum whose primary matter he already has from Cicero. This is not to deny the learned reconstruction of Krieger and others before him. Varro may well have written of Punic barbarity, having read of it in some junior annalist. But the cruelty of Hannibal and his fellows is so commonplace that one can easily imagine this being retold or additional episodes invented in the rhetorical schools or declamatory halls. A more concrete check on the reconstruction of sources and of Varro in particular comes in two cases of misattribution (Krieger led astray in his enthusiasm for Varro at 2.1.10 and 4.3.14) and two cases of doubtful attribution (5.6.4 and 2.8.2). The historicity of young Roman nobles singing the praises of their ancestors while at dinner need not concern us here. In the *Tusculans* (1.3 and 4.3) Cicero tells this story, invoking the elder Cato as his authority. Varro tells much the same in a fragment preserved by Nonius (77.2–5). Riposati reasserts the clear and usual conclusion that Cicero's version is being followed; Valerius shows no trace of Varro's mention of *pueri modesti* and their *assa voce*.[81] In the second case, Nonius (532.10–12) again has a very brief fragment of Varro, on Pyrrhus' attempt to corrupt the Romans—the story told by Valerius at 4.3.14, which along with the second half of 4.3.6, a story of Fabricius Luscinus, he may have take from Trogus (Justin 18.2.6–8); compare Livy 34.4.6 and 11. These two exempla display Valerius at his characteristic composition, using Cicero, Trogus, and perhaps Livy, even if the scholar of Reate may have treated the episode with greater concern for historical accuracy.

Riposati's estimation of the use of Varro, far more conservative and credible than Krieger's, reflects an appropriate diffidence. The variety of ancient treatments not just for the major figures of Roman history but for those "minor" figures whom we may know about only from one or two incidental notices must be kept in mind. Two cases where Krieger is surely wrong to assert Varro as source underscore this. A praetor Aelius had a *picus* perch on his head. The *haruspices* advised that to kill the bird would bring ruin to his family but great success to the Republic, to spare it the reverse. Riposati has discerned well the pitfalls of

81. Riposati 1939, 63.

trying to reduce all extant accounts to stemmatic lines leading back to Varro, for discrepancies in the name given the praetor impede resolution. Varro (preserved by Nonius at 518.37) calls him P. Aelius Paetus; Valerius (5.6.4) has simply *Aelio praetore*; Ps. Frontinus (4.5.14) following Valerius has L. Aelius; Pliny the Elder (*NH* 10.41) calls him Aelius Tubero.[82] Pliny and Valerius do not at any rate seem to be following Varro.

The sheer variety of sources available to Valerius also makes Riposati skeptical of Krieger's attribution to Varro of 2.8.2, where after the defeat of the Carthaginians off the Aegates Islands, the praetor Valerius conducts a rival triumph while the consul Lutatius parades in the official celebration. Nonius (552.22) mentions the wounding of this same consul at the Aegates Islands and refers it to the third book of Varro's *De vita populi Romani*. Riposati argued that this event must have been told at the end of Varro's work where a full-scale treatment, such as Valerius', would not have been appropriate.[83] The story, he suggests, would also have been available in nearly all other ancient historians. Certainly, no direct evidence indicates that Varro wrote of the praetor's private triumph. The slender clue that the praetor Valerius did figure in Varro's work cannot displace all the sources for the Punic Wars that Valerius had at hand.

The temptation to ascribe what seem isolated notices to the one source we know treated this material is strong. This tendency figures in the attribution of 2.8.6 to Varro. The subject is the practice of the Roman triumphator on the eve of his triumph to invite and disinvite, immediately, the consuls to dinner, a custom described by Valerius, by Nonius (94.13), and by Plutarch (*Quaest. Rom.* 80). As Riposati pointed out, Kettner had long since argued that this was common knowledge.[84]

Rather than drag the reader on a labored march through all the individual exempla whose subject might or might not be Varronian, this

---

82. Riposati 1939, 64–65. On the uncertainty of the identification of this praetor, see "Quintus Aelius Paetus," *RE* no. 103.

83. Riposati 1939, 66.

84. H. Kettner, *M. Terentii Varronis de vita populi romani ad Q. Caecilium Pomponianum Atticum librorum quattuor quae extant* (Halae, 1863), 15 cited in Riposati 1939, 69.

study will consider three areas where Varro had material to offer Valerius that elsewhere he would not have found or would not have found in so convenient a form. These are the chapters Valerius devotes to triumphal practice (2.8), the history of the theater (2.4.6), and the ancient institutions of 2.1 and 2.2. Riposati follows Mercklin in locating Varro's treatment of triumphal matter in the *Antiquitates,* although he suggests Valerius may have used Verrius Flaccus.[85] Cichorius concluded Valerius took his theatrical material from Varro's *Libri de scaenicis originibus.* Varro's *Antiquitates* could have inspired the chapter title for 2.1 (*De institutis antiquis*) and certainly some of its contents. Varro, however, will not be found to have supplied the matter or the theme for these chapters—unlike, for example, Cicero who clearly supplies title, theme, and exempla for the chapters *De amicitia* and *De senectute.*

In the case of 2.8.6, the triumphator's dinner invitation, the commonplace nature of this notice suggested that no particular source was needed. This exemplum is the most general of the series of this chapter: it is devoid of any particular names or dates that could tie it to a specific author. Riposati has argued that the other exemplum from this chapter that Krieger attributes to Varro, although full of detail and not by any means a general notice, was also commonplace, available in many ancient historians. This is the story considered previously of the praetor Valerius' private triumph (2.8.2). Other exempla from this chapter do not display Varronian accuracy: at 2.8.3, where the praetor Cn. Fulvius Flaccus rejects a triumph, Valerius may well be confused. Livy knows nothing of this; he does relate this praetor's defeat and exile (26.2–3). Kappius suggested Valerius has confused Fulvius with M. Fabius, who did reject a triumph (see Livy 2.47).[86]

That Valerius has made an error is clearer at 2.8.5, where Marcellus is wrongly said to have been denied a triumph like P. Scipio (for whom see Livy 28.38), for campaigning without official magistracy. Livy (26.31) makes clear that the triumph was denied since the war had not

85. L. Mercklin, "De Varrone coronarum Romanorum militarium interprete praecipuo" (Dorpat, 1859), 13ff., cited in Riposati 1939, 63.

86. Io. Kappius, *Valerii Maximi factorum et dictorumque memorabilium* . . . (Lipsiae, 1782). Kappius' notes can be found in later editions, perhaps most conveniently in the Delphin Edition of 1823.

been completed. The final exemplum of this chapter with its names of civil war victors and Valerius' lament for these wounds of the Republic is, as Guerrini has shown, indebted to Sallust. Varro is, therefore, not a likely source for any of this triumphal chapter.

If one then searches Valerius' pages for other triumphal exempla, Varro's influence is still undetectable. Papirius Masso celebrates a private triumph at 3.6.5. Pliny writes of the same event: "L. Piso writes that Papirius Masso, whose triumph over the Corsicans was the first held on the Alban Hill, used to attend the games wearing a myrtle crown." Kettner referred the story to Varro. Krieger proposed, after Mercklin, Varro's *De bello et pace*.[87] Riposati, who does not cite the Pliny parallel, suggested Verrius since Paulus at times preserves his influence: "Papirius wore a myrtle crown because he had conquered the Sardinians in fields of myrtle." Valerius' version is closest to Pliny's: "For when Papirius Masso had not secured a triumph from the senate for his good service to the Republic, he began the innovation of triumphing on the Alban Hill and left this as a precedent for others. While attending some public games he wore a crown of myrtle instead of laurel."[88] Perhaps both Pliny's and Valerius' sources (Pliny again may simply be using Valerius) were unclear about what festival Papirius with his myrtle crown was attending. One may be hesitant to name Valerius' source as Piso, but at least he complicates the evidence. All lines do not lead to Varro.

The theater at Rome is a somewhat recondite topic for the declaimer, except as it provided exempla for the commonplaces of Rome's moral degeneration or its leading citizens' grand ambitions. This chapter can be attributed to Varro (i.e., divorced from Livy) only by the most fastidious invention of discrepancies. Krieger attributed 2.4.2, 4, 6, and

---

87. Kettner 1863, 13. Krieger 1888, 55 (Mercklin 1859, 6).

88. The Paulus and Valerius passages are discussed by Riposati 1939, 63. Pliny, *NH* 15.126: *L. Piso tradit Papirium Massonem, qui primus in monte Albano triumphavit de Corsis, myrto coronatum ludos circenses spectare solitum.* Paulus 144.13: *myrtea corona Papirius usus est, quod Sardos in campis Myrteis superasset.* Valerius 3.6.5: *Nam Papirius quidem Masso, cum bene gesta re publica triumphum a senatu non impetravisset, in Albano monte triumphandi et ipse initium fecit et ceteris postea exemplum praebuit proque laurea corona, cum alicui spectaculo interesset, myrtea usus est.*

7 to Varro. The subject of the first theater at Rome (2.4.2) is given a brief notice in the epitome of book 48 of Livy. Krieger argued that the abbreviator's version of the theater being destroyed "by Scipio in accord with the senate's decree" (*Scipione auctore . . . ex senatus consulto*) is at variance with Valerius' words "that Scipio conducted the public auction of the theater's goods." Valerius' words show clear parallels: *Auctore P. Scipione Nasica omnem apparatum operis eorum subiectam hastae venire placuit, atque etiam senatus consulto.* The epitomator has omitted the colorful but anecdotal detail of Scipio Nasica auctioning off the goods. Valerius' account in its clear opposition of Scipio Nasica and the censors is in complete accord with Livy's emphasis on these factional combatants.

In the next exemplum (2.4.3) the survival of Livy's text (34.54) reveals the nature of at least some of Valerius' "discrepancies." Valerius derives this account of the division of the senators' seats from the passage of Livy. His discrepancies seem errors of memory: he identifies the occasion not as the Megalensian games but the games in honor of the mother of the gods, and he misidentifies the consul as the younger rather than the elder Scipio. These errors are understandable ones, and there is no need to credit "variant detail" to an unknown source.

Not merely verbal echoes but their parallel sequence—the very structure of the story—reveal that Livy 7.2 is the source for 2.4.4. The passage is a clear pastiche, a reworking of Livy with rhetorical amplification. Krieger errs here as elsewhere in his championship of Varro partly because he believes Valerius is *always* compressing, abbreviating his source. Valerius has in fact added two glosses: the name of the festival, *Consualia*, and the Lydian origin of the Etruscans. Krieger thought he had discovered a verbal echo of Varro (*De lingua latina* 6.20) in the case of the first gloss. The echoes are *Consualia* and *virgines Sabinae raptae*. Of course, "the Rape of the Sabine Women" is no verbal echo but the natural name of one of the most famous incidents in early Roman history. The extremes to which Krieger's thesis force him do not stop here: his investigation of Nonius revealed that Varro wrote of these games (Nonius 530 *sub "intra,"* a reference to Varro's notice of these *ludi* in *De vita populi Romani* 1). Valerius, however, has used the seventh book of Livy but has not augmented this with a reading of two separate works of the great republican scholar.

None of this elaborate reconstruction is necessary if one believes Valerius knew the name of a Roman festival, referred to the rape of the Sabine women as such, and repeated the common hypothesis of a Lydian origin for the Etruscans. This sort of source criticism, which seeks testimony that an ancient author did treat a particular subject, results in a series of separate attestations whose accumulated mass can easily eclipse their narrow authority. This technique reaches an extreme in 2.4.6, a brief list of innovators at the Roman theater. Valerius' exemplum is nothing more than a catalog of the famous Romans who gave the games and the innovation then introduced for the first time: for example, Pompey was the first to air-condition the theater by means of a system of water channels, or C. Antonius was the first to cover the *scaena* with silver. Krieger cites Pliny the Elder, Servius, Macrobius, and Augustine in his effort to demonstrate Varro wrote of all of this. The simple title of one of his works, *Libri de scaenicis originibus*, one would think, would have sufficed. Undoubtedly, Varro wrote of these men, their contributions, and more, much more. One can wager with good probability that the scholar's work devoted to the history of the Roman stage did not reduce the subject to the brief list Valerius has passed down. Are we, then, to imagine that for this single exemplum he has read Varro and compressed decades of history to a brief notice? Perhaps he took the list from another source—the subject of the increase of luxury at Rome, of which the theater was thought such a malevolent instance, would have had many spokesmen. Perhaps too the material does derive from Varro, but in that case we must ask what this means in this particular instance, and in answer voice doubt that the passage reveals any evidence of a direct reading of Varro. A list of Roman nobles subsumed under one rhetorical category is material meant to be memorized by the declaimer. The point is not that Valerius has not read Varro for this notice, but that the evidence, this rather general string of names, is so suited for declamation that it will not reveal its origins. Indeed, those origins may be another declaimer who spoke this series. Ultimately, the stuff of the series is the fruit of antiquarian research, but this does not tell where Valerius found the names.

Lastly, 2.4.7 retails very briefly that the sons of Brutus gave at his funeral the first gladiatorial games at Rome, a fact told by the epitome of Livy's book 16 as well. Krieger's suggestion of a Varronian source is made possible by the abbreviated state of both extant accounts.[89] Nothing suggests that Livy has not been used.

Trying to catch the genuine Varronian trail, the source hound must return where he started, to those arcane exempla from the beginning of book 2 that mirror Varro's expertise in early Rome. Here Krieger, ever the boldest of the reconstructers, pronounced that all the matter "*de nuptiali ritu*" was Varro's. The criterion for genuineness cannot, however, be simply a congruence of subject matter, especially when that congruence extends only to an item in a list. Thus at 2.5.5 the diet of the early Romans is not sufficient to establish Varro as source. Valerius' words, however, do contain an echo of Varro's: compare 2.5.5, "For men of the highest station were not ashamed to breakfast and dine in the open air" (*Nam maximis viris prandere et cenare in propatulo verecundiae non erat*), with Nonius 83 *sub "chortes,"* "Varro in the first book of the *Life of the Roman People*, 'During winter and cold weather they dined before the hearth, during the warm season in the open air'" (*Idem de vita populi Romani lib. I: "ad focum hieme ac frigoribus cenitabant; aestivo tempore in loco propatulo"*). Two sentences later Valerius continues, "they were so intent upon frugality that they used porridge more often than bread" (*erant adeo contentiae adtenti, ut frequentior apud eos pultis usus quam panis esset*). From the correspondence of Pliny the Elder (*NH* 18.108) and Nonius (152 *sub "pinsere"*) on the subject of the old Romans pounding spelt (the prime ingredient of what I have translated "porridge") and the latter's identification of his source as the first book of the *De vita populi Romani*, Krieger had argued that at 18.83 Pliny the Elder (and, from the similarity of diction, Valerius too) is using Varro: "It is clear that for a long time the Romans lived on porridge not bread since even today the name for condiments and appetizers eaten with bread comes from the word porridge" (*Pulte autem, non pane vixisse longo tempore Romanos manifestum; quoniam inde et pulmentaria hodieque dicuntur*). Is Pliny's final phrase (*pulmentaria hodieque dicuntur*) a close echo of Varro's original? Valerius had written in 2.2.6, perhaps taken from the *De vita, qui hodieque senaculum appellatur*. At any rate, two passages from Paulus (in the epitome of Festus), 245 on *puls* and 141 on *mola*, the

89. Krieger 1888, 63.

latter paralleled by Valerius' "And so what is called *mola* in sacrifices is made from grain and salt" (*ideoque in sacrificiis mola quae vocatur ex farre et salo constat*), may also be from Varro.[90] In the case of this exemplum, the assembled testimonia reveal a substantial and some slight verbal agreements. Perhaps, Valerius' account of old-fashioned eating derives from the *De vita populi Romani*. The fatal combination of wine and early Roman womanhood at 6.3.9, reinforced by a parallel from Pliny the Elder, pointed to Varro's *De vita*. So too a number of parallels with Carvilius (2.1.4, the first to divorce at Rome) suggested that Valerius took his entries on the early family from Varro. Dining and women appear together in a number of the exempla of this chapter (2.1). Wine and the idealized Roman matron recur at 2.1.5 while 2.1.3 proclaims the feminine ideal Augustus promulgated as *univira*; old-fashioned dining practices of men and women are at 2.1.2. Apparently, each case has to be scrutinized on its own since at 2.1.10, as we have seen, Valerius took the story of Roman youths at early banquets from Cicero and not Varro. The influence of Varro over the entire chapter cannot be ruled out from this single preference of Cicero; elsewhere Valerius, though he found two stories adjacent in a single source and used that source for the first, prefers a different source for the second.

Valerius has combined sources in just this way in this first section of book 2. In order to demonstrate that Valerius' use of Cicero at 2.1.10 (where Varro supplies the same story) does not preclude use of Varro in the adjacent exempla, the later testimonia must be marshaled to establish Valerius' subjects as Varronian themes and to detect any verbal echoes. Then the particular arrangement of Valerius' chapter will prove another clue in the reconstruction of sources.

Parallel passages for the first exemplum of the chapter are lacking, though the subject, the vestigial title *haruspex* at a Roman wedding, and scholarly method, antiquarian exegesis of an obsolete word, are typical of Varro. A passage from Nonius suggests that Valerius' account of old-fashioned open-air dining at 2.5.5 derives from Varro's *De vita populi Romani*. Isidore provides a parallel for the similar subject of 2.1.2. Here Valerius' theme is not simply archaic dining but the relation of man and wife in early Rome: "Women used to dine sitting while the men

90. Krieger 1888, 36.

reclined" (*feminae cum viris cubantibus sedentes cenitabant*). Isidore attests to Varro's fuller treatment (*Orig.* 20.11.9): "They were called seats since there was no practice of reclining while dining among the ancient Romans, and hence they were said to be 'sitting at dinner.' Afterward as Varro says in the *Life of the Roman People* the men began to recline, the women sat because a woman reclining was a shameful sight."[91] In the succeeding exemplum (the honors of the *univira*, a topic with a rather general parallel in Plutarch's *Quaest. Rom.* 105), scholars have been divided only by the issue of which work of Varro provided the source, with Krieger asserting the *De vita populi Romani* and Riposati reasserting the *Aetia* (which Thilo first proposed, adducing Macrobius *Sat.* 1.15.21, which cites Varro as the source for the same subject).[92] Thus for the first three exempla direct citations of Varro establish at least the subject of the latter two as Varronian. The evidence for 2.1.4, the divorce of Carvilius, has already been presented. As with 2.1.3 no one doubts Varro treated the subject, but there is a division of opinion on whether Valerius drew from the *De vita populi Romani* or another of Varro's many books, here possibly the *Antiquitates*.

Parallels are next of service at 2.1.5: the wineless women of old Rome who follow immediately upon the divorce of Carvilius in both Valerius and Dionysius of Halicarnassus (see my earlier discussion). The final indication of the correspondence of the exempla of this section with a treatment of Varro is a passage of Paulus (62) that, like 2.1.6, treats of the divine marriage conciliator, the *dea viriplaca*. I cease the rehearsal of later sources here because the first six exempla are clearly a distinct, cohesive unit. The *iunctura* of 2.1.7, Valerius' transition to a different theme, reveals the structure of composition: "Such was the moral conduct between husband and wife" (*Huius modi inter coniuges verecundia*). The *verecundia* of father and son, of older and younger males rounds out the chapter; though Varro may have been used, the male is clearly a subject that did not require such a specialized source. The first six exempla, however, display a remarkable similarity of subject and even

91. *Sedes dictae quoniam apud veteres Romanos non erat usus accubandi; unde et considere dicebantur. postea, ut ait Varro de vita populi Romani, viri discumbere coeperunt, mulieres sedere, quia turpis visus est in muliere adcubitus.*

92. Riposati 1939, 56.

date. This close connection of theme and time suggests that one source is being copied out, that Valerius is not sifting and rearranging his material, which surely was his characteristic technique in composing a chapter. For elsewhere his chapters typically move chronologically, draw from a number of authors, and have a specific, often rhetorical or moral category as organizing rubric. None of these is true for the present chapter. The chapter's subject is vague and, more to the point, of uncertain usefulness to the declaimer. "Dreams," "Ingrates," "Exceptional Deaths," "Friendship" are clearly useful and usable matter for the speaker. "Ancient Institutions" is material at a less digested form; a string of these exempla seems harder to memorize since their rubric is less specific and unifying. Individual exempla may prove of use, but the title, the category, is too general and too historical. Varro does seem to have generated this chapter for Valerius, but it is the least declamatory of the collection. Or, at any rate, it has not been altogether reduced to declamatory commonplace—for example, the decline of morals or, in the case of Egnatius' wife, unusual deaths. For the reconstruction of Valerius' sources, 2.1.1–6 is most instructive. Individually, perhaps only 2.1.2, with its indication of verbal and substantial dependence, would elicit confident conclusion of direct reading of Varro. Collectively, these exempla suggest Valerius is nonetheless working from Varro, culling and reworking what the scholar had to offer on the relations of the early Roman husband and wife.

These exempla provide a significant test for the assertion of the influence of lost sources for which we can rely only on later ancient attestations. An examination of the allegedly Varronian in Valerius makes the critic cautious but not overly skeptical. Varro has been used but only for a very specific topic, perhaps one where other sources failed. Later citations of Varro or any other author on a subject that is clearly familiar and famous cannot suffice for proof of influence without the corroboration of verbal echo or some clue from Valerius' own arrangement and presentation. Finally, it is important to note how slight the borrowings are, both in number and in size. These six exempla from book 2 have borrowed very little, if one were able to count words from Varro. That is, the verbal borrowing, once Valerius' lead-in sentence (his transition), his rhetorical embellishment, and especially his moralizing comment (which often constitutes the final sentence) are discounted, amounts to little more than a single sentence per exemplum. Varro has provided the theme and the germ of the individual exemplum, but Valerius' composition cannot be considered a close copy of the original. This is in striking contrast with many passages drawn from Cicero and Livy where one can see Valerius mining the original for phrase and event and which, despite his stylistic reworking, quite often follow the sequence and syntax of a lengthy paragraph. Varro may not have offered such sustained stylistic treatment as Livy or Cicero, or perhaps his more factual glosses lacked the comment, the category by which a historical exemplum was to be understood and to be inserted into a speech, that Livy and Cicero did provide.

Valerius Antias

There is little evidence that Valerius read Valerius Antias. Where Helm suggests use of Antias, he cites immediately the dissenting opinions of Peter and Mommsen. Where Helm's successor in source criticism, Fleck, asserts use of Antias, he is forced, like Helm's old opponents Klotz and Bosch, to conjure up a lost intermediate source. Fleck does differ from these latter two in significant ways: he demonstrates Klotz's reconstruction of Hyginus' *Exempla* to be erroneous, and he notes the important influence, in questions of source, of the rhetorical schools.[93] Fleck's belief in a prior collection of exempla as a source for Valerius, essentially a revision of the theories of Klotz and Bosch that allows direct use of Livy and Cicero, is germane here as it reveals his methodology: variant details are deemed the clues to different versions. Where Valerius and Livy do not agree, even in very common stories, the discrepancy is evidence of a different source. In the case of Valerius Antias, this invention of sources is compounded (indeed, made possible) since so little of the annalist survives.

Helm had suggested that Valerius on occasion used an annalist who contradicted Livy.[94] The primary observation on which this conclusion hangs is valid and important: Valerius Maximus' versions of republican events on occasion do differ from what Livy has written. Helm laid the

93. Fleck 1974. On Hyginus, see in particular 22.
94. Helm 1955, 106.

source of that difference to an annalist and suggested Valerius Antias; Fleck has inserted but not named an intermediary. Maslakov, following L. R. Taylor's suggestion for a single exemplum, suggests that the antiquarian Valerius Messalla replace Valerius Antias.[95] These suggestions will in the end be of more use in delineating what Valerius Antias and Valerius Messalla may have written than what Valerius Maximus read and excerpted.

The particular exempla that have generated all this inquiry are only six: 6.5.1, 1.8.6, 4.3.6, 2.4.3, 4.5.1, and 2.9.3. In the first of these Helm is moved to acknowledge Mommsen's dissenting opinion.[96] The offer to poison Pyrrhus should, as Mommsen thought, be traced to Livy, not Antias. This is the sole case where substantial passages can be compared. Despite this, the most recent critic relies on analyses of historiographical versions rather than attempting a stylistic comparison. This method in this particular exemplum is no doubt adopted in default of any sure conclusion from comparison of the passages of Valerius Antias, Cicero, the *Periochae*, Valerius Maximus, and later authors. At this point, historiographical versions are deduced that take on a permanence and reality that do not correspond to their slim origins. The four chief passages are these:

> When King Pyrrhus was in Italy and had fought two successful battles and the Romans were in difficulties and most of Italy had defected to the king, a certain citizen of Ambracia, Timochares, a friend of the king, came in secret to the consul C. Fabricius and asked for a bounty and, if that were agreed on, promised to poison the king. He could do this easily, he said, because his son was the royal cupbearer. Fabricius wrote of this affair to the senate. The senate sent envoys to the king and charged them to betray nothing about Timochares but to warn the king to act with greater caution

95. G. Maslakov (1978, 68) suggested that Valerius 2.4.5 (on the secular games) was from Valerius Messalla, not Valerius Antias. Bosch (1929, 1) had made the general suggestion to substitute Messalla for Antias as a source for Valerius.

96. Helm 1955, 107, citing Theodor Mommsen, *Römische Forschungen* II (Berlin, 1879; rpt. Hildesheim: G. Olms, 1962), 500.

and to guard his person from the plots of his intimates. (Valerius Antias [Gell. 3.8.1])[97]

Our ancestors established the greatest example of justice shown an enemy: when a deserter from Pyrrhus promised the senate that he would poison the king, the senate and C. Fabricius handed the deserter over to Pyrrhus. Thus they did not approve the immoral destruction of an enemy, even though he was powerful and bringing war of his own accord against them. (Cicero, *De off.* 1.40).[98]

However, that was the judgment on many occasions and again in the Pyrrhic war it was the judgment of the consul C. Fabricius and the senate. For when King Pyrrhus had brought war of his own accord against the Roman people and the struggle for empire was with a king noble and powerful, a deserter from him came to Fabricius' camp and promised that if a bounty were offered him he would return to the camp of Pyrrhus as secretly as he had come and poison the king. Fabricius had this man returned to Pyrrhus, and the senate praised his action. (Cicero, *De off.* 3.86)[99]

When the man who had deserted Pyrrhus promised the consul C.

97. *Cum Pyrrhus rex in terra Italia esset et unam atque alteram pugnas prospere pugnasset satisque agerent Romani et pleraque Italia ad regem descivisset, tum Ambraciensis quispiam Timochares, regis Pyrrhi amicus, ad C. Fabricium consulem furtim venit ac praemium petivit et, si de praemio conveniret, promisit regem venenis necare; idque facile factu esse dixit, quoniam filius suus pocula in convivio regi ministraret. eam rem Fabricius ad senatum scripsit. senatus ad regem legatos misit mandavitque ut de Timochare nihil proderent, sed monerent uti rex circumspectius ageret atque a proximorum insidiis salutem tutaretur.*

98. *Maximum autem exemplum est iustitiae in hostem a maioribus nostris constitutum, cum a Pyrrho perfuga senatui est pollicitus se venenum regi daturum et eum necaturum, senatus et C. Fabricius perfugam Pyrrho dedidit. ita ne hostis quidem et potentis et bellum ultro inferentis interitum cum scelere approbavit.*

99. *Quamquam id quidem cum saepe alias, tum Pyrrhi bello a C. Fabricio consule iterum et a senatu nostro iudicatum est. cum enim rex Pyrrhus populo Romano bellum ultro intulisset, cumque de imperio certamen esset cum rege generoso ac potenti, perfuga ab eo venit in castra Fabrici eique est pollicitus, si praemium sibi proposuisset, se, ut clam venisset, sic clam in Pyrrhi castra rediturum et eum veneno necaturum. hunc Fabricius reducendum curavit ad Pyrrhum, idque eius factum laudatum a senatu est.*

Fabricius that he would poison the king, he was returned to the king with evidence [of his treason]. (*Periochae* 13)[100]

The relation of these and of Livy's original to Valerius' exemplum 6.5.1 is the vexed question. Valerius is characteristically expansive:

> What I have told of up till now is contained within our city walls and closest territories; the following has spread through the entire world. Timochares a citizen of Ambracia promised the consul Fabricius that he would poison Pyrrhus through the agency of his son who was in charge of [the king's] drinking. When this was reported to the senate, envoys were sent to warn the king to be more cautious for plots of this kind, for the senate bore in mind that a city founded by the son of Mars ought to wage war by arms, not poison. Moreover the senate suppressed the name of Timochares, pursuing a policy of justice to both parties because it did not wish an evil precedent either in destroying an enemy or in betraying one who had been prepared to serve Rome well.[101]

There can be no question that the closest verbal similarity of the extant passages is that between the two Valerii. However, the Ciceronian passages must be considered in full, not in Fleck's brief allusion, for in the case of Valerius rhetoric as well as history is influenced by a source. Intent on historiographical versions, the critics have missed Valerius' debt here to Cicero. The *De officiis* provides category and the concluding *sententia*. Fabricius for Cicero is the third and greatest example of justice—the category is declared both in the introduction to the specific exemplum and at the end of this section (1.41: *De iustitia satis dictum*).

---

100. *cum C. Fabricio consuli is, qui ad eum a Pyrrho transfugerat, polliceretur venenum se regi daturum, cum indicio ad regem remissus est.*

101. *Moenibus nostris et finitimis regionibus quae adhuc retuli *** , quod sequitur per totum terrarum orbem manavit. Timochares Ambraciensis Fabricio consuli pollicitus est se Pyrrum veneno per filium suum, qui potionibus eius praeerat, necaturum. ea res cum ad senatum esset delata, missis legatis Pyrrum monuit ut adversus huius generis insidias cautius se gereret, memor urbem a filio Martis conditam armis bella, non venenis gerere debere. Timocharis autem nomen suppressit, utroque modo aequitatem amplexus, quia nec hostem malo exemplo tollere neque eum, qui bene mereri paratus fuerat, prodere voluit.*

De iustitia is, in fact, Valerius' chapter heading. Cicero's second notice of this episode in the same dialogue offers a slightly fuller and slightly different version; here the conflict of *utile* and *honestum* has Fabricius as its first illustration. Cicero's exemplum admittedly is not as close to Valerius as is the fragment of Valerius Antias. The evidence that Valerius was reading this particular passage and work of Cicero comes one section later in the *De officiis* (3.87). Before passing to his second historical example of the Romans' disdain for the advantageous, Cicero seals the example of Fabricius with a rhetorical question: "*Utrum igitur utilius vel Fabricio, qui talis in hac urbe, qualis Aristides Athenis, fuit, vel senatui nostro, qui numquam utilitatem a dignitate seiunxit, armis cum hoste certare an venenis?*"[102] Valerius has not voiced the dichotomy of the just and the advantageous; he has preferred Cicero's earlier category, justice or equity. His debt to this rhetorical question is clear from his own seal on the exemplum: "*urbem a filio Martis conditam armis bella, non venenis gerere debere.*"

The most troubling concern for the source critics had been that no single source or reconstructed version of this event seemed the model used by Valerius Maximus. The imprint of the schools and in particular Cicero's influence both on what made an exemplum and how it was used have been neglected. Gellius provided the seeds for division by relating two annalistic versions. The differences are striking. Valerius Antias reports that the senate sent messengers to warn Pyrrhus without mentioning names. Timochares of Ambracia is the conspirator. Claudius Quadrigarius has the consuls send a letter, which he quotes, with names of the conspirators and their plan. Nikias is the arch conspirator. Here Fleck minimized the differences so as to posit a common annalistic version. This version identified the traitor as a friend of the king; the traitor's son was the royal cupbearer; Pyrrhus was warned by Roman envoys. Fleck then locates the "purest" version of the historiographical tradition in opposition to this annalistic account. This is Eutropius' report (2.14): Pyrrhus' physician comes by night to Fabri-

---

102. "Was it, therefore, more advantageous, either for Fabricius, a man for this city such as Aristides was for Athens, or for our senate, which has never separated the calculation of advantage from that of dignity, to struggle against an enemy with arms or with poison?"

cius who sends him back bound to the king. Fleck's next step is to make this Livy's version, for Eutropius wrote from the epitome of Livy.[103] At this point the rush of reconstruction pauses as Fleck acknowledges that the emphasis on the individual to the exclusion of the senate is the mark of the rhetors. The final source is then inserted in the reconstructed stemma: Cicero has combined the versions. His *perfuga* corresponds to the annalistic version, his emphasis on Fabricius to the Livian. This is a far stretch, for Cicero's first version in the *De officiis* mentions the senate, and the second does not state, like Eutropius, that Fabricius personally resolved the issue by sending the traitor back bound. Rather Cicero writes *reducendum curavit* and has the general's action approved by the senate—purposefully vague, since Cicero does not wish to relate all the details. These do not serve his point, his criticism of a single individual (Julius Caesar) for failing to distinguish the just from the advantageous in his precipitous quest for glory.

The clearest conclusion about the historiographical versions of this episode is that they differ from the start. Second, they have been influenced by the speakers who used them as exempla, certainly by Cicero, and probably by the schools. Far from representing the last genuine traces of Livy's version, the fourth-century Eutropius with his physician-poisoner represents the end of this rhetorical tradition. The physician sounds like a rhetorician's or a declaimer's fiction, like Alexander's physician in Valerius. The *Rhetorica ad Herennium* (3.33) has a vivid, visually mnemonic exemplum of a physician poisoning his patient. The same Roman anxiety had been voiced by Cato who advised his son to distrust the Greeks, especially their doctors.[104] The father of the cupbearer has become the king's physician, another likely poisoner.

Cicero's passages in themselves show that the discrete versions imagined by modern historiographers were not directing the ancient authors. The senate's decision has not been altogether displaced by the general's justice. Cicero has pushed the senate to the background, but this clearly reflects his particular purpose, not another historiographical version. Equally clearly, Cicero was a source for this particular story for Valerius Maximus. Category, valuation (Cicero calls it the greatest

103. Fleck 1974, 96–97.
104. Pliny, *NH* 29.14

example of justice, and Valerius' opening transition asserts its universal, global fame), and concluding *sententia* have all been drawn from the
De officiis. Cicero has then provided the frame: chapter heading, introduction, and conclusion. His treatment is too brief to appeal to Valerius, and so the rhetorician turned elsewhere, perhaps to Valerius
Antias. At this point, the verbal dependence of the Valerii reveals the
techniques of Valerius Maximus' composition. The omissions are as
telling as the parallels. Valerius Maximus omits the historical context,
the first words of the passage as preserved by Gellius, for he already
has his introduction from Cicero. He takes the traitor's name from Antias but not the identification of Timochares as the king's friend. Such
a detail does not matter for the exemplum's point. Similarly, the furtive
meeting is omitted. As in the first passage of the *De officiis,* the reader
has been led very quickly to the promise to poison Pyrrhus. Here like
Cicero and unlike Antias, Valerius uses *pollicitus* (not *promisit*) and the
future participle *necaturum,* but his *per filium suum* is closer to Antias'
filius suus. The strongest syntactic parallel, demonstrating use of Antias,
is the succeeding sentence, which begins *eam rem* in Antias, *ea res* in
Valerius. The borrowings and omissions are now increasingly clear. Valerius has made of Antias' *legatos misit* an ablative absolute: Antias is
being compressed to a single period. His *mandavit* is cut, but Valerius
is once again borrowing syntax as well as diction. Antias' *monuit . . . ut
cautius se gereret* is echoed in *monerent uti circumspectius ageret,* but the
explanation that follows in Valerius is based on Cicero's *sententia* in the
paragraph of the *De officiis* immediately after his second account of
Fabricius. Quite possibly Valerius had before him the same extract of
Valerius Antias that Gellius preserves. He certainly has not used any
more Antias than we have. His usual practice, to seek Livy where Cicero
fails him, may be at work here, but even the ingenuity of the source
critics cannot here reveal what Livy transmitted.

The process of his composition, however, is revealed, to a degree.
Cicero failed him by reason of his slim account: no name of the traitor,
few details, all the focus on Fabricius—in sum a cursory reference to a
famous story.[105] Livy may not have satisfied Valerius, if, as the *Periochae*

105. The conditional clauses of Cicero and his emphasis on secrecy and the
reward reveal that he too had the same passage of Antias in mind. Cicero's

indicates, the historian had the traitor returned bound and identified to the king. This is the justice for which Cicero and probably Livy praised Fabricius. In addition, Livy may have identified the poisoner as the king's physician (42.47.6), which does not fit with Cicero's account. A new *color* has crept in with Valerius Maximus. Following Valerius Antias' version, the justice now consists, in addition to preferring the *honestum* to the *utile*, in not harming the one who tried to do Rome a service. Such was the rhetorical advantage offered by Antias. Cicero was not concerned with the identity of the fellow he calls simply a *perfuga*. Subsequent rhetoricians were: even in a brief reference, Seneca refers to him as a physician.[106] Valerius has suppressed all reference to the reward and the secret meeting not because he had not read of these in Cicero and Antias but because they were to the discredit of Rome's would-be ally, who experiences something of a rehabilitation in the hands of the rhetoricians. Clearly, the story enjoyed no canonical version, and Valerius was not interested in settling issues of historical details. Without book 13 of Livy we cannot know where Valerius Maximus found the passage of Valerius Antias. Certainly, his is not an unmediated reading or use of Valerius Antias. And, as the following alleged parallels will make clear, this use of Antias, with or without the use of other sources, is exceptional.

The remaining exempla where use of Antias has been alleged can be examined quickly. We need not retrace the steps of Helm who demonstrated that Livy and not Antias was being followed in a number of exempla. Two instances of his method should suffice. At 1.1.12 Valerius writes of the two coffins found in Numa's tomb: in one was the corpse, in the other twice seven books. Antias (fr. 8, Pliny *NH* 13.87) numbers the volumes as two dozen. At 2.4.5 the claim that a Valesius was the founder of the Secular Games and the appended story of Valerius Poplicola do derive ultimately from Valerius Antias, but the notice comes in a series on the theater that was taken from Varro. The

---

technique, however, especially at this late date, was not to look up sources for his exempla. These he had collected and memorized. The similarities of his exempla reflect this memory technique, not the repeated use of a written source.

106. *Ep.* 120.6.

criteria for positing Antias as source is not simply coincidence of subject but the presence of numbers (often exaggerated) and the praise of Valerii. The unreliability of such criteria is manifest. Livy also communicates troop numbers, perhaps taken from Antias, and Valerius did use Livy. Even if both Valerius Maximus and Antias agreed upon the contents of Numa's coffin, this would be but a slender indication that the former was using the latter. The second supposed link is even more uncertain: the mention of any patrician house could be laid to that family's flatterers, if not a particular historian, at least the lost funerary eulogies. Even if an annalist or a descendant did overpraise a republican noble, a string of intermediaries winds down to the Tiberian declaimer.

For instance, in 1.8.6 father Mars appears to encourage and assist the Roman forces in battle. Fleck argued that the list of numbers, casualties, captives, and standards won indicated use of an annalist. Münzer had already suggested that Livy was the intermediary for an annalist of Sullan times.[107] The hidden criteria for Fleck's assertion of Valerius Antias seem to be the figure of Fabricius, this particular annalist's predilection for exaggerated numbers, and the absence of Livy's text for this passage (cf. *Periochae* 12), none of which can reestablish Antias.

Fleck's methodology is all the more confusing in the final Fabricius exemplum (4.3.6). This, he ultimately acknowledges, may not derive directly from the annalist, and he postulates that the rhetorical schools may have been responsible for this particular version.[108] In fact, we can be much more accurate in the case of this Fabrician exemplum. Both verbal similarity and the conjunction of a story about Manlius Curius with that of Fabricius demonstrate that Cicero's *De senectute* 43 is Valerius' source. Fleck concedes the verbal similarity but objects that the accounts differ. He then misrepresents the difference. According to Cicero, M'. Curius and Ti. Coruncanius, hearing of Epicureanism from Fabricius (who had heard of it in Pyrrhus' camp), wish Pyrrhus and the Samnites would become converts (so that they would be en-

107. Fleck (1974, 104 n. 16) cites Münzer, *Beiträge zur Quellenkritik der Naturgeschichte des Plinius* (Berlin 1897), 232.

108. Fleck 1974, 105.

ervated). Cicero mentions nothing of Fabricius' criticism of this philosophy to Pyrrhus. Valerius does but mentions nothing of M'. Curius'
and Coruncanius' recommendation of it. Valerius' omission hardly
equals a new source. Further, he has omitted details prejudicial to Curius, the subject of his preceding exemplum. Surely Curius has made
him recall the second story as told in Cicero, but he has then omitted
the detail in it about Curius as not germane to the protagonist of this
story and as not conducive to patriotism. Fleck has misstated the case:
Fabricius' statement (urging the king not to be corrupted by philosophy) has not been, in Cicero's treatment, attributed to his two friends.
They, in Cicero, say something altogether different from Fabricius in
Valerius. Fabricius does not speak in Cicero, but his action is clearly
understood to be the same as in Valerius; that is, he is a foil to his two
friends. Again, Cicero and Valerius are not the conduits of differing
historiographical versions. Cicero is Valerius' source, but a source subject to omission and abridgment and rhetorical amplification.

In his consideration of 2.4.3 Fleck ultimately returns to the traditional and straightforward identification of Livy as Valerius' source.[109]
The exemplum concerns the occasion of the first division of the senators' seats from the people's. Any theatrical or histrionic subject en-
tices the connoisseur of source criticism to resuscitate the names of all
the ancients who wrote on this topic, Varro first and foremost. Once
again, variant versions appear: Livy dates the division of seating to the
Roman Games (34.54.3); Cicero, like Valerius, to the Megalensian
Games (*De harus. resp.* 24). Asconius seems to correct Cicero in his commentary on the *Pro Cornelio* by invoking Antias as the authority for
locating the first division of the senators' seat at the Roman Games.[110]
Valerius was not interested in correcting Cicero, though he was at times
in augmenting him. Verbal parallels link the Livian passage with Valerius' entry. But no contamination of sources need be posited here,
for, as Fleck at his argument's end concedes, Zschech had long since
pointed out the source of Valerius' error: at 34.54.3–4 Livy's text provides the explanation for Valerius' confusion ("The curule aediles A.
Atilius Serranus and L. Scribonius Libo were the first to put on plays

109. Compare Zschech 1865, 37.
110. Asconius, *In Cornelianam* 69.

at the Megalensian Games. The Roman Games of these aediles was the
first occasion the senate sat apart from the people").[111] Cicero may have
been confused, or he may have misremembered at which games these
aediles instituted a change. Valerius has simply confused or conflated
the actions of these men, perhaps from an error of memory or more
likely from an error of compression in his notes.

This same theatrical subject leads Fleck to posit Valerius Antias as
Valerius' source at 4.5.1, an exemplum that begins by dating the same
division of seating to the consulships of Scipio and Tiberius Longus.[112]
This is only the introduction to his proper subject, the honor shown L.
Flamininus, the brother of the "liberator," by the people. Cast out of
the senate by Cato the censor, he took a seat among the common folk,
but their vociferous objection returned him to the senators' rows. Fleck
maintains that since Valerius mentions Scipio's fellow consul and Livy
did not, Livy cannot be the source. This reasoning cannot stand for a
number of different reasons. First, a source is hardly needed for what
is clearly the background, the orienting introduction, to an entirely separate story. Further, Livy is the source for Valerius' knowledge of the
division of seating, as is clear from 2.4.3. Because this particular incident about Flamininus is told elsewhere only by Plutarch (*Cato Maior*
17.6 and *Flamininus* 19.4), in Fleck's argument the source remains unknown; certainly the division of the seating is at best (as we have already
seen) an unsteady link to Antias. Fleck is conscious of this difficulty
and so postulates a lost intermediate biographical source between Valerius and Antias. This is meant to resolve both the difficulties of 4.5.1
and those of the colorful tale, at 2.9.3, of Flamininus' high-handed execution of a captive.

The confident separation of the strands of historiographical versions
and the concomitant faith that these were and remained discrete for
the Roman author are nowhere more ill-applied than in this final case
of alleged use of Antias. The same brother of the "liberator" of Greece
is again the subject of this story, although in Valerius the proper subject

111. Fleck 1974, 109–10, following Zschech, 37. Livy: *Megalesia ludos scaen-
icos A. Atilius Serranus L. Scribonius Libo aediles curules primi fecerunt. horum ae-
dilium ludos Romanos primum senatus a populo secretus spectavit.*

112. Fleck 1974, 111–12.

is not the disreputable noble Flamininus but his critic, the severe and admirable censor Cato. Indeed, since 2.9.3 is not devoted to Flamininus, he consequently receives no more than cursory treatment. Valerius' reference to him is so brief that the source critic may not have the material with which to seek a source. The wealth of sources available has, however, obscured such a straightforward approach. Livy is ultimately responsible, for he, in an effort to correct Valerius Antias and no doubt the orators who were even freer with the details of the story, cites Antias so as to castigate the annalist while championing his own version on the authority of Cato's speeches. Helm had already, quite sensibly, noted that the brevity of Valerius' account and the inclusion of this episode as a declamatory theme (Seneca, *Contr.* 9.2) make it difficult to assert the direct use of Antias.[113] Nonetheless, Fleck distinguished two historiographical strands and tried, on the basis of comparison with Plutarch (*Flamininus* 18), to tie Valerius with the earliest extant source for this story, Valerius Antias. Cicero (*De sen.* 42), Valerius, and Seneca the Elder all belong to the wrong fork—the tradition condemned by Livy and derived from Antias. Plutarch follows Livy who has his matter from Cato. The difference of the two accounts is one of stage set, not of plot or context: the version Livy corrects has the banqueting Flamininus kill a condemned criminal as a favor for a disreputable woman; the version Livy endorses has a different scene (a gladiatorial contest), character (the ill-famed lover is here a boy), and victim (a Gallic deserter). So far can Livy direct us. Cicero had told the incident in a single sentence: "For when he was consul in Gaul, a whore at a dinner party begged him to strike with an ax some fellow in chains, condemned for a capital offense."[114] Valerius' single sentence is "Just as Porcius Cato [thought] L. Flamininus [unworthy of the senate house] whom he removed from the senators because he had beheaded with an ax some condemned man in his province, having let a common woman, with whom he was enthralled, set the time of execution in accord with her fancy and for her sport."[115] This one sentence does not betray any

113. Helm 1955, 108.
114. Cicero, *De sen.* 42: *Ille enim, cum esset consul in Gallia, exoratus in convivio a scorto est ut securi feriret aliquem eorum qui in vinculis essent, damnati rei capitalis.*
115. Valerius 2.9.3: *Sicut M. Porcius Cato L. Flamininum, quem e numero sena-*

great knowledge: it will not resolve whether Valerius read Antias or whether he read Antias in Livy. Certainly, he has made no use of the names and colorful details of either of the versions that Livy presents. Cicero is a sufficient though hardly the necessary source, for the most important single source for the investigator of the sources of the anecdotes of Flamininus is Seneca's testimony that this particular story was a declamatory theme. Valerius Maximus' reference to a "certain" man as the victim may be a borrowing from Cicero, but, like its appearance in the *De senectute,* this very inexactness reflects not the reading of historical sources but the quick-moving memory of a speaker— or of an author unconcerned with the minor characters who do not affect the point of the exemplum.

Minor Authors

After discussion of a Greek encyclopedic historian, a Roman antiquarian, a Roman annalist, and the historian who ranked with Livy in the Romans' judgment, it is abundantly clear that Valerius has not used several "probable" sources. More exactly, his use of Diodorus Siculus, Varro, Valerius Antias, and Sallust is at best occasional, indeed so occasional that sustained or even direct reading of the works seems unlikely. The pattern of his preference—Livy and Cicero above all others and apparently to the exclusion of these mostly lost sources—and the influence of the rhetorical schools make one even more suspicious of the minor authors whose use has been alleged. This final group is made up exclusively of lost works: the history of L. Coelius Antipater, the memoirs of M. Aemilius Scaurus, the fourteen or more books of the annalist Q. Aelius Tubero, the *Exempla* of Cornelius Nepos, the speeches of the younger Cato, his biography written by his friend Munatius Rufus, the history of C. Asinius Pollio, the *Exempla* of the librarian C. Julius Hyginus, the work of his fellow freedman and Augustan scholar Verrius Flaccus, and the otherwise unknown collection of examples of a Pomponius Rufus.

---

torum sustulit, quia in provincia quendam damnatum securi percusserat, tempore supplicii ad arbitrium et spectaculum mulierculae, cuius amore tenebatur, electo.

Citation of any of the first three of these, Coelius, Scaurus, or Tubero, would lend an aura of old-fashioned authority. Valerius does
name Coelius and perhaps Scaurus for just such a purpose. He has
borrowed the reference to Coelius (1.7.6) from Cicero's *De divinatione*
1.56. Notably, the alleged uses of Scaurus, Tubero, and Pomponius Rufus all occur in a single chapter, 4.4. In this chapter on poverty, Valerius
proceeds chronologically through a series of famous if impoverished
Roman generals and statesmen. Where he can, he joins instances of
men from the same *gens*; so the *nomen* Atilius joins two exempla (4.4.5
and 4.4.6) while the Aelian clan connects 8 and 9. In a discussion of
this chapter Maslakov has suggested that the ultimate source for this
Aelian material was the historian Q. Aelius Tubero, the descendant of
the like-named subject of Valerius' exemplum, although he proposes
that the second half of the ninth exemplum, in which Valerius dilates
on the morality of old Rome, may derive from the (lost) section of book
46, where Livy wrote of Aemilius Paullus' *abstinentia* (the beneficent
Paullus is reported by Valerius as having given his son-in-law Tubero
five pounds of gold).[116] Maslakov also points out that Valerius Messalla
"was interested in the *Aelii*."[117] The disposition of lost annalists and
antiquarians to the Aelii will not much illuminate Valerius Maximus.
He is interested in the easy verbal link that the Roman *nomen* offered.
He does not relate much about either of these families; a real reader
of Tubero might well have found and reported more. Connection of
material by a proper name may well reflect Valerius' system of taking
notes and not the order of material in one source. This is hardly conclusive argument, but the source investigator should be most circumspect in this particular chapter. Prior critics have suggested Tubero for
two of this chapter's exempla; for the final exemplum Valerius himself
names the first book of Scaurus' autobiography. This sort of exact reference, as we have seen from the case of Coelius Antipater, does not
necessarily indicate a Valerian source. Valerius' text here, however,
does reveal two novelties: first, he does not follow Livy where he clearly

116. Maslakov 1978, 208.
117. Maslakov (1978, 210 n. 1) draws this conclusion from the evidence of
Pliny, *NH* 7.173.

could have, and second, he refers to the totally obscure Pomponius Rufus, a citation not at all like the naming of Coelius and Scaurus.

In the first exemplum of the chapter "On Poverty," Lucius Junius Brutus and the end of the Roman kings are mentioned to set the scene for the subject at hand: the public funeral of Valerius Poplicola. Little in the way of historical circumstances or individual events is to be found. The arrogance of Tarquinius was responsible for the termination of the monarchy; this must suffice to jog the reader's memory. Instead of giving the names or motives of the participants, Valerius simply begins: "When the rule of the kings had been brought to an end by the excessive pride of Tarquinius" (*Regio imperio propter nimiam Tarquinii superbiam finito*). It is noteworthy that Valerius uses the abstract noun *superbia*; not an individual agent but a moral category prompts the fall of the kings. Having set the time and mentioned Poplicola's colleague, Valerius has only two more details of substance to add: Poplicola's four consulships and his burial at public expense. Valerius has no interest in further historical niceties, so he declares, "it is not for us to inspect with any greater inquiry the poverty of so great a man" (*non adtinet ulteriore disputatione tanti viri paupertatem scrutari*). Dionysius of Halicarnassus had no such scruples; he dilated on Poplicola's poverty.[118]

Of the potential sources for Valerius 4.4.1, only Livy is extant. The Livian passage is a brief note inserted in the narration of the Sabine Wars; Valerius' passage follows for comparison.

P. Valerius, by common consent the leading citizen in all techniques of war and peace, died in the year following the consulships of Menenius Agrippa and Publius Postumius, a man of immense fame but of such straitened circumstances that he lacked the means for a funeral; they were provided at public expense. The women mourned as for Brutus. (2.16.7)[119]

When the excessive pride of Tarquinius had put an end to the rule

118. Dionysius 5.48.1.

119. *P. Valerius, omnium consensu princeps belli pacisque artibus, anno post Agrippa Menenio P. Postumio consulibus moritur, gloria ingenti, copiis familiaribus adeo exiguis, ut funeri sumptus deesset; de publico est datus. luxere matronae ut Brutum.*

of the kings, Valerius Poplicola along with Junius Brutus took the auspices at the first consulship. Afterward he served three consulships most pleasing to the Roman people and augmented the legend of his ancestors' epitaphs with the ornament of his many great deeds; nevertheless when that pinnacle of the consular lists died, his estate did not suffice for the price of the funeral, and so this was given at public expense. It is not for us to inspect with greater inquiry the poverty of so great a man: for it is abundantly clear what he possessed alive who dead lacked a funeral bier and pyre. (4.4.1)[120]

Valerius' notice of the consul's financial straits has a content common with Livy, but no resounding verbal concurrence. The story was probably well known; the sources, equally probably, were many. However, Valerius has given a clue to his source or at least to the other versions known to him: he declines further discussion (*disputatione*) of Poplicola's straitened circumstances.

Ogilvie, in his note on Livy 2.7.5–12 on Poplicola's unpopularity, argues that the historian is not following Valerius Antias.[121] In his note on 2.33.10 regarding the public funeral of Menenius Agrippa, Ogilvie writes, "it is significant that the only other cases of this custom concern Valerii, L. Valerius in 3.18.11, and P. Valerius Publicola in Plutarch, *Popl.* 16: ? Valerius Antias."[122] Certainly this passage of *Memorable Deeds and Sayings* should be added to Plutarch's. Further, Valerius Maximus' implicit notice of more detailed accounts suggests the work of Valerius Antias, the historian bent on making much of his connection to the Valerii.[123] It seems plausible then that Valerius is not following Livy, a

---

120. *Regio imperio propter nimiam Tarquinii superbiam finito consulatus initium Valerius Poplicola cum Iunio Bruto auspicatus est idemque postea tres consulatus acceptissimos populo Romano gessit et plurimorum ac maximorum operum praetexto titulum imaginum suarum amplificavit, cum interim fastorum illud columen patrimonio ne ad exequiarum quidem inpensam sufficiente decessit, ideoque publica pecunia ductae sunt. non adtinet ulteriore disputatione tanti viri paupertatem scrutari: abunde enim patet quid vivus possederit, cui mortuo lectus funebris et rogus defuit.*

121. Ogilvie 1965, 251.

122. Ogilvie 1965, 321.

123. Hans Volkmann, "Valerius Poplicola," *RE*, A.15, 182 (no. 302).

source he knew and used elsewhere, nor other sources with fuller details such as Plutarch and Dionysius of Halicarnassus used. Valerius Antias is the likely candidate as source for these last two.

Neither Livy nor Valerius Antias provided the model for 4.4.1. This passage seeks to imitate neither the narrative style and diction of Livy nor the tendentious details of Valerius Antias' account.[124] The style Valerius chooses to imitate is the epigraphical and not merely the epigrammatical, as so often. Poplicola is said to have increased *titulum imaginum suarum* and to be *fastorum illud columen*. This latter term does mean the crowning glory or even a prop or pillar; so Catullus calls Peleus *Thessaliae columen*,[125] and for Horace Maecenas is *Grande decus columenque rerum*.[126] No doubt the poetic term is ultimately Homeric: Hector is Τροίας ... κίονα in Pindar's *Olympian* 2.81–82 as Ajax was ἕρκος Ἀχαιῶν at *Iliad* 3.229. Valerius may have had the Catullan or Horatian phrase in mind, but what he means can best be understood visually. Poplicola is the first of the *fasti*—that is, at the head of the consular lists. The reader is to visualize the list of consuls inscribed and to see Poplicola (with Brutus) at the top of that list. As the first, he is both the topmost glory and the column on which all else rests.

Statuary and inscriptions are a plausible source of names, dates, and achievements for the Roman historian, especially if he needs to know of early republican figures. Further, there are inscriptions for Valerius Poplicola of both types implied by Valerius, the lists (*fastorum*) and the portrait inscription (*titulum*). Poplicola's death is recorded in the *Fasti capitolini*,[127] his triumph in the *Acta triumphorum capitolina*,[128] his name on a headless herm.[129] These and similar inscriptions would have provided not the source but a stylistic analogue for this passage. Valerius here seeks the brevity and spareness of an inscription; he offers an expanded *titulus imaginis* and, as a consequence, does not dwell on the

124. For these, see for instance Valerius Antias' frag. 17p and Ogilvie's notes, 1965, 251.

125. Catullus 64.26.

126. Horace, *Odes* 2.17.4.

127. *CIL*, I.1, 16.

128. *CIL*, I.1, 43.

129. *CIL*, VI.1, 292.

poverty of an *imperator*. Augustus had erected in his own forum statues of republican *imperatores* complete with archaizing inscriptions of their offices and achievements.[130] Valerius is in a small way following suit by celebrating in spare fashion the venerable consul and keeping unsuitable material at a distance. He has been caught up by Augustus' propaganda, which identifies "republicanism" with a remote past, the common possession of all Romans.

This discussion of the first exemplum of the chapter is not meant to multiply the possible sources or compound the difficulties of the source critics, but to underscore the peculiar qualities of Valerius' composition. The theme of the chapter, the preference of old-time frugality to modern decadence, the satirist's delight, was hackneyed at best. Every schoolboy would have been able to trot out such exempla. Cincinnatus and Fabricius are the stuff of lore, not antiquarian or historical research. The one unusual element in this chapter comes at the very beginning, the reference to Pomponius Rufus and the *sententia* he put in the mouth of Cornelia (*"Haec," inquit, "ornamenta mea sunt"*). This citation is unlike those to Coelius and Scaurus simply because Valerius writes that he has read the author. That is, this is a first-person pronouncement: "We have found in Pomponius Rufus' work *Selections*, 'Children are a wife's greatest treasure'" (*Maxima ornamenta esse matronis liberos, apud Pomponium Rufum Collectorum libro * sic invenimus*). Valerius does not write that he has read the other two; he merely states "Coelius . . . scribit" (1.7.6) and "Scaurus . . . refert" (4.4.11). *Collecta* is an odd title. What was this unknown author gathering? Most likely, Valerius was reading a collection either of exempla, if it is the case that he took the whole anecdote from his source, or of *sententiae*, the sort of collection book to which Seneca the Elder refers and which his work in part was. The *sententia* that Valerius reports smacks of the rhetorical schools as does the category of the chapter. Perhaps, Pomponius Rufus' work was a gathering from or for declaimers. Valerius may even have found the reference to Scaurus or the rest of the chapter's material there, but the most striking indication of source remains the categories of this chapter. Poverty is the general rubric, but the first two examples are of men buried at public expense. The fourth example is also distant

130. For a recent treatment, see Sage 1979, 192–210.

from the rubric, and all category, those summoned from the fields to
be consuls; it names no individual, although it does anticipate the case
of Atilius Regulus Serranus (4.4.5). Nameless heroes, led from the plow
to *imperium*, are most plausibly derived from the schools.

Of the remaining Latin authors, a number can instantly be recognized as borrowed references.[131] Valerius does cite the lost speeches of
Cato (8.1.2); this notice derives directly from Cicero's allusion to the
Origines in the *Brutus* (89). The *Brutus* throws more light on Valerius'
reading. This dialogue (227) provided the source for the reference at
8.10.3 to Cicero's lost *Pro Gallio* and makes unlikely Valerius' reading
of Scaurus; for at *Brutus* 112 Cicero says that no one reads Scaurus'
memoirs. Münzer long ago made the case that Valerius' reference to
Hortensius' speech for Messalla derives from Cicero's *Consolatio*. The
appearance of massive and wide learning dissolves yet further, and
we are left with the picture of a diligent reader of Cicero. Indeed, one
can only suspect that Valerius' reference (9.5.ext.4) to C. Gracchus'
speeches is a similar borrowing.

Valerius' citation of Asinius Pollio (8.13.ext.4) is suspect on a number
of grounds. The form of the citation is like those to Coelius and Scaurus: *Pollio . . . commemorat.* Moreover, this particular exemplum comes
in a chapter of borrowed references. Third, the theme, long-lived men
and in particular kings, may well have been a declamatory commonplace. The variety of opinion regarding Valerius' source here does not
take these considerations into account. Instead, Münzer had argued
that Cicero and Asinius Pollio were being combined, and Fleck denied
such contamination by answering that the whole chapter derived from
a lost source that supplied Cicero and Asinius Pollio.[132] In truth, all
argument must stem from a single sentence in Cicero's *De senectute*
("For as I have read there was a certain Arganthonius of Gadis who
ruled 80 years and lived 120"),[133] and from Valerius' passage, which

131. See Fleck 1974, 9.
132. Münzer 1897, 106. Fleck 1974, 11.
133. *De sen.* 69: *fuit enim, ut scriptum video, Arganthonius quidam Gadibus, qui
octoginta regnaverat annos, centum viginti vixerat.* Valerius 8.13.ext.4 citing Pollio:
centum illum et xxx annos explesse.

reports the same figures, then in a new sentence appends the authority of Asinius Pollio, and quotes his words as "he lived 130 years." What has been overlooked in the passage from Valerius is that he himself attests to the variety of sources: *cuius rei certi sunt auctores* precedes the mention of Asinius Pollio. Valerius had used a very similar formula in referring a story to Varro (3.2.24). Such a formula clearly does not imply an unmediated reading of Pollio. Further, the very first exemplum of the chapter cites the *De senectute* as its source. The structure of Valerius' chapter points to a combination of sources: first comes material in form and content very like Cicero's, then mention of the reliable authors, the name and words of Pollio. The foreign examples of this chapter are notable for their similar citations of learned and abstruse authorities (Aristoxenus Musicus in ext.3 or Hellanicus and Damastes in ext.6). Indeed, ext. 5, 6, and 7 refer to two or more sources each. Valerius does quote the exact words of these authorities, but the form of the quotation is always the same: the number of years lived. Valerius has not read all of Herodotus or even the Egyptian *logos* in order to quote the length of the Ethiopian king's life (8.13.ext.5), and Asinius Pollio should be judged on the same terms as his neighboring authorities. Valerius is concerned to give an aura of learned authority to these tall tales of longevity. References if not sources are combined to create the impression of erudition. Cicero's *De senectute* has clearly been consulted, and in all likelihood a borrowed reference to Asinius Pollio has been appended. The more exotic authority is then cited.

Munatius Rufus, though named by Valerius as his source in 4.3.2, also in all probability belongs to the list of borrowed references.[134] Peter denied that Plutarch, who also cites Rufus (*Cato Minor* 25 and 37), had read this particular champion of Cato.[135] The number of sources for Cato's life was simply too many (since *Catos* and *Anti-Catos* had become the vehicle for political polemic) for one to believe that Valerius or Plutarch had read Cato's contemporary's account, a version that did not survive and, more important, seems to have had no influence.

134. Fleck 1974, 11.
135. Peter 1906, vol 2, LVIIII and CXXX–CXXXI.

Conclusions

The parade of potential sources has slimmed. We cannot say that any has been altogether eliminated, but rather the patterns and preferences of Valerius' reading have become clearer. His reading of Diodorus Siculus has been seen as a scholar's fancy: examination of Valerius' alleged borrowings from the Greek historian revealed instead his preference for Cicero and Livy. Foreign material has been taken from late republican and Augustan Latin texts, chiefly the theoretical works of Cicero and the work of Pompeius Trogus. No reconstruction of sources can prove exhaustive; this can hardly be the scholar's aim. Still, we should resist the tendency for *Quellenkritik* to become *Quellenforschung*. The first was and is devoted to the elucidation of a text; the latter became an academic division in itself and sought a written source for every variant detail. Where no work or name survived, the source searcher had but to conjure up a lost intermediate source. In Valerius' case in particular, this approach ignored his preference and actual practice of reading and the contemporary influences of declamation and the rhetorical schools. It imposed a model of composition tied to "historiographical versions," which was far more rigid than the fluid medium of rhetorical illustration could ever abide.

Valerius' versions of history are indeed shifting. On close examination they may betray, to the professional historian, the patchwork quality of anecdotal, traditional material. We have seen that Valerius is not writing history and that he is not tied to or directed by "historiographical versions" or historians. Nonetheless, he is occupied in the commemoration of the past, with the praise and vituperation of past men, and in communicating this set of paradigms to the present. Valerius' particular interests have of course guided his handling as well as his selection of this material. His treatment of history, the extent of his historical knowledge, the judgments of the past that he makes and implies, and the peculiar treatment of recent history constitute the next subject of investigation.

4 Valerian Historiography
The Case of the Civil Wars

In the reigns of the Julio-Claudians the historian had at least two great burdens—the 142 books of Livy and the prospect or problem of imperial attention. Both might be avoided by dedication of the work to one's sons, the strict maintenance of the pretense of pedagogic purpose, and a choice of subject or genre on the margins of history proper; such was the course taken by Seneca the Elder and Asconius. One burden could be embraced and the other avoided. Velleius Paterculus in the *festinatio* of his breviary history praised Tiberius while studiously avoiding any rivalry with the scope and labor of Livy's project.[1] Other historians avoided not Livy's genre but his subject by writing of contemporary history, especially the German Wars (Aufidius Bassus, Pliny the Elder, and Nero's general and victim Corbulo). To engage both Livy and the Caesars was a daunting, indeed disastrous choice. Such anyway is the usual wisdom on the republican history of Cremutius Cordus, condemned on a charge of treason for his version of the Republic's fall.[2] Even those within the imperial family had to be

---

1. On *festinatio* in Velleius, see Woodman 1977, 198–99, and 1975, 3.

2. Cordus was prosecuted for calling Brutus and Cassius the last of the Romans (Suetonius, *Tiberius* 61; according to Tacitus, *Annales* 4.34, he was prosecuted for praising Brutus and calling Cassius the last of the Romans). His cause has, since Tacitus, been taken up as one of the first and most prominent (literarily and socially) cases of censorship. Tacitus has Cordus maintain what was obvious to all readers of history: Augustus had tolerated much greater dissent from other historians. The reason for Cordus' demise may have nothing to do with his writing; his conflict with Sejanus (Cassius Dio 57.24; Seneca, *Ad Marciam* 1.2 and 22.4), the public slighting of this man who sought to tie the aristocracy to himself with the appearance of *amicitia*, may have been his real crime. If imperial anger really was aroused by Cordus' writings, the reason

circumspect: Claudius had to abandon his projected history of the years 44–31 B.C.[3]

Those who have chosen to treat the era of historiography between Livy and Tacitus have split the historical authors into imperial panegyrists and republican dissenters. In addition, the writers of Tiberius' reign have all been tainted by the disparagement that this emperor's literary tastes, to say nothing of his supposed character, have earned him from antiquity.[4] Goodyear has labeled this emperor's literary influence abysmal,[5] although Butler had attempted to redeem the emperor's reputation and Tiberius has certainly had his rehabilitators.[6] Since the demise of Maecenas, the swiftest route to literary success had been the unmediated path, and direct solicitation of the emperor marks the surviving literature of Tiberian times. We need not imagine literary success and imperial patronage in terms of the delicate and independent relations of Horace and Augustus, but in the far more mundane, material ways that the sole evidence (a premium paid for an outlandish dialogue) for Tiberius' patronage presents. Again, not the

---

cannot be, as Tacitus suggested, that Tiberius was less tolerant of what Augustus had tolerated. In writing of the last of the Romans, Cordus was not following Livy's Pompeian sympathies. Tiberius' rule, like Augustus', depended on the pretense of continuity with the republican past. The imperial declaimer could acknowledge the decline in Roman morals but not the end of the Roman era.

3. Suetonius, *Claudius* 41.2.

4. Woodman (1977, 37–38) rightly emphasizes "the domination of Augustus" as the crux of the historians' difficulty. He defends Velleius from the charge of "panegyrist" by arguing that encomium was a fundamental feature of Roman historiography and that Tiberius is not cast in altogether rosy light (52–56). Goodyear (1982, 639–66) takes up the defense of Velleius.

5. Goodyear (1984, 603, 604) finds the emperor guilty: "Tiberius most directly influenced literature by inhibiting it," and "He alone could have sustained freedom of speech and checked the contagion of flattery. He did not."

6. Butler (1909, 1) was concerned in particular to explain the state of poetry and strove to avoid blaming the Principate "as the *fons et origo mali.*" He sensed the same cultural wasteland (1909, 2) as the later critics: "The principate of Tiberius is notorious for the silence of literature," but declared unclear whether Tiberius' character or "the exhaustion of genius" was responsible.

profession of poet but the career of bureaucrat may have enchanted an ambitious schoolman. Or, if Valerius Maximus was a teacher of rhetoric, imperial recognition would ensure students.[7] Since Tacitus, however, literary historians have focused on those members of the equestrian and senatorial classes whose literary efforts were the pretense of treason trials. The authors of this period who have received any literary celebration are the historian Cremutius Cordus and the author of a *Cato,* the Stoic secessionist senator Thrasea Paetus, while Velleius Paterculus and Valerius Maximus, too minor in talent or social class to merit recognition from Tacitus, are made to do as examples if not of Sejanus' satellites at least of the imperial believer and beneficiary.

In truth the picture of historical writing is far more complex than this vision, the Tacitus-influenced program, implies.[8] Julio-Claudian historiographers include historians of the German Wars, Curtius Rufus the biographer of Alexander, the antiquarian Fenestella, and the historical commentator Asconius. They will not as easily fit the dichotomy of republican dissent and imperial flattery. Indeed, the affinities of Tiberian writers could be better described in terms of their practical, even encyclopedic literature. For example, Celsus, Velleius Paterculus, and Valerius Maximus all share an interest in being useful to a broad audience, in offering the subjects of education in an easily digested, Latin form. And they differ from Cremutius Cordus, Corbulo, and Thrasea, so familiar thanks to Tacitus, since they are also nonsenators.

Valerius' "history" belongs to this more mundane sphere of literature. It is not a connected vision meant to offend or a program marshaled solely to win imperial recognition. For a writer of Valerius' nonsenatorial status either attempt seems to have been pointless. The chief feature of Valerius' history is its variability. Eclectic in source, *Memorable Deeds and Sayings* clearly and understandably fails as a homogeneous history. Quite expectedly, no comprehensive account of the First Punic War emerges from the collection book, but the collector, had he aimed at projecting a consistent and cohesive view of the process

7. He was clearly a client of the proconsul of A.D. 24/25, Sextus Pompeius, but notably does not, unlike the writers of an earlier generation, dedicate his work to a man of only consular rank.

8. A convenient review is Wilkes 1972.

and periods of history, could have suppressed variant stories about the same historical figure or omitted material critical of the Caesars. Consistency of outlook and unanimity of presentation do not necessarily serve the declaimer, or the lawyer. Valerius, however, is not simply a sophist: he does have favorite figures, heroes and villains, from history and does advance a certain program of what is valuable and paradigmatic from the past. The type of book he wrote did not necessitate a consistency of historical event or of outlook, which is what modern historiographers have often tried to distill when assessing an ancient historian's "historiography."

The present discussion of this quality of Valerius' history—of this particular historical attitude—begins with his visions of Marius in part because earlier historiographical analysis has focused on Marius and, more important, because while not Valerius' favorite historical character, Marius represents all that is difficult and disturbing in a Roman past, which is always paradigmatic, which cannot be denied. He is a figure of ambition, success, civil conflict, bitter revenge, and cruelty for an ambitious and politically perilous age. He is also the outsider recognized as Roman, the Italian municipal who excelled all Romans in his share of Roman office. Valerius could find rich and contradictory material in prior treatments of the new man and seven-times consul who plunged Rome into civil war.[9] After Valerius' all-time favorite Scipio Africanus the Elder, Marius figures fifth (Caesar, Hannibal, and Pompey are each mentioned 38 times, Marius 37), and Sulla is a not-so-distant seventh (28 mentions).[10] Not content with these statistics (based as they are on "significant" mentions of a figure—the criterion Kempf used in his index of names), Carney found that just under 10 percent of the exempla are "relevant" to Marius (94 of the 968 exempla).[11] Unlike these criteria or the numbers advanced, Marius' prominence in *Memorable Deeds and Sayings* cannot be contested. Traditionally, Roman historians have surveyed this prominence only to glean facts—

9. This multifariousness of Valerius on Marius is the distinctive feature with which Carney begins his 1962 study.

10. Carney 1962, 289 n. 2.

11. Carney 1962, 289 n. 3.

has Valerius preserved some event or detail omitted by the other sources for the late Republic?

At the outset of his article Carney had maintained that Valerius' great value for Marian studies lies in his absence of bias. This is of course the reflex of the familiar criticism that Valerius is an undiscriminating borrower. Valerius is imagined to preserve the truth where the more biased chief authorities, Sallust, Cicero, and Plutarch, have suppressed the facts in order to present a consistent and distorted view of the unsavory general.[12] He therefore, according to Carney, differed from Cicero or Plutarch in his attitude toward Marius—or perhaps in his lack of attitude. A reader will readily grant that Valerius' criteria for telling a particular story were not Plutarch's or Cicero's; still his principles of inclusion, like his choice of sources, are not the haphazard and hence "objective" practice that earlier scholars imagined.

Carney's chief concern was, of course, Marius, not Valerius. His study built upon his prior work, "Cicero's Picture of Marius,"[13] and sought primarily to glean fresh historical data or at least historical perceptions from a neglected and different source. Carney was interested in the historical record, including the dating of "accretions" to the Marian tradition. Despite his keen awareness of Valerius' peculiar imprint on the historical material—"[Valerius'] contribution to the conceptualization of Marius as the type-figure of the paradoxical working of fortune was to have a markedly distorting effect upon the whole subsequent tradition"[14]—Carney's purpose (to augment the historical record as he had in his earlier study from Cicero) led him to "rehabilitate" Valerius, with the consequence, as Maslakov observed,[15] of wrongly

12. Carney 1962, 289. For Valerius the sources would have been of the same highly charged and conflicting sort he found with the Gracchi. The difficulty of the Roman historian in judging ancient authors on a politically and socially controversial figure is well stated by Earl 1963, 5: "I am convinced that the whole of our literary tradition with regard to T. Gracchus' tribunate is to be approached with extreme caution; that all ancient versions, both hostile and favourable, are so corrupted by contemporary and later propaganda as to be, in themselves, very uncertain guides as to what actually happened in 133 B.C."

13. Carney 1960.

14. Carney 1962, 291 n.9.

15. Maslakov 1984, 448.

making the author of exempla as consistent in his viewpoint as the ear-lier orator or subsequent historian. Neither consistency of viewpoint nor objective reporting, however, mars Valerius' work.

Maslakov's work emphasized Valerius' uniqueness—his essential dif-ference from those who wrote before him—which Maslakov deemed the attitude and product of one who is a "witness of an age of transi-tion."[16] For the present purposes, Maslakov's work is of great interest as a corrective to the concept, which Carney took as axiomatic, of a unified picture of a historical figure in Valerius.

Maslakov's attitude to Valerius has benefited emphatically from the work of Bliss (clarification of Valerius' imitative aesthetic), Fleck (em-phasis on the influence of the rhetorical schools), and Carney (inves-tigation into Valerian historiography). In his detailed examination of a few, particular subjects (e.g., the Gracchi), Fleck described Valerius' debt to the rhetorical schools—a feature often recognized but here spe-cifically argued. Maslakov develops in a more theoretical fashion the premises of these studies, asserting, for instance, like Fleck, that "These exempla developed in the environment of rhetorical education: nurtured by rhetoricians—absorbed, abridged or elaborated by their students."[17] Maslakov then, however, turns to consider the process of this rhetoricization of historical material. Here too he takes issue with Carney, both generally by maintaining Valerius' peculiar differences from Cicero or Sallust and in particular by stressing that Valerius' words reflect not the *nobiles'* attitudes but the public's conception of history and historical figures. As a rhetorician, Valerius was undoing the work of the antiquarians: "Rhetoric tended to abstract and frag-ment a particular career. As a result, only a deliberate effort of enquiry . . . could bring a particular exemplum in line with the historical tra-dition."[18] Maslakov sees Valerius' principal vices as the inevitable prod-ucts of such a methodology applied to a great variety, in kind and number, of sources. So Valerius will confuse Scipios and incorporate the highly tendentious accounts of family histories.[19] The scope of Va-

16. Maslakov 1984, 454.
17. Maslakov 1984, 445.
18. Maslakov 1984, 444.
19. Maslakov 1984, 442–43.

lerius' collection is also responsible for the inclusion of ideologically contradictory material. These then are the three elements contributing to an understanding of Valerian historiography that Maslakov considers in his sample analyses of single Valerian exempla: the quite unhistorical demands that the exemplum imposes as a discrete and self-contained unit, the easy interpolation of conflicting material occasioned by a work of such dimensions, and the peculiar interests of this Tiberian author and rhetorician.

The actual analyses are grounded on the probability that Valerius used primary sources firsthand. Throughout, Maslakov lays emphasis on the realities of Valerius' Rome, on the intellectual, social, and political environment of the capital under Tiberius. So in his analysis of the story of Tarpeia (9.6.1),[20] Maslakov does not treat Valerius' text solely as a stylistic variant of Livy (after Bliss), nor does he attempt to deduce the attitude of Valerius as historian to this particular villainess (after Carney). Departures from Livy's account are interpreted, quite rightly, as the stripping away of antiquarian or historical details. Maslakov attributes the taste for such a vision of the past to Tiberian Rome. A "stark moralism" is seen as the guiding light.[21]

This is all no doubt true, but not sufficient; a strong if not overriding guiding principle is the theme that Valerius has set himself. By moving from earlier historiographical versions to Valerius' categories and instances, the critic is comparing unlike or at least discontinuous traditions. The models of Valerius' understanding are not simply historians' narratives but the techniques and categories of a rhetorical educational system and of declamation in particular. Prior schoolmasters and declaimers had embellished many of the stories told by Valerius. Thus, for example, the trial of Horatia according to Valerius (6.3.6) most reasonably does not point to lost versions but to the school's free play with history. Legal niceties did not make good fodder for schoolboys or the declaimers' hearers. Thus in the tale of Horatia, as Maslakov sug-

20. Maslakov 1984, 461–64.
21. Maslakov 1984, 464. A "stark moralism" is, like an elevated style, an impression Valerius strives to communicate. For the essentials of these codes—what sort, and whose values or behavior the *Memorable Deeds and Sayings* creates and projects—see my chapter 6.

gested,[22] Valerius omitted the legal circumstances provided by Livy. And surely Livy has provided us with far less than Varro would have or than Livy's source did. The point is not that time and historical accuracy here exist in some inverse relation, but that the various writers have at least equally varied interests.[23] Just as the antiquarian is at a far remove from the historian, so Valerius departs from Livy. His departure cannot always be attributed to other sources or to the rhetorical tradition. We must ask why he has in this particular case abandoned the historical in preference for a different sort of source or a different impulse in composition. Even if a rival source were the sole explanation for the presence and state of a particular version in Valerius, the preference in itself is of the greatest interest for the cultural and literary historian. At a certain level an old-time morality is Valerius' guide, or at least his avowed intention. The closer guide is, however, the chapter heading: "Betrayal" is the chapter for Tarpeia, "Severity" for Horatia. Legal studies have little interest here.

Valerius is after all not just an excerptor; he is a binder of stories. Thus bitter enemies, republican and Caesarian, must peaceably cohabit, adjacent witnesses of some trite theme. The binder strives to make the most of his theme: to bring under the same lexical classification the most famous or distinctive examples. Factual inconsistencies are not as important as is making the whole a connected, monumental work. Marius' deeds and the anecdotes that cluster about them will therefore be shuffled to fit the theme of the moment, and the particular text will arise not simply from a reworking of a model and the influences of a rhetorical tradition but also from the very immediate de-

22. Maslakov 1984, 464–71.

23. Maslakov (1984, 471) argued that Valerius and the rhetorical tradition had recourse to "material of considerable antiquity, drawing on moral principles and standards of conduct going back to Fabius Pictor, Cato and Piso Frugi." If there were extant some early account of Horatia's trial, we would hardly wonder that Livy has not further spiced his account with antiquarian knowledge. This Augustan historian is interested in setting his figures in their historical context, in including them in the chronological narrative, and also in depicting their thoughts and motives—the psychological motivation of a Horatia or a Tarpeia.

mands of the chapter's lexical category and even from the preceding exemplum, for the reader must be pulled along from one story to the next. The abstract process of the creation of exempla from historical and oratorical narratives is not the sole influence on a story; the creation and relation of the categories that the exempla are to illustrate are also essential.

Maslakov's work is, then, chiefly germane to the present study for his assessment of the underlying assumption of Carney's inquiry. Their debate turned on the possibility of Valerius' presenting a unified picture of any historical figure: the inconsistencies of Valerius' representation are too great, so Maslakov argued, to support this premise, and it is Valerius' heterogeneous wealth of sources that accounts for these disparities. Maslakov asserted, "One gets a very strong impression that [the exempla] come from a variety of contexts with different perspectives and aims, with the compiler failing to impose an historical pattern on this material."[24] In short, Valerius' methodology precludes a unified picture. Perhaps Carney has really erred only in not sufficiently stressing the difference between the unified picture a scholar can derive from Valerius' kaleidoscope and the picture or, more properly, pictures of Valerius' actual representations. He had certainly recognized the inconsistencies of Valerius' view, though he ascribes these to a lack of cross-references in the collection; and he concludes in general that Valerius' "presentation of Marius is not seriously marred by factual contradictions."[25]

Carney charged Valerius not with partisan reporting but with "antithesizing oversimplification" and a certain historical naiveté. The latter is the true historian's complaint: factional politics meant nothing to Valerius, who had "little appreciation for the intrigue-ridden relationships of republican family life."[26] The issue of a unified portrayal, of whether the contradictions of Valerius' text are so serious as to preclude the possibility of a unified representation, is not so easily resolved; Carney himself returns at the end of his article to address these problematic and undeniable inconsistencies, "Valerius' depiction of Marius'

24. Maslakov 1984, 448–49.
25. Carney 1962, 292–93.
26. Carney 1962, 293–94.

character is marred by much inconsistency, as might be expected from an excerptor who has to make facts fit into certain predetermined categories." The final flaw discovered in Valerius is that his methodology is not the historian's: "Valerius' nationalistic and conservative attitudes and general moralising bent make him regard certain actions of Marius in an emotional rather than intellectual fashion."[27] Nonetheless, Carney believes that historical fact can be winnowed from the rhetorician's accretions and the author's fiction. This is unquestionably the achievement of Carney's work, but to remove an author's bias and distortions hardly produces that author's unified view of anything. Indeed, the removing of contradictions—by calling them bias and distortions—in order to arrive at a consistent attitude and a kernel of historical fact is a far from reliable procedure.

Valerius is not a less biased source for Marius. His value for Marian studies, which Carney has convincingly demonstrated, arises from his choice and use of sources, a process no less systematic than, but programmatic (aesthetically and politically) in a fashion far different from, Cicero's or Sallust's. For example, popularist and optimate are factions and biases that belong to preceding generations. Without doubt they live on in Valerius, since they were enshrined in canonical works that Valerius has plundered for his own purposes, but the points of view they represent are no longer a living controversy. One particular version may come to exclude another, but primarily for stylistic or thematic reasons, not for its original political proclivity. Further, the sources are not the sole important controlling element in Valerius' composition. He does make personal pronouncements (authorial intrusions into the text) about Marius, Cinna, and Sulla: that is, Valerius does come to a judgment about these men and their actions, and his judgments can neither be simply laid to the vagaries of his materials nor be divorced, as rhetorical flourish, from the stuff of his exempla. Valerius' attitudes (*pace* Maslakov) can be known. This is not to deny that historical matter, obscured or ignored by other ancient authors, can be gleaned from Valerius, but is rather to shift the emphasis of inquiry. The present approach examines the kaleidoscope of melodrama—ever-shifting to the demands of the theme at hand—that Valerius offers on the revo-

27. Carney 1962, 333.

lutionary and reactionary trio of Marius, Cinna, and Sulla. This entails an analysis of Valerius' techniques of melodrama or rhetoricization and the attempt to discern any unity or consistency in Valerius' judgments and approaches. That Valerius is quite capable of at least a small consistency is hinted at by, for example, his consistent malediction of the popularist pretender Equitius (who maintained he was brother to the dead Gracchi) and his consistent ambiguity of judgment (the noble beginnings, wretched outcomes of the Gracchi)—especially if these suit a rhetorical purpose.

The following sections, then, have as their subject Valerius' methods and conclusions regarding these Marian and related exempla. They ask what Valerius made of this, one of the most unpleasant stages of Roman history. The examination begins with what Carney dismissed—Valerius' explicit judgments—and considers his comparisons also, the most characteristic and distorting habit of his thought and composition. The "unified" pictures that Valerius seeks to give, the exempla that review the careers of the three principals Marius, Cinna, and Sulla, conclude this first section. Next comes, in very brief compass, a treatment of his choice of themes, especially those two chapters devoted to the events of this era's civil conflict. From this study of 9.2, "Cruelty," and 9.7, "Revolution," we move to the material most "dangerous" (to a writer of imperial times and sentiment) and most upsetting (to the traditional Roman historian), the deaths of the proscribed, where a source less biased to Marius than Cicero or Plutarch (as Carney declares Valerius to be) would surely bowdlerize. We shall see that Valerius' explicit comparisons and judgments, especially when assembled, reveal a general antipathy to all three civil troublemakers. So too his treatments of the proscribed and his choice of themes, with their implicit comparisons and judgments of these men, contribute to the conclusion that these three are mostly antitypes. Undoubtedly the views expressed are Valerius', for these attitudes are gleaned from the sections and aspects of the *Memorable Deeds and Sayings* that most clearly reveal his hand at work, that is, from his articulation of the organization of the work—the choice of themes, the arrangement of exempla, the junctures, and the rhetorical closures. Of course, considering an assembled series of exempla, no matter what their theme, is altogether different from reading Valerius' collection, which in its scope and variety tends to preclude consistent synthesis of men or events. What becomes clear from such an artificial act of collection is Valerius' categorizations, and not some hard, historian's unity.

Valerius' Explicit Judgments

The very brevity of Valerius' comparisons of the famous men of the late Republic is important; Valerius indulges neither erudite historical allusion nor the precipitous haste of his contemporary Velleius. The figures of Marius, Cinna, and Sulla have become types and consequently often need only the barest mention. In the exempla considered, Marius is compared and contrasted with Cicero (2.2.3) and with Cato (3.1.2). Sulla is contrasted with Caesar (Augustus) (9.15.5) and with Rutilius (6.4.4). Marius and Cinna are presented as antitheses to the orator M. Antonius (8.9.2). Finally, the three are noted in a chapter on triumphs (2.8.7), which involves, as seems unavoidable, comparison with Augustus.

In only a single instance (2.2.3) does any of the characters receive praise, and this, as has been seen, is of a neutral, apologetic sort. The adducing of his fellow townsman Cicero in an exemplum occasions parallel praise of Marius as Valerius contrasts Roman virtue (Marius' antique severity, his ignorance of Greek) to vice suffered from contact with Greece.[28] But this is clearly a reaction to an unusual context. Valerius' "true feelings" about Marius, Cinna, and Sulla are clear from the remaining comparisons. Or, rather, the rhetorical possibilities evoked by mention of these three, while various, are unequivocally negative. The association of Cicero and Marius did once lead to praise of Marius, but this is not the rhetorician's usual connection. Most of the time, these three figures appear only as negative foils to Valerius' main interest. This is contrast of the simplest kind. So as the second illustration of "The Power of Eloquence" (8.9.2), following the happy solution to the first secession of the plebeians, Marius and Cinna serve as the villains, foils to the proscribed M. Antonius and his eloquence. The exemplum begins, "Eloquent words checked even Marian and Cinnan

---

28. See my chapter 2, on the composition of this chapter (2.2).

daggers raging with their passion for civil blood" (*Quae etiam Marianos Cinnanosque mucrones civilis profundendi sanguinis cupiditate furentes inhibuerunt*), but rhetoric enjoys only a short respite, no victory: Antonius dies. The important point is, of course, the stereotype, the rhetorical abstraction that two historical persons and their partisans have become. Valerius does not restrict this sort of treatment to one side. The high virtue and wrongful exile of Rutilius are succinctly established and given rhetorical closure by comparison, in the final sentence, with Sulla: "indeed what Sulla stole, Rutilius deserved" (6.4.4: *quod quidem Sulla rapuit, Rutilius meruit*). Partisan spirit does not animate this author. No discussion of the illegality of Sulla's hold on Rome, no constitutional review ensues.

Politics can infiltrate these comparisons, but such cases are restricted to exempla connected with the Caesars (though even here the exempla are not cast in political terms). Rather, in these exempla Valerius has discovered his greatest moral heroes and the greatest contrasts with his three villains. Caesarian equity is invoked at 9.15.5 as a counterbalancing abstraction for Sullan violence. The reader will not be allowed the parallel of Augustus with the earlier autocrat. The allusions to Julius Caesar here and to the Augustan house at 2.8.7 do cap a series, but do so by way of strong contrast so as to deny any continuity or likeness of development in the reigns of the Caesars. No doubt, the rule of Augustus and Tiberius made the subject of 2.8.7 (civil war victors who did not celebrate triumphs) a dead issue. The exemplum, which begins with Scipio Nasica and Tiberius Gracchus, must be derailed before it reaches Julius Caesar or Augustus. In the sequence of civil victors Valerius does approve all the optimate heroes, who so brutally crushed the rebellious popularist leaders, and saves his fiercest reproof for our final three troublemakers: "L. Cinna and C. Marius had avidly spilt civil blood," and finally "L. Sulla, who caused and conducted the most civil wars, whose successes were the cruelest and most domineering."[29] Then the list is brought up short: "It is irksome and tiresome to proceed further through the wounds of the Republic" (*Piget taedet-*

---

29. Valerius 2.8.7: *L. Cinna et C. Marius hauserant quidem avidi civilem sanguinem, . . . iam L. Sulla, qui plurima bella civilia confecit, cuius crudelissimi et insolentissimi successus fuerunt. . . .*

que per vulnera rei publicae ulterius procedere). The terminus has been reached, and Valerius diverges to praise the serene, citizen-saving house of the Augusti. The whole passage has been a comparison—in form a chronological crescendo with Sulla as its evil climax but in theme simply varied instances of the same point.[30] Comparison of the different historical figures is unavoidable, until it is choked off. No historical details arise that might offer some contrast, in motive, faction, or circumstance, between the exemplars. Only comparison with the Caesars is a special case, one that requires the assertion of a radical break with the Marian and Sullan past. Valerius' abstraction of these figures is particularly vivid and significant here. Marian and Cinnan daggers were the ready foil for Antonius' eloquence just as Sulla provided a moral antitype for Rutilius. Marius, Cinna, and Sulla have become metaphors for civil violence, and are comfortably used this way; this abstraction then needs no further scrutiny. With mention of the Caesars a different, but likewise moral, abstraction can be promulgated, and comparison can be carefully channeled.

This elevation to stereotype, to abstraction, is most vivid in two comparisons that involve Valerius' radical fiction. In these exempla (5.3.5 and 3.1.2) Pompey's and Cato's actions are analyzed by contrast and comparison with an earlier figure who has clearly passed the boundary between historical person and rhetorical type. In the first exemplum Valerius betrays his embarrassment about this subject ("Ingrates") and the particular instance (Pompey's assent to Cn. Carbo's murder) and so voices his difficulty to the great man himself: "How I shall now treat you, I do not know." The truth will out, and Valerius does find his way to reprimand the general: "you made use of the violence of Sulla rather than the restraint of Pompey."[31] The act has become an aberration in moral behavior and is explained by reference to the archetypal personification of civil bloodshed. The direct address to a figure long dead, this imaginative form of anachronism, is a familiar feature of declamation. Schoolboys did not just dream of accompanying Hannibal

30. For echoes of Sallust in these passages, see Guerrini 1979 and my comments in chapter 3.

31. Valerius 5.3.5: *Quo te nunc modo, Magne Pompei, attingam nescio . . . plus L. Sullae viribus quam propriae indulsisti verecundiae.*

through the Alps and Alexander in his conquests; their set exercises were to counsel these men in their most crucial moments. Such a conceit characterizes these comparisons of Valerius.

In his chapter on "Youthful Promise" (3.1), Valerius introduces the young Cato visiting Sulla at his home. The Stoic suddenly can bear the tyrant no longer, and his pedagogue must intervene to restrain the young man's righteous ardor. Valerius concludes with this comment: "Had you put Marius in his place, Marius would have sooner thought of his own escape than of Sulla's murder."[32] This comparison involves two sorts of fiction that were the standard fare of declamation: the aforementioned anachronistic insertion of the speaker and audience into the deliberations of the past and the imaginative and fictitious meetings or confrontations of famous men. Antony never offered Cicero a deal ("Burn your writings or die"), but such wranglings were often heard in the generations after the orator's death. In this exemplum Valerius imagines the unhistorical meeting of Sulla and Cato; he then analyzes Cato's behavior by reference to another famous Roman and suggests the dramatic or declamatory possibilities.

In these two cases, fiction set the scene for a comparison between a good man and Sulla. But fiction also infected Valerius' explicit judgments about Marius, Cinna, and Sulla. Carney, while maintaining that Valerius' presentation of the actual facts could be accepted, found his interpretations very dubious material: "an attitude of some reserve must be adopted towards his ascriptions of motivation or his explanation of facts."[33] The problem, according to Carney, was that Valerius' political "*naïveté* renders many of Valerius' subjective reconstructions valueless," that is, for the historian intent on reconstructing the events of the late Republic. Let us begin with the most historically valueless and irrelevant judgment about these three men, an effusion kindred to the declamatory comparisons just considered. In his chapter on "Devotion to the Fatherland" (5.6), Valerius had told of Brutus' death in battle with the Etruscan prince and Curtius' plunging into the chasm that had so inconveniently split the forum. The third and fourth ex-

---

32. Valerius 3.1.2.: *ipsum Marium illo loci statuisses, celerius aliquid de sua fuga quam de Sullae nece cogitasset.*

33. Carney 1962, 294.

empla belong to that strange, though, to the Romans, very serious side of public life: prodigies and their expiation. Genucius Cipus, while praetor and about to leave the city, suddenly sprouts horns. Similarly disfavored, the praetor Aelius, engaged in his official, judicial role, had a woodpecker light upon his head. The respective responses were: if Genucius returns to the city, he will be king; and the bird, if spared, will bring good to the praetor's family, harm to the state; if killed, the reverse. The exemplary outcomes: Genucius departed the city in perpetual, self-imposed exile; the bird was delivered up to the senate for execution, the Aelian clan lost seventeen good men at Cannae, and the Republic came to empire. Dividing these stories from the subsequent tales of the ritual self-sacrifice of the Decii is this outburst: "No wonder Sulla and Marius and Cinna ridiculed these exempla as stupid!" (5.6.4: *haec nimirum exempla Sulla et Marius et Cinna tamquam stulta riserunt*). This is all Valerius has to say. These three self-serving interlopers need only be mentioned to throw selfless patriotism into relief. The brevity of reference assumes recognition of a stereotype, not just of three particular men but of these civil wars in general.

  Valerius' judgments reveal a fixed, rhetorical image of civil strife. Causes, motives, or connections are not plumbed. Instead, these years are remembered as an unholy time, whose leaders sneered at piety. This impiety, according to Valerius, was directed against the gods as well: the fourth illustration of "Necessity" (7.6) begins, "Moreover, when the consuls Marius and Cn. Carbo were in conflict with L. Sulla in civil war, when victory was not sought for the Republic but the reward of victory was the Republic, the gold and silver decorations of the temples were, by the senate's decree, melted down so that the troops might be paid."[34] The proscriptions are some bad memory, but the recurring feature of Valerius' memory of them is the indiscriminate blame he showers on all three men. Those years of civil strife and proscriptions have become "that storm that C. Marius and L. Cinna had inflicted upon the Republic" (4.3.14: *In illa quoque procella, quam C. Marius et L.*

---

34. Valerius 7.6.4: *C. autem Mario Cn. Carbone consulibus civili bello cum L. Sulla dissidentibus, quo tempore non rei publicae victoria quaerebatur, sed praemium victoriae res erat publica, senatus consulto aurea atque argentea templorum ornamenta, ne militibus stipendia deessent, conflata sunt.*

Cinna rei publicae inflixerant). Sulla likewise does not escape Valerius' condemnation, nor his abstraction, even in death; Valerius affixes as his rhetorical close to the exemplum that narrates the ever-fuming Sulla collapsing in a fit this rhetorical *dubitatio*: "therefore it is a matter of some doubt whether Sulla or Sulla's anger was first snuffed out" (9.3.8: *igitur in dubio est Sullane prior an iracundia Sullae sit extincta*). These judgments of Valerius are rather small stuff; they are so frequent and so obviously rhetorical that it it is tempting to dismiss them as the offhand by-product of Valerius' composition. They depend on and represent, however, consistent rhetorical classifications whose form and use are peculiarly suited to the early imperial rhetorician. This by no means denies Valerius' or the declaimers' interest in these men or their violent times; rather, it begins to describe that interest. At times, his fascination with what he considered evil may seem trivial, as, for instance, when Valerius tells of Marius dressed as Liber (3.6.6) or Sulla in Greek costume (3.6.3). Certainly, such rhetoric, so insistent in its types, becomes glib and, no doubt far worse in the declaimers' opinion, predictable, and thus boring. When Valerius retails that Marius' son escaped "Sullan cruelty" by death (6.8.2), the reader may well tire of the clichés. For Valerius, however, these moral abstractions will recognize no generational limits; this is precisely the quality that makes the exemplum useful.

In a writer so generous in his reception of anecdotes, a great difficulty must be their selection and arrangement. Valerius has a wide range of stories about Marius, not all of which are fallow fields awaiting his moral indignation. Tales of a muddy Marius dragged from the swamps or of the diffidence of his Cimbrian executioner are, by their subject, suited to different themes—especially to that rhetorician's delight, the mutability of fortune. But for Valerius, gathering many of his illustrations from such formerly politically controversial material as the actions of the participants in civil war and the instigators of widespread civil murder, an eclectic or indiscriminate compilation would undermine the consistency of his moral types. Valerius' imprint on his received material, however, is not that of a thoroughgoing, systematic propagandist. He does engage in imperial panegyric and repeats in the appropriate places praises of the Augustan house as maintainer of civil peace. But he does not suppress dissonant material; his strategy is to denounce the negative: he will not celebrate civil agitators, especially since their proscriptions had earned the opprobrium of his predecessors. Divergent points of view do occasionally slip through, in part because, as with the Gracchi, partisan sentiment led to partisan records and because great, venerable Romans had been on the "wrong" side.

At 3.8.5, for example, Valerius seems to offer and approve a divergent account of Marius. This is the judgment Scaevola refuses to give of Marius. Valerius has just related in this chapter on "Constancy" Metellus Numidicus' steadfast preference of exile to compromise:

> But though I may rank no one before Metellus, nonetheless I would be right to compare the augur Scaevola to him. After shattering and routing the partisans of his enemies and occupying the city, Sulla assembled the senate by force of arms and was passionately proposing to declare C. Marius a public enemy as quickly as possible. No one opposed him except Scaevola, who when questioned declined to answer. Indeed, when Sulla pressed him even more vehemently, he said, "You may show me the columns of soldiers by which you have encircled the senate house, time and again you may threaten me with death, but never will you bring me, for the sake of my scant and aged blood, to declare my Marius, the savior of the city and of Italy, a public enemy." (3.8.5)[35]

Scaevola's opposing viewpoint receives no explicit comment from Valerius, but the classification of the event is quite clear: an instance of fidelity, second only to the much vaunted resolution of Metellus. The heroic sole dissenter and true friend here makes his appearance, not the political ally of Marius. Valerius proffers no political or historical justification; like the stories of Tiberius and Gaius Gracchus' friends,

---

35. *Ceterum ut neminem ei praetulerim, ita Q. Scaevolam augurem merito conparaverim. dispulsis prostratisque inimicorum partibus Sulla occupata urbe senatum armatus coegerat ac summa cupiditate ferebat [sic Gertz] ut C. Marius quam celerrime hostis iudicaretur. cuius voluntati nullo obviam ire audente solus Scaevola de hac re interrogatus sententiam dicere noluit. quin etiam truculentius sibi instanti Sullae "licet," inquit, "mihi agmina militum, quibus curiam circumsedisti, ostentes, licet mortem identidem miniteris, numquam tamen efficies ut propter exiguum senilemque sanguinem meum Marium, a quo urbs et Italia conservata est, hostem iudicem."*

faithful even after their patrons' deaths, this exemplum is cast only in moral terms.[36] Sulla is the insistent, threatening bully (*truculentius sibi instanti Sullae*) to whom Scaevola can utter his grand and memorable reply. Scaevola's speech relieves Valerius of any need to defend Marius, who is in effect hailed as the father of his country, the distinction he won by his military exploits against the Cimbri and the Teutones. In short, such an anecdote is shaped by and satisfies Valerius' categories for canonization: the story can be set in moral terms (that is, it can illustrate a moral, lexical category); its agents are famous Romans; and the story includes a famous, pointed *dictum*. Any inconvenience of subject is skirted by adhering to these moral lines and in stressing, as in the actual *elogium* of an epitaph, titles and military distinctions.

The scene has thus become the spirited reply of the augur to the menacing general. The melodrama of the confrontation and the famed jurist's pungent words have recommended this anecdote. The particular origin is not known, but there are a few clues to suggest that Valerius was working from one of his customary, canonical sources and not culling material from some partisan, pro-Marian author. First, as to the genuineness of Scaevola's words, there is the slight argument that elsewhere—for example, Scipio Aemilianus' verdict on the murder of Tiberius Gracchus—Valerius' version of a famous *dictum* is supported by Livy, Cicero, or Plutarch; in these matters he does not engage in wholesale fiction. In addition, Scaevola was known for his pithy if not exactly eloquent expression: Cicero pronounces of Scaevola, "he had

---

36. Although *amicitia,* for Scaevola and Marius as for the agrarian reformers a generation earlier, meant factional as well as familial and cordial ties, and although Scaevola's "constancy" did involve *amicitia,* the bond that this popularist politician strengthened by the marriage of his granddaughter to Marius, Valerius has been naive in these matters, as Carney pointed out. But this is a sort of willful, or at least purposeful, ignorance. Sulla's march on Rome in 88 and the familial and political connections of the augur and Marius demand explanation (e.g., for the former: Sulpicius' extraordinary maneuvers, which resulted in the replacement of Sulla by Marius in the eastern command), an explanation that would undermine the pious theme. It would be much better for Valerius' purposes (and an easy insertion into a declamation) to set the scene as "After shattering and routing the partisans of his enemies and occupying the city, Sulla . . ."

many finely reasoned arguments and many succinct and apt expressions" (*De am.* 1: *multa ab eo prudenter disputata, multa etiam breviter et commode dicta*). Further, the senate's judgment, though not Scaevola's speech, is recorded in the epitome of Livy: "from [the faction of Marius and Sulpicius] the senate declared as public enemies twelve men including C. Marius, both the father and the son" (77: *ex qua duodecim a senatu hostes, inter quos C. Marius pater et filius, iudicati sunt*). This notice, in itself, seems slim evidence; the verbal parallel of "judged a public enemy" is, after all, official language, the sort of thing any teller of this event might repeat.

This phrase does recur in Valerius' version of Marius' omen at Minturnae. The substance of this particular exemplum is Marius' observation of an ass's preference of water (to hay), and his own interpretation and imitation of this (flight by water to Africa). The date is set as "the time when he was judged a public enemy" (1.5.5: *quo tempore hostis a senatu iudicatus*). Now, the event that chronologically preceded this episode of Marius' escape is also narrated (though elsewhere) by Valerius, and here a dependence on Livy is established by verbal agreement with the *Periochae*. The epitome relates: "C. Marius the Elder, when hiding in the swamps of Minturnae, was dragged out by the townspeople, and when the Gallic slave sent to murder him fled out of terror of the grandeur of such a great man, he was placed at public expense aboard ship and transported to Africa."[37] Valerius is, quite understandably, fuller, dilating as usual on the upheavals of Marius' fortune; the passage of this exemplum that derives from Livy is:

> The public slave, a Cimbrian, sent to murder him when hidden in a private residence in Minturnae, though brandishing a drawn sword, did not dare approach a man old, unarmed, and filthy, and blinded by the fame of the man dropped his sword out of astonishment and fled in a tremble. (2.10.6)[38]

37. *Periochae* 77: *C. Marius pater cum in paludibus Minturnensium lateret, extractus est ab oppidanis, et cum missus ad occidendum eum servus natione Gallus maiestate tanti viri perterritus recessisset, impositus publice navi delatus est in Africam.*

38. *missus enim ad eum occidendum in privata domo Minturnis clausum servus publicus natione Cimber et senem et inermem et squalore obsitum strictum gladium tenens adgredi non sustinuit et claritate viri obcaecatus abiecto ferro attonitus inde ac tremens fugit.*

In his "lead-in" sentence, but two words before this, Valerius has referred, like the epitome, to Marius' *maiestas*. The outcome of Marius'
escape from the assassin—his flight to Africa—is not narrated here by
Valerius (as in the epitome of Livy) but at 1.5.5: "straightway he em-
barked upon a small boat and carried by her to Africa escaped the
victorious arms of Sulla" (*protinus naviculam conscendit eaque in Africam
pervectus arma Sullae victricia effugit*). Of all this, the surest evidence of
Valerius using Livy is 2.10.6, Marius and the Cimbrian slave. In the
other passages, as in 3.8.5 (Scaevola's reply to Sulla) he may well have
had Livy before him or Livy's version foremost in his mind. The recurrence in Valerius of the diction of the epitome may seem slight, but
at times the indirectness of the relation of exemplum and source is a
sure proof of Valerius' use of that source. That is, when for instance
at 2.10.6 Valerius writes *maiestatis* not, as his source did, in the narration of the event, but in his rhetorical introduction, this argues that he
was working from Livy. The accidental intrusion or, if deliberate, the
employment of a key word displaced from its original sequence is the
result of a compiler reading one passage and composing another. The
fact that a key phrase such as "deemed a public enemy" recurs in Valerius suggests that he was using one source for several exempla. This
is not surprising, especially if Livy is the source, since narrative must
be broken into separate blocks to become exempla. Exact verbal alignment cannot be expected in such a manner of composition, which, of
necessity, expands from the original.

The figure of Scaevola offers additional illustration of Valerius' relation to his sources for this period. At 9.11.2 Valerius cites as a "Criminal Act" (*Dicta improba aut facta scelerata* is the chapter heading) the
wounding and attempted prosecution of the augur:

> Not as harsh [as Servius Tullius' daughter's order to drive over her
> father's corpse] were the deed and words of C. Fimbria, but judged
> on their own, each is the most brazen. He had arranged to have
> Scaevola assassinated at C. Marius' funeral. After he learned that
> Scaevola had recovered from his wound, he resolved to prosecute
> him before the people. When asked what he would say to the dis-
> credit of this man whose integrity could never be worthily praised,
> he answered that he would charge him with insufficient bodily re-

ception of a weapon. Unrestrained madness ought to be met by the Republic's lament! (9.11.2)[39]

The source for this exemplum is clearly a passage in Cicero's *Pro Sexto Roscio Amerino*:

> We had once in this nation a man by far the most brazen and, as all agree who are not themselves insane, the most insane—C. Fimbria. During the funeral of C. Marius he had brought about the wounding of Q. Scaevola, a man of the greatest integrity and distinction in our nation, about whose praises neither is the present the place to dilate nor can there be more told than Rome already remembers. He lodged a suit against Scaevola after he learned that he might live. When it was inquired of him with what he would accuse a man whose dignity no one could even sufficiently praise, they say the fellow, as he was enraged, answered "incomplete bodily reception of a weapon." (33)[40]

Valerius' changes at first seem to be these: *iugularetur* for *vulneraretur*; for Cicero's extravagant praise of Scaevola (the passage that builds from superlatives and develops to a *recusatio*), a more compressed denial of the possibility of sufficient praise. In addition, for the simple *postea quam comperit eum posse vivere* Valerius has *postquam ex vulnere recreatum conperit*, a change necessitated by his choice of the more vivid,

---

39. *Non tam atrox C. Fimbriae est factum et dictum, sed si per se aestimetur, utrumque audacissimum. id egerat, ut Scaevola in funere C. Marii iugularetur. quem postquam ex vulnere recreatum conperit, accusare apud populum instituit. interrogatus deinde quid de eo secus dicturus esset, cui pro sanctitate morum satis digna laudatio reddi non posset, respondit obiecturum se illi quod parcius corpore telum recepisset. licentiam furoris aegrae rei publicae gemitu prosequendam!*

40. *Hominem longe audacissimum nuper habuimus in civitate C. Fimbriam et, quod inter omnes constat, nisi inter eos qui ipsi quoque insaniunt, insanissimum. is cum curasset in funere C. Mari ut Q. Scaevola vulneraretur, vir sanctissimus atque ornatissimus nostrae civitatis, de cuius laude neque hic locus est ut multa dicantur neque plura tamen dici possunt quam populus Romanus memoria retinet, diem Scaevolae dixit, postea quam comperit eum posse vivere. cum ab eo quaereretur quid tandem accusaturus esset eum quem pro dignitate ne laudare quidem quisquam satis commode posset, aiunt hominem, ut erat furiosus, respondisse: "quod non totum telum corpore recepisset."*

and fatal sounding, *iugularetur*; he avoids the proper legal idiom, *diem dixit*, in favor of the grander circumstance of a trial before the people (*accusare apud populum instituit*). Finally, Valerius has couched Fimbria's insolence in indirect discourse. These changes can be simply described as a more vivid vocabulary, the streamlining of authorial judgment, and a syntactic subordination.

The source of these changes, Valerius' reworking of Cicero's text, is more interesting. The need for compression and the ensuing syntactic subordination and preference of, for example, an abstract noun in lieu of the original verbal phrase are self-evident. The more lively diction is, upon closer scrutiny, not his own but Cicero's, borrowed from the passages of the *Pro Roscio* that immediately precede and follow the short exemplum. Valerius calls Fimbria's action and words *audacissimum*—the superlative Cicero had used of Fimbria. *Iugularetur*, the colorful though less accurate substitute for *vulneraretur*, is borrowed from Cicero's rhetorical question to Roscius' accuser that immediately precedes this historical exemplum.[41] The entry in *Memorable Deeds and Sayings* begins, *non tam atrox*; Cicero had used the same words, after the historical digression, to characterize Chrysogonus' attack upon his client: *in hoc tanto, tam atroci, tam singulari maleficio. . . .* Valerius has transferred this beginning from its original context to the historical illustration.

This is not conclusive proof that at 3.8.5 (the reply to Sulla) Valerius was using Cicero or Livy but does suggest that Valerius followed both, often quite closely if not exactly, in the stories of Marius and Scaevola. The decision to include Scaevola's judgment of Marius, which is in strong contrast to Valerius' judgments and comparisons, is therefore not an act of partisan politics, nor is it subversive of his rhetorical types, his consistency, or unity of judgment. Scaevola, for Valerius as for the schoolboys and all who read Cicero and Livy in early imperial times, was the much-lauded augur of Ciceronian fame. Valerius' consistent interest is in what labels to give the agents of his exempla: good or bad, constant or faithless, *augur* or *imperator*. Scaevola's refusal to proclaim

---

41. *Rosc. Amer.* 31: "Have you come with sword and arms right to the jurors' seats that you might either slit the throat or secure the condemnation of Sextus Roscius?" (*etiamne ad subsellia cum ferro atque telis venistis ut hic aut iuguletis aut condemnetis Sex. Roscium?*)

Marius a public enemy is thus doubly attractive: all the criteria for a successful exemplum are present (e.g., melodrama, pithy sayings, a classical stylist's treatment, the paradox of a "good" man praising a "bad" because a worse is involved), and the anecdote turns upon a label—what to call Marius.

Valerian Overviews

Valerius' interest is not limited to single anecdotes—the odd and colorful details of these men's lives—or to brief judgments made in passing. The final three selections of exempla examine Valerius thinking and writing of these men more directly and extensively. First, he actually does offer "unified" pictures of Marius and Sulla: he devoted individual exempla to reviews of their careers. Further, in two chapters these figures are the central concern, the dominant figures, not cited in passing (as with the comparisons) nor inserted to explain the context (as at 7.3.6 where Sertorius is introduced and defended: "forced by the Sullan proscription to be the leader of the Lusitanians").

The reviews of Sulla and Marius are of the briefest sort—swift rehearsals of signal deeds. Valerius does not depart from the famous and the familiar; no new historical details emerge, and even the rhetorical categories with which he represents the facts are commonplace. At 6.9.6 Sulla's career and future achievements follow the introductory foil of Marius' resentment at receiving a dissipated junior officer:

L. Sulla, right up to his election as quaestor, led a life of debauchery, stained with lust, drink, and the theater. Thus, it is said, C. Marius as consul, conducting the harshest of wars in Africa, was irked that he had received by lot so effeminate a quaestor. Sulla's manhood, having as it were shattered and cast off the bars of its jailer sloth, manacled the hands of Jugurtha, tamed Mithridates, quieted the waves of the Social War, broke the tyranny of Cinna, and forced the man who had disdained him as quaestor in Africa to seek that same province a condemned exile. If anyone should wish to weigh in his own mind with a more exact comparison such different and so contradictory events, he would believe there were two Sullas in one body, a disreputable youth and a man, I would say brave, if he had not preferred to be called fortunate. (6.9.6)[42]

A reprimand for the proscriptions, for the civil loss that Valerius elsewhere deems Sulla's work, is noticeably absent. Just such an omission seemed to Sallust reason for a candid portrait of Sulla. In his introduction of Sulla as a principal in the Jugurthine War, Sallust objects to L. Sisenna's history as too favorable to the young quaestor: "he seems to me to lack candor" (95.2: *parum mihi libero ore locutus videtur*). Sallust's corrective passage shares the opening and concluding points of Valerius' exemplum: "Sulla . . . was passionate for pleasure but even more for fame, leisure brought dissipation" and "for this man, the luckiest of all before victory in the civil war, fortune was never greater than his due, and many wondered whether he was braver or more fortunate." But Sallust's crucial difference from Valerius falls between these judgments: he faults Sulla's marital relations and to complete the character sketch, offers the historian's verdict, "as to what he did afterward, I am not sure whether shame or disgust attends further inquiry."[43] Moreover, Valerius may have chosen to take only the facts from Sallust—that Sulla went as quaestor to Marius in Africa, that he, "raw and unacquainted in warfare, was soon the most skilled of all"[44]—but these facts,

---

42. *L. vero Sulla usque ad quaesturae suae comitia vitam libidine, vino, ludicrae artis amore inquinatam perduxit. quapropter C. Marius consul moleste tulisse traditur, quod sibi asperissimum in Africa bellum gerenti tam delicatus quaestor sorte obvenisset. eiusdem virtus quasi perruptis et disiectis nequitiae, qua obsidebatur, claustris catenas Iugurthae manibus iniecit, Mitridatem conpescuit, socialis belli fluctus repressit, Cinnae dominationem fregit eumque, qui se in Africa quaestorem fastidierat, ipsam illam provinciam proscriptum et exulem petere coegit. quae tam diversa tamque inter se contraria si quis apud animum suum attentiore conparatione expendere velit, duos in uno homine Sullas fuisse crediderit, turpem adulescentulum et virum, dicerem fortem, nisi ipse se felicem appellari maluisset.*

43. *B.I.* 95.3–4: *atque illi, felicissumo omnium ante civilem victoriam, numquam super industriam fortuna fuit, multique dubitavere fortior an felicior esset. Sulla . . . cupidus voluptatum sed gloriae cupidior, otio luxurioso esse. . . . nam postea quae fecerit, incertum habeo pudeat an pigeat magis disserere.*

44. *B.I.* 96.1: *rudis antea et ignarus belli, sollertissumus omnium in paucis tempestatibus factus est.*

his rank and life-style, were common knowledge. Sallust has drawn attention in this very passage to a prior historian's treatment and, more important, to the triteness of Valerius' theme: *many,* he says, have wondered whether Sulla was braver or luckier. Those many go unnamed, but their query is in the form (an alternative question) so dear to declamatory debate—that is, to a *controversia* that turns on the meaning of a word, the applicability of a term or label.

This rhetorical query ("brave or fortunate"), which ended 6.9.6 and which properly pertains to Sulla, also is echoed at the end of Valerius' review of Marius' career. The likeness of this Marian exemplum to the Sullan (narrated eight exempla earlier) is quite striking, especially since they have this same rhetorical ending and a similar, unadorned sequence of their subjects' distinctions:

> Now C. Marius in his struggle with fortune endured with the greatest bravery all her attacks by the strength of his body and mind. Deemed unfit for public office at Arpinum, he dared to stand for election to the quaestorship at Rome. By tolerating defeats, he rather broke into the senate house than arrived. Having suffered a similar token of the electorate's disdain in his campaigns for the tribuneship and the aedileship, he slipped by as the final candidate for the praetorship, which he won at some risk: accused of bribery he was acquitted barely and with difficulty. From that Marius so humiliated at Arpinum, so undistinguished at Rome, such an inconsequential candidate, emerged the famous Marius who subjugated Africa, who drove King Jugurtha before his triumphal chariot, who destroyed the armies of the Teutons and the Cimbrians, whose double trophies the city witnessed, whose seven consulships can be read in the official records, who after exile became consul, after proscription the author of a proscription. What is less fixed or more changeable than this man's state? If you will include him among the despised, he will be found the most despised; if among the fortunate, the most fortunate. (6.9.14)[45]

---

45. *iam C. Marius † maximae fortunae luctatione: omnes enim eius impetus qua corporis qua animi robore fortissime sustinuit. Arpinatibus honoribus iudicatus inferior*

This exemplum would be more like Sulla's (6.9.6) if it began from the fourth sentence (*ex illo Mario . . .*). That is, Valerius seems by comparison hostile to Marius, for Sulla escaped without historical censure; but in truth, where the sixth exemplum had, as foil to his subsequent great good fortune, Sulla's dissipated youth, the fourteenth has only Marius' early political setbacks, and this material is only included because the theme to be illustrated is "Change of Customs or Fortune." Proscription is not of interest in itself or adduced as commentary on Marius' excesses, but rather provides Valerius with the climax to the list of Marius' *res gestae*—doubly attractive as Valerius has it combine two figures, paronomasia and oxymoron ("for the proscribed to make a proscription"). Marius' electoral difficulties are of equal value, to Valerius, as the African campaigns: the rags-to-riches story must have both. Not only such detail, but this theme is trite: Cicero had already (in the *Pro Plancio*) juxtaposed the vicissitudes of the candidate.[46]

This exemplum, therefore, like the review of Sulla's career, cannot be called a "unified" picture, if by this is meant the recurrent, deliberate shaping of a complex tradition for a particular historiographical vision. These exempla present a range of the men's activities with the extremes

---

quaesturam Romae petere ausus est. patientia deinde repulsarum inrupit magis in curiam quam venit. in tribunatus quoque et aedilitatis petitione consimilem campi notam expertus praeturae candidatus supremo in loco adhaesit, quem tamen non sine periculo obtinuit: ambitus enim accusatus vix atque aegre absolutionem ab iudicibus impetravit. ex illo Mario tam humili Arpini, tam ignobili Romae, tam fastidiendo candidato ille Marius evasit, qui Africam subegit, qui Iugurtham regem ante currum egit, qui Teutonorum Cimbrorumque exercitus delevit, cuius bina tropaea in urbe spectantur, cuius septem in fastis consulatus leguntur, cui post exilium consulem creari proscriptoque facere proscriptionem contigit. quid huius condicione inconstantius aut mutabilius? quem si inter miseros posueris, miserrimus, si inter felices, felicissimus reperietur.

46. *Pro Plancio* 51: *et C. Mari, qui duabus aedilitatis acceptis repulsis septiens consul est factus.* Valerius may have had some of the details from Livy, but the incidents are too famous and Valerius' expression too terse to identify any sure sources. Marius in his triumphal splendor, for instance, was fully drawn in Livy's epitome (*Periochae* 67), and this event never lost its appeal for the Romans. Velleius (2.12.1), Plutarch (*Marius* 12), Pliny the Elder (*NH* 33.4.12), and Florus (1.36.17–18) all tell of Jugurtha's humiliating participation in the triumphal procession.

not of political behavior but of personal habits and fortunes singled out. Selection of incidents or character traits is neither partisan (like Sisenna) nor balanced (as Sallust assures his reader), but the most apt, as Valerius can make them, for his theme. An odd consequence of this declamatory manner of presentation is that Marius receives Sulla's epithet (*felicissimus*—the most blessed by fortune). These bitter enemies have lost much of their enmity when the rhetorician instructs his students to place both in the same categories. This juxtaposition of contraries, like a reliance on synchronisms, may offend the historian as melodramatic; the virtuoso declaimer delights in the unexpected combination.

Quite often Valerius has joined Marius and Sulla either for their historical association and conflict or for their suitability to the intended theme. These two considerations do, of course, overlap: the contrast of enemies is the more striking when they share the same abstract category, for example, when they both illustrate fickle fortune. Equally, the theme is better established—a more convincing element in the declaimer's performance—if it can call to witness such antithetical examples. These men's repeated appearances in Valerius are, then, no surprise. The likening of opposites and the reversals of fortune share the appeal, for performers and audience alike, of the unexpected, though not necessarily of the novel. The appearance of Marius and Sulla in a chapter such as "Change in Customs or Fortune" offered little that would not be familiar to the declaimers and audiences of Tiberius' day. Or at least, this is the impression of a reader of the undiluted series that is Valerius' work. Actual declamation involved a variety of presentations and especially of rhetorical figures, which the book of exempla cannot reproduce. Nonetheless, declamation contented itself with the same (recurring) historical figures. A desire for novelty of subject did not impel the declaimer to antiquarian investigation but to a novel category and its appropriate incidents.

Such a method of composition develops to a limiting process, as category and instance fuse in rhetorical tradition and popular memory. Marius and Sulla as types for the whims of fortune are already quite familiar, though not yet fossilized. Valerius' eclectic habit of composition works against such radical simplification; the search for famous examples of unusual themes will preserve odd details such as the Teuton women's request to Marius (6.1.ext.3) or his rewarding on the field of battle of two Camertine cohorts with Roman citizenship (5.2.8). Where, however, Valerius considers these men's lives in review or compares the two (i.e., where some judgment is required), the rhetorical classifications are recurring, simplifying, and enduring.

Chapters of Civil Strife

Valerius' review of Marius' and Sulla's deeds, encapsulated in a chapter devoted to the reversals of fate, has already been examined. The remaining categories in which Marius and Sulla are of focal, shaping concern to Valerius are the chapters detailing civil strife (9.7) and cruelty (9.2). Both draw their material from the civil wars, and in the latter Valerius indulges in his severest castigation of Sulla. The first illustration of this chapter succinctly declares the reasons for Marius' and Sulla's popularity with the declaimers: Sulla is the most abundant figure for praise and for blame. Panegyric and invective are, after all, the stock in trade of the declaimer, and Sulla offered the greatest subject for both.

Sulla's preeminent position in the list of cruelties is no surprise (9.2.1).[47] Sulla, it could be argued, is a remarkable figure, one who requires special treatment, and Valerius could have been carried away by the possibilities of this subject to incidents and themes that bring no credit to the Republic. His interest in the period cannot, however, be so easily tied to one man or even to the villainous trio of Sulla, Marius, and Cinna. Sulla undoubtedly provided the shaping, generative impetus for the chapter on cruelty, but Valerius must always move to other instances. In addition, the horrors of civil strife do not suggest themselves solely upon mention of Sulla; they are not associated with a single figure. Indeed, Valerius knows and tells more of the civil conflicts than the occasional connection of thought or theme would produce; this material does not simply arise accidentally or digressively. His range of knowledge and his familiarity with the proscribed (and with a variety

47. See chapter 2 for discussion of Valerius' composition in this chapter and the central role of this Sullan exemplum.

of information about the proscriptions) cannot be so explained. Valerius is, of course, ever ready to revile vice, wherever it can be found. In the exempla that relate the fates of the proscribed, Valerius' attitude is not novel; indeed, it has already been made quite clear in an exemplum such as the young Cato's visit to Sulla or in the rhetorical lead-in to 4.3.14 where the whole period is the "storm that C. Marius and L. Cinna had inflicted upon the Republic." In writing of the deaths of the proscribed, a certain sympathy is required; charging the victims with partisan politics hardly evokes an audience's sense of pathos. For the same reason, the Samnites of 9.2.1 were not identified as Rome's bitter enemies, but as the victims of the perfidious Sulla. The proscribed will not be discussed, then, to gauge the range of Valerius' knowledge but the peculiar uses he makes of this.

Valerius can be, it is true, rather indiscriminate in the identification of the victims of Marius, Cinna, and Sulla. At various times, he sees the whole Republic, the temples of Rome (7.6.4), or the Penates of one family (9.15.5) falling to the iniquity of one or more of these villains. Not content with these general pictures, Valerius also retails the deaths of individuals: C. Caesar, L. Petronius, and P. Caelius, the consul Octavius, M. Antonius, and Marius' legate Gratidius. Individual victims, the defeated partisans serve Valerius' need for pathos, blackening the reputation of the civil agitators and arousing pity.

There is little heroization here, though some idealization. For the most part Valerius does not portray these as heroes' deaths—no celebration of one side's martyrs is to be found. Rather, M. Antonius is eloquence embodied (8.9.2); L. Petronius and P. Caelius, defeated by Cinna's army at Placentia, are included for the by now familiar theme of true friendship unto death (4.7.5)—a theme that has allowed Valerius to include others of unorthodox politics (e.g., the friends of the Gracchi).[48] In the first exemplum about the proscribed considered here, Valerius finds what good he can; the people in their abstinence

---

48. Similar is the exemplum of Sulla's execution of the slave who betrayed the demagogue Sulpicius (6.5.7). The issue of a slave's loyalty to his master, like that of friendship, seems to Valerius of greater importance than any question of politics.

provide a hero, but of a negative sort. In this double exemplum Valerius has already noted the people's rejection of Pyrrhus' bribe:

> In that storm as well that C. Marius and L. Cinna had inflicted upon the Republic, the restraint of the Roman people was magnificently displayed: for when they threw out the Penates of those they had proscribed for the people to despoil, no one could be found who sought profit from civil loss: everyone abstained from these as if from the sacred temples. And indeed the sympathetic restraint of the people was the silent cry of reproach against the cruel victors. (4.3.14)[49]

Here Valerius stops. Velleius Paterculus was not so circumspect; the ambiguity of this heroism is spelled out in his history:

> Everything in the Republic was rushing to disaster; nonetheless no one was found so brazen as to distribute or so unfeeling as to attempt the property of a Roman citizen. Afterward, it did happen that avarice provided the pretext for this outrage. (2.22)[50]

Velleius seems to be embellishing Valerius, making the latter's clause, *inveniri nemo potuit, qui civili luctu praedam peteret,* into a more pointed, balanced *sententia, nec tamen adhuc quisquam inveniebatur, qui bona civis Romani aut donare auderet aut petere sustineret.*[51] The telling difference is clear: Valerius here sees fit to ignore the subsequent facts of history, that stage when wealth became reason enough for proscription, when "Abstinence and Continence" no longer held good.

---

49. *In illa quoque procella, quam C. Marius et L. Cinna rei publicae inflixerant, abstinentia populi Romani mirifica conspecta est: nam cum a se proscriptorum penates vulgi manibus diripiendos obiecissent, inveniri nemo potuit, qui civili luctu praedam peteret: unus enim quisque se ab his perinde ac si a sacris aedibus abstinuit. quae quidem tam misericors continentia plebis tacitum crudelium victorum convicium fuit.*

50. *Omnia erant praecipitia in re publica, nec tamen adhuc quisquam inveniebatur, qui bona civis Romani aut donare auderet aut petere sustinet. postea id quoque accessit, ut saevitiae causam avaritia praeberet. . . .*

51. The relation of these two passages will not be discussed at length: any of four possibilities can be argued (Velleius using Valerius, vice versa, both following a common source, or coincidence).

This later period is touched upon, though not comprehensively addressed, in a group of three contiguous exempla illustrating "Violence and Sedition" (9.7). In lieu of the usual foreign material, Valerius has substituted Roman military examples, all three of which are drawn from the conflicts of Sulla and Marius. This section spans their conflict—from the Sulpician law wresting Asia from Sulla to the death of a Sullan partisan at Volaterrae in 81 B.C. The three exempla relate violent, lawless actions of three different armies: first, Sulla's legions butcher Gratidius, the envoy of Marius; then the soldiers of Cn. Pompeius do likewise to the consul and colleague of Sulla, Q. Pompeius; finally, C. Carbo[52] is killed in a mutiny of his soldiers. All these passages offer a good insight into Valerius the nonpartisan. He does not take sides, nor does he understand or at least advocate any of the constitutional or legal issues. The closest he comes to partisanship is the rhetorical question that closes the first exemplum. Here he deplores the incident from a social point of view: "Who can bear a soldier correcting the decrees of the popular assembly by the destruction of an envoy?" (9.7.Mil.Rom.1: *sed quis ferat militem scita plebis exitio legati corrigentem?*). This piece of condescension suffices to dismiss the subject and move on to the next.

Valerius may have found this material, though hardly this easy judgment, in Livy. The epitome of book 77 has mention of the circumstances of 9.7.Mil.Rom.1 (though not of Gratidius' death) and of the death of Q. Pompeius (9.7.Mil.Rom.2). This concurrence of subject matter, hardly conclusive in itself, is not supported by substantial verbal parallels simply because so many events are packed into the abbreviation. However, the parallels of topics are not limited to the two episodes of army outrages. Individual exempla in Valerius retell all but three incidents related by the *Periochae*. These exceptions are instructive. Valerius does not tell of the (relatively unimportant) crossing of the younger Marius to Africa (though he mentions the elder's escape and other incidents of the younger's life). He does not tell of two social and constitutional reforms that clearly had no interest except for the true historian: the Sulpician Law's provision for the recall of exiles and

52. *RE* 18.3, 1020–21 (no.34), a Sullan sympathizer, unlike his brother the consul.

for the creation of new tribes and Sulla's constitutional reform and plans of colonization. The remaining incidents and their reappearance in Valerius are listed in table 5. Particular exempla (e.g., 6.5.7, 8.2.3, 2.10.6) demonstrate a direct dependence on Livy, but this table of general agreements offers an unusual insight into Valerius' exploitation of a single book and his treatment of a single period of history. Valerius does not differ with the prior historian's general outline of the period. Of course, his sequence does not follow Livy's, and Valerius does relate some unattested information (Sulla in Greek dress at 3.6.3); but this is the sort of colorful detail that, though it does not do the historian much good, is the favorite of a gossip, or of a declaimer. Valerius uses Livy here in an exhaustive fashion, taking the events of one book to exemplify a number of topics. Valerius has not included dissenting information (which might have undermined Valerius' generalized picture of this time and of its leading actors). No incidents (such as Sulla's autobiography would undoubtedly have contained) glow with credit for the dictator, nor is there the abject vituperation derived from the political invective of Sulla's contemporaries. While Valerius does not simply reproduce Livy's picture and attitude, he was content with the received and respected version of events. This material could then be mined for any variety of topics and could always be augmented by the more vivid fare and fiction of the declaimers.

Valerius' accounts of the deaths of the individuals proscribed reinforce this conclusion; for here too, while the *Periochae* is again most compressed, agreement of subject matter, though not always of the actual wording, demonstrates that Valerius has not preserved a partisan source contemporary with Sulla and Marius. Additionally, the classical treatment of Cicero and perhaps the contemporary of Velleius were available for this subject. The entrance into Rome of Marius and Cinna—"as if to a captured city," the epitomator writes—was soon followed by the first proscription, an outrage seized upon by writers for its break from all precedent and for the gruesome precedent it set for the coming generations of civil strife. Unlike Valerius, Velleius, and Cicero, the epitome gives only the names of the first victims:

> The consul Cn. Octavius was killed and all the nobles of the opposing side were slaughtered, including M. Antonius, a man of the

TABLE 5. *Valerius and Livy's abbreviator on Marius and Sulla*

PERIOCHAE	VALERIUS
Sulpician law grants Marius Sulla's army and province	9.7.Mil.Rom.1
Q. Pompeius' death	9.7.Mil.Rom.2
Sulla's capture of Rome	3.8.5; implied by 6.4.4, 6.9.6
Sullan senate's declaration of public enemies	3.8.5, 8.2.3
Sulpicius' death	6.5.7
Sulla's execution of the slave who betrayed Sulpicius	6.5.7
The elder Marius in the swamps	8.2.3
His "Gallic" executioner terrified	2.10.6
The elder Marius flees to Africa	1.5.5, 6.9.6
Mithridates invades Phrygia	9.2.ext.3 (his butchery of Roman citizens; 9.7.Mil.Rom.1 mentions the war)

greatest fame for eloquence, and C. and L. Caesar, whose heads were placed on the rostra. The younger Crassus was killed by Fimbria's horsemen; the elder, to avoid any indignity, committed suicide. (80)[53]

Immediately following this passage, the *Periochae* narrates the next year's events: the extralegal self-election of the consuls and Marius' murder of the senator S. Licinius. Cicero also gives a rapid review of these victims. In the third book of the *De oratore* he recounts the deaths of the participants of his dialogue—with an optimate twist: L. Crassus should be deemed happy in his death for he did not live to see the flower of the nobility ruthlessly murdered,

We preserve in memory Q. Catulus, a man outstanding in every

---

53. *Cn. Octavio cos. occiso et omnibus adversae partis nobilibus trucidatis, inter quos M. Antonio, eloquentissimo viro, et C. L. ⟨que⟩ Caesare, quorum capita in rostris posita sunt. Crassus filius ab equitibus Fimbriae occisus, pater Crassus, ne quid indignum virtute sua pateretur, gladio se transfixit.*

branch of distinction, who, though he was begging not for acquittal but for exile and flight, was compelled to take his own life. Already, on the very rostra, where as consul he had most adamantly defended the Republic and which as censor he had adorned with his victor's spoils, was placed M. Antonius' head, by which the heads of many citizens had been saved; and not far from this lay the head of C. Julius, betrayed by the crime of his Etruscan host, alongside that of his brother L. Julius, so that Catulus, who did not see these things, seemed to live and to die with the Republic. Nor did he see his relative P. Crassus, a man of outstanding courage, killed by his own hand nor the image of Vesta stained with the blood of his colleague the pontifex maximus [Cicero continues with the deaths of C. Carbo, Cotta, and Sulpicius]. (3.9)[54]

The final complete version of these events comes from Velleius:

Among these [prominent Romans killed on Marius' return] the consul Octavius, a man of the gentlest disposition, was killed at Cinna's order. Moreover, Merula, who upon Cinna's arrival had resigned his consulship, opened his wrists, and stained with his blood the altars at which as *flamen dialis* he had often prayed to the gods for the safety of the Republic; after invoking these gods to curse Cinna and his partisans, he gave up a life that had deserved only the best from the Republic. M. Antonius, the leading citizen of the state and of eloquence, at Marius' and Cinna's order was stabbed, the soldiers' weapons delayed by his eloquence. Q. Catulus, of great renown both for his other virtues and for the fame

---

54. *tenemus enim memoria Q. Catulum virum omni laude praestantem, cum sibi non incolumem fortunam sed exilium et fugam deprecaretur, esse coactum ut vita se ipse privaret. iam M. Antoni, in eis ipsis rostris in quibus ille rem publicam constantissime consul defenderat quaeque censor imperatoriis manubiis ornarat, positum caput illud fuit a quo erant multorum civium capita servata neque vero longe ab eo C. Iulii caput hospitis Etrusci scelere proditum cum L. Iulii fratris capite iacuit, ut ille, qui haec non vidit, et vixisse cum re publica pariter et cum illa simul exstinctus esse videatur. neque enim propinquum suum, maximi animi virum, P. Crassum suapte interfectum manu neque collegae sui pontificis maximi sanguine simulacrum Vestae respersum esse vidit. . . .*

of the Cimbric War, which had been his and Marius' joint respon-
sibility, when he was sought out for execution, shut himself up in
a newly plastered room and had a fire brought into the force of
the vapors, at the same time breathing in the fatal air and choking
off his own, he died a victim rather to his vow than to his enemies'
sentence. (2.22.2–5)[55]

The odd figure is Q. Catulus: not mentioned here by the *Periochae*, but
at the head of Cicero's list and the end of Velleius'. Cicero retails the
fact but not the story of his death at *Tusculans* 5.56. In the review of
Marius' misdeeds in the chapter on "Cruelty," Valerius mentions the
murders of C. Caesar and M. Antonius (9.2.2). Antonius had already
appeared (8.9.2) as a demonstration of the power of eloquence (a customary connection—Cicero and Velleius had both remarked on his
eloquence). Valerius had also already used the death of the consul Octavius, or rather the prodigy presaging his death (1.6.10). C. Caesar
like M. Antonius is included under two headings; his first appearance
(5.3.3), which described his betrayal by his host (just as in the *De oratore*), exemplified "Ingrates." In the final exemplum of these proscribed
aristocrats, Q. Catulus does appear, to be followed by Merula (whose
death Velleius set just before Catulus), both for a rather predictable
theme, "Extraordinary Deaths" (*De mortibus non vulgaribus*, 9.12.4
and 5).

The various proscribed do not, despite the different authors, present
any pleasing variety. The familiar quality of all this, from Antonius and
his eloquence to heads fixed on the rostra, makes the line from models

---

55. *in iis consul Octavius, vir lenissimi animi, iussu Cinnae interfectus est. Merula
autem, qui se sub adventum Cinnae consulatu abdicaverat, incisis venis superfusoque
altaribus sanguine, quos saepe pro salute rei publicae flamen dialis precatus erat deos,
eos in execrationem Cinnae partiumque eius tum precatus optime de re publica meritum
spiritum reddidit. M. Antonius, princeps civitatis atque eloquentiae, gladiis militum,
quos ipsos facundia sua moratus erat, iussu Mari Cinnaeque confossus est. Q. Catulus,
et aliarum virtutum et belli Cimbrici gloria, quae illi cum Mario communis fuerat, ce-
leberrimus, cum ad mortem conquireretur, conclusit se loco nuper calce harenaque per-
polito inlatoque igni, qui vim odoris excitaret, simul exitiali hausto spiritu, simul incluso
suo mortem magis voto quam arbitrio inimicorum obiit.*

to imitation very difficult to discern. Nonetheless, this is an instructive difficulty. If these stories had been rarely told, the line of dependence would have been clearer. Valerius is neither distorting these historical events nor following some aberrant source. His historical memory is not failing, though it is highly characterized. His interest remains in the mainstream, mostly here with Marius, Cinna, and Sulla. At the same time, he is concerned neither to plumb nor to alter the historical record. His recurring interest is what name to give these men, whether they are *felix* or *fortis*; what strange category he can invent for them. Marius he includes so often because the consul-exile fits so well in a theme such as 8.6.2, "Those Who Themselves Suffered What They Inflicted Upon Others."

Despite his stated distaste for the subject of this civil conflict and its chief agents, Valerius has found it fecund and appealing material. Marius and the period as a whole contribute most to his chapters on cruelty, friendship, and the mutability of fortune. For Maslakov, Marius was the case that proved Valerius' ignorance of factional alliance and his fragmentation and moralization of history. Valerius certainly has avoided explanation by reference to factional motivation. Marius is a test case—but of Valerius' choice and use of historical material for the censure of this ambitious *homo novus*. Marius in Valerius, however, fails to be a political precedent just as Valerius' evocations of his times fail to be a bridge to the present. The failure of political relevance and its eclipse by a new paradigmatic are the single most striking features of Valerius' characterization of Marius. Valerius' choice of theme constitutes the form by which Marius the proscriber and autocrat is sundered not only from his contemporary context but from his successors. For in the next stages of Roman history, the end of the Republic and its "restitution" by Augustus, Valerius is even more circumspect in his handling of political partisans and their motivations. It is important to realize that his techniques, which succeed in divorcing Brutus or Cassius from their political and social interests, are not invented for this particular historical moment. There is a unity to Valerius' picture of Marius or of Brutus, a unity not necessarily of source or of historical version but of the techniques of commemoration. Nonetheless, the more recent history remained a challenge to Valerius as to any writer or public speaker of the early Principate. In the reliving and retelling of the times and characters who brought Julius Caesar and his adopted son to power, the Caesars and their critics waged a war for legitimacy, for their own "Romanness."

5 The Fallen Restored and the Republic's Restorers

Greater heroes than Valerius' Scipio Africanus and worse villains than his Marius-amid-the-proscriptions are a burden to the imaginations of reader and author alike. Nonetheless, in the exempla drawn from the late Republic, Valerius, with a new, panegyrical impetus, does not balk at such extremes. The figures from Pompey to Brutus do, however, have far more in common with Marius, Cinna, and Sulla than with any Scipio of the distant Republic: their actions and his memorializing of them involve both praise and blame. In the chronology of Roman civil conflict, the struggles of Marius and Sulla give way to the civil war of Pompey and Caesar and then to the various alliances and contentions of Caesar's aspirant successors. But like his contemporary Velleius, Valerius does not make even these simplifying distinctions: from Caesar's falling out with Pompey to the establishment of Octavian is a single civil war.[1] For Valerius this strife and period are distinguished and defined by their end point—the Caesars. Any objection that the final history of the Republic is not so teleological—for instance, that even Octavian may not have had the actual result as his cherished and constant aim—has nothing to do with Valerius.

These same individuals set a precedent for revolution at Rome. The perilous connection of some of these precedents to the imperial regime is, by reason of time, faction, and kin, far closer than Marius and his period. Specific precedents like the tradition of dissent (*libertas*) toward Pompey and general, overriding considerations such as the rise to power and consequent legitimacy of the imperial family are new concerns that Valerius does not eschew. Valerius has seemed almost unconscious of the continuity of social and political strife in the final century of the Republic. The imperial author's attitudes to revolution, to single power, and in particular to that stage of republican history

1. Woodman 1983, 78.

whose leading protagonists dramatized the Republic's collapse might be a touchstone to guarantee his republicanism or conversely his imperial sycophancy. Valerius, of course, will prove no republican, a stance probably only possible for the senatorial historian (e.g., Asinius Pollio or Cremutius Cordus), and his pictures of this era and of its rivals for power will be no more unified than his versions of Sulla. And yet Valerius is faced with a novel dilemma: this admirer of the emperors Augustus and Tiberius writes of what his favorite Cicero deemed the death of the Republic. Issues of composition are again of far more than formal interest. Valerius' manner and scope of depiction, the shape he gives to anecdotes, the controlling rubrics he assigns, and the comparisons drawn and judgments delivered all create visions of the past—more immediate and potentially perilous (as Cremutius Cordus indicates) than the veneration of Scipios or the vituperation of Marius and Sulla.

The events and personalities that do emerge are drawn from the noble families and the familiar, leading protagonists of the last decades of the Roman Republic. Valerius really does not offer new information. The occasional detail, unattested by other sources, is included not to throw novel light on the historical process but for the sake of the bizarre and the extraordinary. So from Valerius alone we learn that the plebeian aedile M. Volusius escaped his proscription through disguise (7.3.8). Equally typical of Valerius, the famous are well represented: for example, Brutus' suicide at Philippi is included, an instance of "Error" at 9.9.2. Valerius does offer a new understanding and appropriation of this time and its agents. He represents neither the Augustan propagandist nor the senatorial republican; rather, his work reflects and communicates the terms of acceptance of the new social and political reality. A new audience, one without historical ties, familial or factional, to Augustus and Julius Caesar or Cato and Cicero, has come to share in the Empire's past, specifically with Valerius in its educational system, its symbols of public behavior and public participation.

Valerius has subjected some of this time's set of characters to a predictable division. His panegyrical devotion to his own emperor has shaped, for example, his treatment of the Caesars (always considered by Valerius as Rome's savior family) and of their most bitter foes. So Octavian receives unmixed praise, and, true to this panegyrical line, Cassius undiluted blame. Yet, outside the vilified and the exalted (the assassins and the Caesars) comes a most interesting set of characters who will be treated here first. Pompey, whose fame can be mitigated but not denied, belongs to this class: the rivals in power and in prestige to Julius Caesar and, in their ardent republicanism and championship of the senate, his historical antagonists, who nonetheless garner Valerius' favorable memorialization. The members of this class later than Pompey are of the greatest importance, for they provided the precedent for dissent in the imperial age—not just the unrealistic example of armed conflict with the Julian house (so Pompey), but the realizable and enduring paradigm of intellectual or ideological dissent. Cato and Cicero were such figures for the Thrasea Paetus of Tacitean fame,[2] but, for Valerius, Cato and Cicero win fame at the expense of partisanship. Valerius has been charged with an ignorance of factional politics.[3] The usefulness of such "ignorance" is manifest here; it divorces Cato and Cicero from their enmity if not entirely from their cause. A neglect of political allegiances and animosities makes possible Valerius' entertaining of opposites, his inclusion of such political antagonists as Caesar and Cato. In the tug between a slavish, imperial flattery and respect for the traditional heroes of republican history (traditional even if as recent as the fall of the Republic, for a canonical literature had raised Cato and Cicero to this stature), Valerius has not been pulled to sole celebration or suppression of either extreme. The new demands of flattery have not worked any great exclusion. The need for inclusion marks Valerius' work far more strongly; he is driven by a desire for wide, encompassing culture. The limits of that culture are the contradictions and conflicts of Roman history, more exactly of the Roman noble families in civil conflict.

The Opponents of Julius Caesar

Cato

Valerius' treatment of the wife of the consistently abused Brutus reveals the narrowness of the class of the vilified. Porcia, in the

2. The danger of such a paradigm is clearly realized, for example, by Nero's flatterer Cossutianus Capito, who condemns Thrasea as an imitator of Cato (Tacitus, *Annales* 16.22).

3. Carney 1962, 293–94.

judgment of Valerius, belongs to the class of her father and not her husband. Even so, the virtues that Valerius has Porcia illustrate are essentially devotion to her husband. Under the rubric "Bravery" Porcia rehearses her suicide (3.2.15). Cassius Dio tells the same story but with a different point: she wounds herself to gain Brutus' confidence.[4] In Valerius she already knows her husband's plan and stabs herself with a pair of scissors as a proof of her devotion to Brutus—to see how calmly she will kill herself should the conspiracy miscarry. Her contemplated suicide is no political act, no attempt to learn of the plans for Caesar's murder, but pious preparation for widowed love. Valerius tells of her actual suicide for the sake of this same moral. Comparison of her suicide (at 4.6.5) with her father's finds hers motivated by an admissible sentiment, "Conjugal Love"—the chapter heading. Valerius praises her act as an imitation of her father's, and not her husband's, noble end.

Valerius is intent on blood connection as the justification for her inclusion, as this comparison with her father and the two Porcian exempla that frame the rehearsal of her suicide demonstrate. The first of these (3.2.14) introduces the Porcian series with Cato at Utica. The last of the three begins: "More fortunate than his offspring was the elder Cato" (3.2.16: *Felicior progenie sua superior Cato*). Fortune's whims are to be blamed for Porcia's death, and her death is but one instance, though the most minor, of the Porcian family's resolution.

Cato himself receives Valerius' highest praise, with neither invidious nor mitigating comparison with Caesar. As is characteristic of Valerius' favorite historical figures, the assembled exempla of Cato offer all the elements of a rhetorical encomium: the subject's genealogical distinction, signal and proleptic anecdotes from his childhood, pithy sayings, unusual and instructive events, offices sought and held, an exemplary death.[5] Valerius is of course even less concerned than an ancient bi-

---

4. Cassius Dio 44.13. In Plutarch (*Brutus* 15) she faints from anxiety and is reported dead.

5. Valerius only occasionally gives a description of his characters, but he is concerned with their *forma*, with their appearance and especially expression (*vultus*) under the public eye. Cato's *forma* is a special case (see my subsequent discussion of Valerius 2.10.8).

ographer with the cement that binds a biography—with presenting the reasons for actions and with asserting an analytic vision of the whole man. Cato has become a rhetorical force, and Valerius is interested in the usefulness and proper use of this. So in bringing the chapter on "Majesty" to an end, with a second exemplum devoted to Cato, Valerius abandons the particulars and engages in laudatory comparison: "To what riches, to what commands, to what triumphs was this [the people's respect for Cato's morals] given?" (2.10.8: *quibus opibus, quibus imperiis, quibus triumphis hoc datum est?*). Not content to leave to his reader the solution of this rhetorical question, Valerius continues the eulogy with the answer, his composite reduction of the younger Cato:

> The man's means were small; his habits honed by restraint, with a small following, a home closed to ambition, with a single great ancestor, not handsome except for a virtue perfect in every aspect. All of which have as result that if anyone wishes to denote a citizen as moral and singular, he calls him a Cato. (2.10.8)[6]

Cato is thus the final and supreme instance of "Majesty." Virtue in place of wealth, honors, family, or beauty is the rhetorician's resort when the usual distinctions fail. In this exemplum this commonplace is more than such an alternate or ancillary mode of praise. Commonplace and example are losing their boundaries. Cato becomes the abstraction as the instance supplants the category. The simile is to be reversed: not Cato like "Majesty" or like "An Outstanding Man," but the lexical classification like Cato. Valerius is ever in search of what *nomen* (name or category) to give a particular person or deed. In Cato he has found an appellation for others, a *nomen* by which to classify men and actions.

This extraordinary rhetoricization—where the individual loses individual features and has as substitute a verbal classification—characterizes Valerius' treatment of Cato. In the string of protests to Pompey's rule, Valerius introduces Cato's dismissal of evidence (a letter

---

6. *exiguum viri patrimonium, astricti continentia mores, modicae clientelae, domus ambitioni clausa, paterni generis una imago, minime blanda frons, sed omnibus numeris perfecta virtus. quae quidem effecit ut quisquis sanctum et egregium civem significare velit, sub nomine Catonis definiat.*

from Pompey praising the guilty defendant) as inadmissible with the following word play: "What am I doing? Freedom without Cato? No more possible than Cato without freedom" (6.2.5: *Quid ego? libertas sine Catone? non magis quam Cato sine libertate*). This *sententia* depends on a similar substitution of the man for the category. While in origin a technique of eulogy, such abstraction substitutes itself for the individual and historical—in this exemplum sufficing as introduction and as the author's explanation of Cato's judicial ruling. The factional struggles for political power have been replaced—superseded by a virtuous abstraction—not simply forgotten.

The historical Cato has not, however, been altogether lost. Valerius knows of Cato's journey to Cyprus and makes three exempla from the successful discharge of this mission and the honors ensuing from the people and the senate (4.1.14; 4.3.2; 8.15.10). The famous suicide at Utica is included (3.2.14) as well as the refusal of the young Cato, in his uncle Livius Drusus' home, to aid the Italians' enfranchisement. The odd details, proof of his eccentricity, are also present: Cato reading Greek in the curia (8.7.2) and wearing no tunic as praetor (3.6.7). His participation in the civil war is not masked: in addition to his death at Utica Valerius offers a trifling detail—the number of slaves he brought on campaign (4.3.12). This last anecdote does not reflect upon the war or Cato's loyalties; rather it follows from the Porcian context of the prior exemplum, which illustrated the elder Cato's moderation.

Cato is clearly of exceptional stature, for Valerius he has even moved from illustration to theme, from instance to category. Writing of Cato's journey to Greece and Cyprus (4.3.2 of "Abstinence and Continence"), Valerius cites as his source, but not as his authority, Munatius Rufus.[7] Cato's continence needs no authority—so Valerius asserts, much as Velleius Paterculus instructs his reader: "It is impious to praise Cato's integrity" (2.45.5: *cuius [Catonis] integritatem laudari nefas est*). The grandness that Cato has assumed in the literary tradition simplifies Valerius' task: the historical character is easily introduced and the point or moral of the incident easily asserted; such a Cato is ready for rhe-

---

7. "And Munatius Rufus, his faithful companion on the embassy to Cyprus, attests to this in his book" (*atque id Munatius Rufus, Cypriacae expeditionis fidus comes, scriptis suis significat*).

torical classification. As always, most nonpersonal historical details need explanation that would lengthen the incident beyond the bounds of the exemplum and could complicate the moral. So no hint of anti-Pompeian measures arises from Valerius' notice that Cato as tribune passed legislation making more difficult the awarding of triumphs (2.8.1). No bribery is suspected nor Caesar's hand detected when Cato loses the race for the praetorship to Vatinius (7.5.6). No Catullan abuse flows from Valerius; instead, he builds a *sententia* that, in his characteristic manner with this subject, depends on an inversion of the man and the abstract noun: "The praetorship was not denied to Cato; Cato was denied to the praetorship" (*non Catoni tunc praetura, sed praeturae Cato negatus est*). Cato has thus been successfully stripped of any political blame. His motives are always those of an abstract virtue; his defeats, the consequences of that virtue. This process has succeeded in setting him apart from the other republican martyrs. Valerius thus groups him not for or against Caesar but with his own family. His companions in Valerius' pages are then the elder Cato and his family. No longer Caesar's antagonist, he is the "greatest glory" of the elder Cato (3.4.6).

Cicero

The Cicero of Valerius' pages is likewise an ornamental figure, marched out to illustrate apolitical themes. The indignation in such a judgment, of course, signals little more than that the historical or historian's Cicero is not to be found in *Memorable Deeds and Sayings*. The reader must dismiss the historical Cicero and yet not substitute any of the leading images—the great statesman or the great stylist—nor supply the intimate picture known to us from the letters. Not only are the exaggerations, either the caricature of his political enemies or the orator's own swollen image, absent (Cicero the fence-sitter and Cicero the country's savior), but Valerius has very little of Cicero's actual relations to Caesar and Pompey. Again, partisan politics are not described, and Cicero's motivation is made to fall outside such sordid concerns. Carney censured Valerius' credulity: the realities of Caesar's power do not seem to occur to Valerius at 4.2.4, where Cicero, his exile and enmity overcome by an extraordinary humanity, defends his former adversaries, Gabinius and Vatinius.[8] Cicero and Cato, however, are not alone in their remove from politics and, more to the point, from political motivation. Cicero's fiery antagonism to Antony has left no mark on Valerius' presentation (quite unlike the declaimers of Seneca's collection), but Octavian, for instance, never even appears. Augustus, in this first stage of his career, enjoys a near complete silence—the triumvirs are mentioned but never named. From Valerius one would not know who the three were. The lack of historical context or understanding is not, in short, whitewash peculiar to the pro-republican figures.

Velleius provides an illuminating comparison at this point, for his periodization of history is remarkably close to Valerius'. The unity of this period, an ignorance or misunderstanding of its factional politics, and the rhetorical (not historical) emphasis in its narrative[9] characterize both Tiberian authors. This period, Woodman concluded, was considered a unity not just by Velleius but by Augustus, Livy, Manilius, "and probably Valerius Maximus . . . and Lucan."[10] In their vision of these years as a simple, almost teleological continuum, Velleius and Valerius may ultimately be following Augustus' lead. Valerius' neglect of the actual motivation of historical figures and his appropriation of language originally and deliberately programmatic indicate the success of Augustus' view, but the vehicle of that success seems to have been declamation. In a note on the final battles of Pompey and Caesar, Woodman remarks on Velleius' emphasis—a way of representing these events that has much in common with Valerius; any historian is easily disappointed in Velleius' accounts of Dyrrachium and Pharsalus, which have "almost

8. Carney 1962, 294 n. 24.

9. Woodman (1983) offered these three conclusions in the course of his exegesis of Velleius' narrative of this period (49–29 B.C.), which agree to a striking degree with Valerius' versions of this time. The second of these observations Woodman offers in a note to Velleius' assertion of Pompey's envy (*invidia* at 44.2, p. 63) for Caesar. Woodman compares Cicero, Velleius, and Seneca the Younger on this point: "All three authors echo the language of the fifties (e.g. Caesar *B.C.* 1.7.1 . . .), but their disagreement over motive is perhaps influenced by the schools of declamation. See esp. Sen. *Contr.* 1.8.10."

10. Woodman 1983, 78. This conclusion, in Valerius' case, should be restricted: Valerius treats only the years from Caesar's death through Octavian's rise as a continuum.

nothing about either campaign." What follows could easily be written of Valerius: "instead he [Velleius] focuses on a colorful episode in each case. . . . Far more time is spent on the aftermath of Pharsalus and Pompey's death, subjects which attracted considerable attention from the rhetoricians, whose topoi Velleius displays in abundance."[11] Coincidence of topoi in Velleius, Valerius, and the declaimers is of interest here not only as the common cultural context of these authors but as the identifiable, actual location where they learned and performed Roman "history." In this context, and therefore not solely or chiefly in the out-of-date contest of Caesarian and republican, we should reunderstand their historiography.

Declamation and the Caesars are both well served by this teleological, simplifying, and even nonhistorical view of the civil conflicts of the latter half of the first century B.C. The consequence of such a view is quite clear, and here two more contemporaries, as recorded by yet another—Seneca the Elder—lend their testimony. Varius Geminus' remarks in the course of the *Controversia* on Cicero's murder (7.2) receive Seneca's stated approval: "Whether actions committed during the civil wars are free from prosecution. Varius Geminus spoke well and correctly on this theme; he said, 'If you make an accusation from those times, you speak of the Republic's, not of a man's, behavior.'"[12] Velleius' and Valerius' views of the conflict may ultimately have Caesar's and Augustus' propaganda as origin, and yet they have come to serve other purposes, ones crucial to declamation. First, the complexity of civil conflict has been reduced to the category of moral aberration of the body politic. As such, it is material for moral themes. In addition, much of the historical pain—proscriptions and conflict—can lose its sting while, perhaps most important, individuals are delivered from blame. This exculpatory result is most surprising as it is most un- or even antihistorical. Again, a propagandistic origin is easily discerned—Caesar's *clementia* would allow no enmity to endure—but the rhetoricians make the action of this quality retroactive. The declaimer, Albucius Silus (ac-

11. Woodman 1983, 91.

12. *Contr.* 7.2.9: *An in bello civili acta obici non possint. honeste dixit, cum hunc locum tractaret, Varius Geminus: "si illa," inquit, "tempora in crimen vocas, dicis non de hominis sed de rei publicae moribus."*

cording to Seneca) proves this point by invoking Cicero himself: "If having been on the other side constituted murder, Cicero would never have defended Ligarius before Caesar. M. Tullius, how light you judged the charge to which you had confessed!" (*Contr.* 10.3.3: *si parricidium esset fuisse in diversis partibus, numquam defendisset apud Caesarem Ligarium Cicero. M. Tulli, quam leve iudicasti crimen de quo confessus es!*). Cicero's change of heart is, as in Valerius' notice of his defense of Vatinius, not plumbed. Further, the applicability of the title and charge of parricide to mere partisans is categorically denied. Praise of individuals—on which Valerius, Velleius, and indeed declamation depend—is thus made possible; indeed, liberation from the charge of parricide is a prerequisite for any treatment of republican heroes, as will be clear from Valerius on the regicides, whose constant branding (as parricides) constricts their usefulness.

Among the republican partisans Cicero is, like Cato, a special case. The general divorce of the partisans from their political cause combined with his special rhetorical elevation augments his usefulness to the declaimers and increases his applicability to various themes. The memorialization thereby achieved remains remarkably self-contained. The historical optimate is forgotten in lieu of a more serviceable abstraction.

Seneca the Elder attests to the attitudes of his contemporaries and offers, in contrast, what Valerius never hazards: criticism of Cicero. Seneca's own high estimation drives him to the historians to clear Cicero from the charge of a cowardly death. In Seneca, however, Cicero has not been so elevated as to become a mere abstraction—the metaphoric substitute, the synecdoche for "eloquence." The orator is, however, so famous that the barest mention suffices for proof; so Calvus is introduced, identified, and dismissed by the following: "Calvus, who long conducted a most unequal suit with Cicero for preeminence in eloquence" (*Contr.* 7.4.6: *Calvus, qui diu cum Cicerone iniquissimam litem de principatu eloquentiae habuit*). As prince of eloquence, Cicero's individual words are, for the orthodox, individual exemplars; he is the guide for diction: even though the school's practice was to avoid ordinary words, the declaimers allowed two exceptions—words made sacrosanct by old practice and by Cicero (*Contr.* 4.pr.9). The *Controversiae* attest to a veneration, in practice and in theory, which has already made

Cicero the (single) canonical orator. Such is no doubt the opinion of Seneca who regrets his missed chance to hear Cicero, "that famous genius, Rome's sole rival to her empire" (*Contr.* 1.pr.11: *illudque ingenium quod solum populus Romanus par imperio suo habuit*).

Valerius is much more clearly part of this adulatory mainstream. That adulation was the rule is revealed not only by Velleius, Valerius, and Seneca, but even more convincingly by the notices of dissent that Seneca transmits, which are given publicity as odd and exceptional. So Cassius Severus singles out for hybris and his own abuse Cestius, whom students are tempted to prefer "even to Cicero" (*Contr.* 3.pr.8). The whole scene is ludicrous—a deliberate mockery of the excess and unreality of declamation: Cassius has interrupted Cestius reading his response to Cicero's *Pro Milone* and proceeds to haul Cestius into court (on grounds as imaginary as many of the declaimers' cases), where Cestius, faced with a forensic reality, knows not what to say. Seneca and Cassius are having good fun with the declaimers' legal fictions, yet the incident does reveal a current of opposition to Cicero. Seneca, like Cassius, was a Ciceronian enthusiast, but this partiality does not induce him to omit material unflattering to Cicero. Indeed, at *Controversiae* 7.3.8–9, a section devoted to clever lines (many from Publilius) Seneca speaks in his own person of examples drawn from Cicero. This section does include material from Pomponius' Atellan farces, some of it at Cicero's expense—for example, "Cicero, it was said maliciously, was a sure friend neither of Pompey nor of Caesar, but a flatterer of both" (*Cicero male audiebat tamquam nec Pompeio certus amicus nec Caesari, sed utriusque adulator*)—which is succeeded by Cicero's witticism to Laberius about Caesar's packing the senate and Laberius' reply on Cicero's fence-sitting.

This opposition to Cicero, however, remained a minority: Romanius Hispo[13] is said to have been the only declaimer to abuse Cicero (*Contr.* 7.2.13). All others rail against Popillius, Cicero's assassin of *Controversia* 7, and in the sixth *Suasoria* only a few take the side prejudicial to Cicero (having him beg Antony for his life). This idea so much offends Seneca that he departs from his proper subject (declamation) to consider the

---

13. On the form of the name of this declaimer, see Goodyear's note to Tacitus, *Annals* 1.74.1 (1981, 158 n. 4).

historical truth behind this theme. The result of the aside, in addition to its intended demonstration of the nobility of Cicero's death, is to single out Asinius Pollio as sole detractor: "He alone gave a prejudicial account of Cicero's death" (*Suas.* 6.24: *Ciceronis mortem solus ex omnibus maligne narrat*). Moreover, Seneca's string of historians offers the proof to another conclusion: that Asinius Pollio wanted the fiction of Antony's wager of Cicero's life for his speeches believed. Seneca explains that Pollio actually did not say this in his speech to Lamia, nor in his histories, but published it afterward (presumably in the speech). The dissent, then, from the elevated view of Cicero is isolated to the malice of Asinius Pollio and to the fiction of a few declaimers; by Seneca's account, it has become a straining after novelty in the declaimers' themes and finds no place in the histories.

Valerius and Seneca have not freed Cicero from all censure, but political criticism is essentially absent. His fickleness does appear—in the already mentioned criticism of Laberius and when Julius Bassus, in an illustration of the imperfect virtue of men, offers three examples for his thesis: "No man is free of fault: Cato lacked moderation, Cicero steadfastness, Sulla mercy" (*Contr.* 2.4.4: *Nemo sine vitio est: in Catone deerat moderatio, in Cicerone constantia, in Sulla clementia*). All three men are victims of this undifferentiating reduction. Bassus' words have diluted historical actions and agents to this abstract and inexact generalization. Both the declaimers and Valerius offer no novel or indeed nuanced treatment for the great orator. Valerius' Cicero strongly resembles his Cato or his Sulla in the way generalizing abstractions subsume his individual actions, whether political or not. The brevity and compression of expression in these themes may be accurately described as epigrammatic, but unlike epigrams, theme and treatment in Valerius do not provoke thought but shut it off, supplying the reader with the analytic category and the proper resolution.

Seneca the Elder provides unique insights into the Cicero of this literary generation. He describes the estimation of Cicero held by the majority of the declaimers: "All that Roman eloquence has to rival or excel impudent Greece flourished about Cicero; all the geniuses whose brilliance illumined our culture were born then; since then there has been daily deterioration." (*Contr.* 1.pr.6–7).[14] Seneca's contemporaries'

---

14. *quidquid Romana facundia habet quod insolenti Graeciae aut opponat aut prae-*

sense of their own inferiority, of cultural decline, was no doubt genuine, and heightened by their practice of canonization—of branding one man as the apogee of each literary genre. As an appraisal of the heights of Augustan literature, Seneca's words are not surprising. The periodization about Cicero, rather than Virgil, is quite natural for a prose rhetorician. After all, the poet would come to be taught as a rhetorician: rhetoric remained the hallmark and fascination of Silver Latin, with different genres collapsing into it. In this passage from the very beginning of his work, Seneca does reveal why Cicero is so especially revered: he has provided the literary achievement to set against the insolent Greeks. One of the most notable characteristics of Velleius, Valerius, Seneca, and the declaimers as a whole is that for the first time at Rome the literary models are preeminently Latin, not Greek. Cicero as Roman champion provides the wherewithal to neglect and ultimately to forget Greek literature.

Valerius had used this patriotic, Greek-balancing attitude to justify the inclusion of politically controversial material. (Republican partisans are celebrated for their friendship, which is set in strong and approving contrast to the Greek, mythic, and further suspect [as homosexual] devotion of Theseus and Pirithous [4.7.4].) The memorialization of Cicero, both in Seneca and Valerius, develops along well-defined patriotic lines. The republican martyrs Cicero and Cato have thus not been rehabilitated into imperial puppets, just as Cicero's overtly political, final works had not been suppressed. Modern analogies of ideology and dissent do not illumine the situation of imperial Rome. In this particular case, Cicero and Cato had never fallen into disrepute—despite even Caesar's pen—and thus can not be said to suffer rehabilitation. Their fame has become a literary creature, subject to the embellishment and fiction of recurring topoi. The attempts to recapture the historical Cicero are exceptional: Seneca's introduction of the historian's judgments and Asconius' commentary were not the rule.

In the examples drawn from Valerius' work, Cicero has been reworked into an elevated verbal abstraction (although, characteristically, Valerius has the unusual detail, which, as unparalleled or first attested,

---

ferat circa Ciceronem effloruit; omnia ingenia quae lucem studiis nostris attulerunt tunc nata sunt. in deterius deinde cotidie data res est, . . .

may be of use to the historian). This reworking closely adheres to the needs of praise. That is, an imperial panegyrist could have found much discreditable to the republican champion (such as the material Seneca is careful to criticize), but Valerius has not taken this path. Cicero has already had his politics subsumed, even overwhelmed, by his books and by the abstraction, *eloquentia Romana*, he has become.

The shaping element in Valerius' depictions of Cicero is the published prose texts: Valerius' knowledge of Cicero depends mainly on the speeches, the rhetorical, and the philosophical works. For Valerius the published words of Cicero had, in the search for anecdote and illustration, the attraction of accessibility and orthodoxy. Valerius did not, however, invariably follow a Ciceronian source for a Ciceronian subject; habitually, he told some famous incidents briefly, for his own point (often the chapter heading), and mingled his sources to produce a pastiche of famous authors. For instance, Valerius exhibits no direct verbal dependence on Cicero at 8.5.5 and 9.12.7, the jury's rejection of Cicero's testimony in the infamous trial of Clodius and the orator's withholding of sentence (when praetor) in the case of the suicide C. Licinius Macer. Valerius devotes the first five chapters of the eighth book to legal examples, but by the fifth he seems to have tired of this subject, introducing the fifth chapter with the perfunctory: "it follows that I should recount examples concerning witnesses" (*sequitur ut ad testis pertinentia exempla commemorem*) and departing in the next chapter from strictly legal matters. This fifth chapter is a string of short notices of unusual witnesses. Cicero is given the same short treatment as the rest:

> Well then, after winning the greatest honors and the most noble rank of dignity in the forensic contest, wasn't M. Cicero rejected as a witness in the very camp of his own eloquence, when he swore that P. Claudius had been at his home in Rome while Claudius was preserving himself from the disgrace of sacrilege by the single argument of his absence? For the jurors preferred to free Claudius from the charge of adultery than Cicero from the infamy of perjury. (8.5.5)[15]

---

15. *Quid? M. Cicero forensi militia summos honores amplissimumque dignitatis lo-*

The compression of this single sentence precludes any substantial direct verbal dependence on a model. Cicero is simply introduced as the height of forensic eloquence; the case of Clodius is not described in any detail; two clauses explain the significance of Cicero's testimony. The outcome is given in a closing *sententia*. The acquittal was, in fact, infamous, and Cicero tried to make it all the more so by dressing down Clodius in the senate house and writing of this to Atticus.[16] Plutarch may have had this letter with Cicero's witticisms available;[17] Valerius probably not. The two sources which he undoubtedly had, *De domo sua* 79–80 and *Pro Milone* 46, make but passing references to the case. Valerius is also interested only in making a passing reference: no need to borrow a lengthy harangue against Clodius—the schoolboys knew the *Pro Milone*, as is clear from the fact that Cestius had been singled out by Seneca for his vanity in replying to this speech and for the audacity of teaching his students to prefer this reply. Valerius is referring to a well-known incident in the orator's career. Cicero is portrayed not as Pompey's henchman or the optimates' spokesman but as the apogee of eloquence suffering an ironic defeat.

The second notice of Cicero that does not directly depend on an (extant) written model is the story of Cicero's timely stay of judgment when the news of the death of the defendant (about to be condemned) is brought before him. In a letter to Atticus, Cicero writes of the popularity of this decision (hinting thereby at the fact that it would be well known).[18] The subject of this exemplum is Licinius Macer and not, predominantly, Cicero, for the theme to be illustrated is "Distinguished Deaths" (*De mortibus non vulgaribus*). Death without condemnation freed Macer's property from confiscation—that is, it ensured the wellbeing of his family and the preservation of his name. These two exempla, a brief illustration of a notable witness and a notable suicide, were well-known subjects that Valerius has not chosen to embellish.

---

cum adeptus, nonne in ipsis eloquentiae castris testis abiectus est, dum P. Claudium Romae apud se fuisse iurat, illo sacrilegum flagitium uno argumento absentiae tuente? si quidem iudices Claudium incesti crimine quam Ciceronem infamia periurii liberare maluerunt.

16. Cicero, *Ad Att.* 1.16.
17. Plutarch, *Cicero* 29.
18. Cicero, *Ad Att.* 1.4.

For the greater part of the Ciceronian exempla Valerius is engaged
in his customary method of composition: borrowing and adapting his
classical source's diction. Even with Cicero as subject and source, however, Valerius does not always keep to his single source. Instead, a contamination of models produces a stylistic pastiche. In addition, Valerius
can be misleading about his source, as, for instance, when he mentions
Cicero's speech *Pro Gallio* as the setting for Cicero's response to the
overwhelming evidence marshaled by the prosecutor M. Calidius. The
story is also preserved in Cicero's *Brutus* where it exemplifies the need
for force (*vis*) in speaking (the orator's duty to move and not merely to
please and to instruct his audience).[19] Cicero in the *Brutus* quotes from
his own speech, but Valerius has only the beginning of this ("If you
were not making this up, M. Calidius, would you behave so?").[20] The
remaining verbal parallels reveal that Valerius had the *Brutus* and not
Cicero's early speech before him. Cicero reminds Brutus of the case:

Why, I remember that, when Calidius in his prosecution accused
Q. Gallius of planning to poison him and said that he had found
the poison and that he and the defendant's handwriting and the
testimony and the evidence and the inquiries signified one thing
clearly and he argued about this with care and in detail, I in response, after I had pointed out, in my argument, the seriousness
of the case, added this as an argument that, though he said he had
clearly discovered and himself apprehended a threat to his life and
proofs of his intended murder, he acted so dispassionately, so
calmly, so listlessly: "If you were not making this up, M. Calidius,
would you be behaving so?" . . . [the quotation from the speech
continues for another seven lines]. (277–78)[21]

19. *Brutus* 276.
20. *Brutus* 278 and Valerius 8.10.3.
21. *quin etiam memini, cum in accusatione sua Q. Gallio crimini dedisset sibi eum
venenum paravisse idque a se esse deprensum seseque chirographa testificationes indicia
quaestiones manifestam rem deferre diceret deque eo crimine accurate et exquisite dis-
putavisset, me in respondendo, cum essem argumentatus, quantum res ferebat, hoc ipsum
etiam posuisse pro argumento, quod ille, cum pestem capitis sui, cum indicia mortis se
comperisse manifesto et manu tenere diceret, tam solute egisset, tam leniter, tam oscitanter.
"Tu istuc, M. Calidi, nisi fingeres, sic ageres?"*

Valerius has compressed this original and rendered it in the third person:

> For M. Cicero indicated in his defense of Gallius the importance of both elements of which we are speaking, when he reproached the prosecutor M. Calidius for employing a blank expression, calm voice, and relaxed style of speaking when maintaining that the defendant's intention to poison him would be proved by witnesses, handwriting, and inquiries, and he both detected the orator's weakness and added an argument to his endangered case by rounding off this passage: "If you were not making this up, M. Calidius, would you be behaving so?" (8.10.3)[22]

Valerius has not only lifted the details and diction of his exemplum from the *Brutus*; the discussion of the orator's fault (*vitium*) comes from here as well, for Cicero, in the passage that immediately follows his quotation from the *Pro Gallio,* had Brutus take up the issue of whether such an even, untroubled delivery was a vice or a virtue.[23] Despite the somewhat misleading reference to the *Pro Gallio,* Valerius is working from the *Brutus,* from a famous Ciceronian text; elsewhere, however, he does allow other versions of famous events to influence his own depiction. At 9.11.3 Valerius retails Catiline's threat to quench his impending demise with general ruin; Valerius seems to have understood the scene as Sallust depicted it but took Cicero as his source for diction and phrasing.[24]

The most striking example of this mingling of sources comes in a series of three consecutive exempla drawn from Cicero's *De divinatione.* The only indications of Valerius' source are the subject of the second (1.7.5: Cicero in exile dreams of Marius) and the direct reference in

---

22. *Nam M. Cicero quantum in utraque re, de qua loquimur, momenti sit oratione, quam pro Gallio habuit, significavit M. Calidio accusatori exprobrando, quod praeparatum sibi a reo venenum testibus, chirographis, quaestionibus probaturum adfirmans remisso vultu et languida voce et soluto genere orationis usus esset, pariterque et oratoris vitium detexit et causae periclitantis argumentum adiecit totum hunc locum ita claudendo: "tu istud, M. Calidi, nisi fingeres, sic ageres?"*

23. *Brutus* 279.

24. See my discussion in chapter 3.

1.7.6 to Coelius Antipater. The expiation for a murdered slave (1.7.4), Cicero's own dream (1.7.5), and Gaius Gracchus' dream (1.7.6) are all taken from one passage in the *De divinatione* (1.55–56). Valerius found the story of 1.7.4 in Cicero (who narrates it sparely); the search for further details brought him to Livy 2.36.1. Unlike Cicero but like Livy, Valerius names the dreamer (T. Latinius) and identifies Jupiter as the source of the dream. Valerius seems to have had the text of Livy before him: not only do these details agree but Valerius' "before the entrance of the procession" (*prius quam pompa induceretur*) is a gloss for Livy's "early in the morning before the games had begun" (*mane . . . nondum commisso spectaculo*). In the final exemplum a parallel of syntax (*quo ipse . . .*) and the mention of Coelius reveal Valerius' return to Cicero, for this reference to the earlier historian is borrowed from Cicero.

Valerius' composition may at times seem a mixture of outright plagiarism and faked footnotes. If an apology is needed, it will help to remember the practice of his contemporaries, Velleius and the declaimers. Seneca does complain of plagiarism; this is in part why he writes: to assure the proper attribution of sayings and colors to their authors.[25] The sixth *Suasoria* (*Deliberat Cicero an Antonium deprecetur*), where the various speakers appropriate Cicero's own words, however, elicits no authorial objection. Seneca has not objected because the speakers intended the borrowings to be recognized as allusions; he may lament that the strange novelties of declamation have been plagiarized—used without proper attribution or without the audience's knowledge of their true origin—but this plagiarism is possible because declamation was an oral performance. The only records were human memory and some commentaries, and the latter, he complains, were few or erroneous.[26] Valerius is as innocent of plagiarism as the declaimers who produced a Ciceronian pastiche. Cicero's words were published, taught in the schools, and above all recognizable. The audience's recognition of these words spurred on the artistry of the speakers in their Ciceronian centos.[27]

25. Seneca, *Contr.* 1.pr.11.
26. Seneca, *Contr.* 1.pr.11.
27. Woodman (1983, 65) has observed the same artistry in Velleius, again on a Ciceronian subject—the struggles of Clodius with Cicero and Cato in 58–

The declaimers, Valerius, and Velleius share this acquisitive habit of composition. Cicero's actions, just as surely as his words, are being reshaped by speakers and writers who combine a peculiar mixture of veneration, which in part takes the form of devotion to stylistic strictures and of adherence to a canon, and license. Admittedly, the step to plagiarism is small (once the reader or listener does not realize the source and the composer has not altered the wording). Valerius is not engaged in literary composition on the same scale as the declaimers or the historian, but his actual composition has much in common with them, especially the strained search for novel fusions, novel junctures, and for reusing the classical in unpredictable ways.

Valerius' direct tie to declamation is evident, for example, in his account of the death of Cicero, a version that no doubt would have provoked Seneca's censure. This exemplum (5.3.4) develops the melodrama and paradox of the confrontation: Cicero's former client volunteers to hunt his benefactor down; the orator's head and peacemaker's right hand are returned to Rome; the dead Cicero requires another Cicero to redress this outrage. Such fictions were responsible for the elder Seneca's digression in which he compares various accounts of Cicero's murder. Valerius has common ground with the declaimers—the paradoxical workings of fortune—and also common fictions. An examination of Valerius' Cicero and Cato is not simply an exercise in demonstrating the historical distortion that results from the contemporary intellectual rage (declamation). Rather, this new age hagiography divorces its subjects from politics through a rhetorical elevation. The result is a new classification of men and actions. Often this tends to a simplifying assignment, a restriction of one virtue (or vice) to one man. So Varius Geminus referred to "Cassius' violence, Brutus' pride, Pompey's stupidity,"[28] and Seneca himself pointed out that genius failed Cicero in poetry, Virgil in prose.[29] A canon of virtues and

56 B.C.: "This section [45] is an excellent illustration of V.'s use of literary allusion. When focusing on Clodius (1), he appropriately echoes Sallust's turbulent narrative; but when referring to Cicero's exile and return (2–3), he echoes Cicero's own speeches for the period in question."

28. Seneca, *Suas.* 6.14.4.
29. Seneca, *Contr.* 3.pr.8.

historical exemplars, like a canon of authors, depends on such clear, one-for-one identities. Complexity of motive, like variety of genius, tends to undermine the simplicity that such elevation demands. The processes by which Cicero and Cato, a generation after their deaths, have become rhetorical exemplars are not merely an obfuscating political reflex, but the various reactions of a particular set of literate men to a changed society; they are their attempts to appropriate a recognizably alien past and to build an enduring, connected, and sustaining memorial of that past.

The Caesars

Valerius is highly selective in the examples drawn from the most recent Roman history. In part the lack of material from his own times is due to methodology: he retold those anecdotes that he found in Livy, Cicero, and Trogus. The extraordinary nature of the contemporary material that he does transmit reflects his method of composition and his veneration for these prose authors. This same restriction on contemporary matter reveals an extreme reticence: only in very specific circumstances is the present allowed as exempla. A very select company can imitate republican exempla in the public, political sphere. Valerius' exactly contemporary references are the invocation of the emperor and the denunciation of Sejanus. The role of the family of the Caesars and of Augustus in particular is the crucial, focal issue for the historian of the early Principate. The depiction of this subject declares the author's partisanship, politically, socially, and literarily, and his ambition. The panegyrist would boast of peace after the decades of strife. The republican critic would lament institutions perished. The omission by the historian of this subject is a third choice, a type of *recusatio* that allows that author to attempt the history of a marginal topic, one that purports to be free of republican-imperial animus: Seneca's history of declamation, Asconius' historical commentary on Cicero's speeches, a number of accounts of the German Wars. Quite understandably, Valerius in his book of examples does not articulate the social and political changes at the close of the first century B.C. and the beginning of the first century A.D. But neither are there exempla from Tiberius' military campaigns or from any of the German Wars. Would not Quinctilius Varus have made an excellent example? Or should not Agrippina the Elder, if she really did address the mutinous troops as Tacitus so vividly portrays, have been included in the chapter on female public speakers? If Valerius is to present the past as paradigmatic, surely there must be a seamless joint with the present, and the Caesars must be that link. He does write of his own age as happy and serene under the parental guide of the Caesars and yet never develops a vague sense of difference, the distance of the present from the severe moral exemplars of the old Republic. The seamless quality of Valerius' "history" is nowhere more apparent than when it touches the time of the Caesars: he never really moves from the fall of the Republic to its restoration. His treatment of material drawn from this time presents no discernible break between the past and the contemporary. The Caesars are the agents of that continuity.

Some continuity of past with present is essential for a historical exemplum to remain a valid means of argument: the reader or audience must have enough in common with the example so that the precedent still offers a basis for behavior, for thought, or for action. Valerius' seamless vision of Roman history ensures the connection of past with present as his chapters' chronologically ordered series of exempla sweep the reader from distant times to the present while his rhetorical techniques, such as apostrophe, involve the audience, anachronistically, in the actions of the past.

Augustus' version of his own rise to power and of his hold on Rome has, however, significantly influenced Valerius' composition, for Valerius transmits the consequences if not the program of Augustan propaganda. The generation of Augustus had heard peace celebrated as Augustus' gift and indirectly as justification for the new political system. Valerius does not feel the need so to defend the Caesars. He recognizes the achievement of pacification and includes it in his imperial eulogy, yet his relatively minor emphasis on the change worked by Augustus and perpetuated by Tiberius attests to the success of the imperial view, to the acceptance of autocracy under the guise of republicanism. In Valerius the rallying cry of peace has been muted, though not through any opposition to the Caesars. Valerius, in an almost naive and not programmatic or problematic fashion, reflects the success of the Caesars' view of themselves as the lawful sustainers of the Republic. Justification is no longer wanted once no novelty or change is discerned. Each Caesar is the legitimate successor to his adoptive father, and the series of Caesars is the legitimate continuation of the Republic.

For some the juncture of the imperial and the republican may seem strained or even strange.[30] The failed fusion of the two eras and ideologies could constitute either outright intellectual dissent (Valerius paying lip service to the Caesars while undermining their claims with republican examples) or some unrealized psychological dissent (where the subject matter unwittingly gives the lie to the panegyric or reflects contemporary doubts or misgivings about the imperial regime). Valerius shows no signs of the former. The difficulty with the second interpretation is that this tension bothers the critic far more than it does Valerius: it is a conflict of underlying fact, not of the fictive weave that is Valerius' work. One may as well object to the tension between Soviet propaganda and historical reality. Those who wrote of the "liberation" of Poland felt no such tension; a reader, especially a historian, might. The ridiculousness of ideology, of any one version of a historical event, while glaringly evident to a certain audience, can be decidedly absent from the author's intent. Valerius does differ from the modern panegyrist in a certain inconsistency: he has not suppressed material that, either by its substance or the intent of the original author, could possibly be viewed as subversive of the present regime. He is equally an ideologue, if we mean by ideology the attempt of one segment of a society to gloss over the contradictions of history and of social structure.

30. Maslakov (1984, 447) raises the historian's objection: "does the collection work to undermine rather than confirm the notion of the continuity of the Roman political tradition?" To address this "tension" in the work, Maslakov examined material prejudicial to Valerius' imperial panegyric (e.g., republican instances of excessive concentration of power within one family (4.1.5) and of the degeneration of a noble family (3.5.1–4)) and concluded (pp. 451–52), "No matter how confidently an image is projected of a *princeps* firmly in control . . . and responsible for the moral climate in which *virtutes* are encouraged to grow and vices are punished, images from the past (of Marius and Sulla, as well as those of external enemies of Rome and their former successes) are forceful reminders of possible challenges to it."

Valerius thus has made a strained and ideological joining of his own age with the past, but this is hardly evidence of dissent.

A tension of subject matters is felt only if one part of Valerius' work is read as commentary upon another. If, instead, each chapter or exemplum is seen as designed for the illustration of a rhetorical topos, the whole will be understood as the patchwork it is. Exempla do vie with each other—as instances of a particular category—but do not compel political action just as they do not promote historical inquiry. These are neither categories to be illustrated nor recurrent concerns for Valerius. Further, his treatment of Julius, Augustus, and Tiberius Caesar, although it shares the features peculiar to his praise of this family, differs only in degree (the Caesars as the apex of Roman history) from his customary composition: the techniques of heroization, elevation, and abstraction recur.

Julius Caesar, Pompey, and the Assassins

Valerius' treatment of Julius Caesar is remarkable and distinctive. Where Marius, Cinna, and Sulla formed a center of sorts for any anecdote that dealt with the eighties (collectively or individually, these men were the point of reference by which to locate and identify a person or event), the decades that follow, as covered by Valerius, have an end point. The Caesars often appear in Valerius as the apex of a chapter, as the culminating and capping figures in a series of exempla. For example, within a chapter praise of Pompey or the mention of one of Caesar's adversaries in any remotely favorable light seems of necessity to occasion the balancing mention of Caesar. Valerius' practice is neither random nor purely chronological—that is, in a series of historical figures Caesar as the most recent is naturally mentioned last. Rather, in the following instances, Valerius displays a characteristic, though intruding, habit of structure and thought: Julius Caesar is conjured up as a sort of balance to the proper subject matter of an exemplum.

The most notable case is the story of Cassius as a schoolboy. Cato and his restraining pedagogue, in the previous exemplum (3.1.2), have set the scene of noble youth's resistance to tyranny. Now Cassius strikes his schoolmate, Sulla's son, for praising the proscriptions and promising to imitate his father. Valerius cannot let the story go with this, but

must add a concluding comment to mitigate his praise of the young
Cassius: "a hand that ought not to have stained itself with public parricide" (3.1.3: *dignam manum, quae publico parricidio se non contaminaret*).
Even the tersest allusion to Julius Caesar has two of the three essential
elements of Valerius' characterization of the founder of the imperial
line: he will be mentioned last as the seal on the civil wars (so as always
to remedy or balance the reader's view of that contest and those con-
tenders) and his death will be consistently represented as parricide
(both to blacken the assassins in the highest degree and to suggest the
familial tie of the Caesars to the state).[31] The epithet *divus*, though not
present in this brief comment, constitutes the final element of Valerius'
rhetoric of the Caesars. The divinization of Julius and Augustus Caesar, an insistent emphasis on the familial connections of the Caesars
and the identification of this family with the state, and the treatment
of this family and its members as the apex of all that has come before
constitute the recurrent essentials of Valerius on the Caesars.

This ideological trinity is hardly surprising, but the context of its
appearances provides an index to the success of the imperial (Augustan) view. Such a story of the young Cassius, of course, cannot resist
embellishment. Plutarch in telling this story has the two boys brought
before Pompey,[32] who is successor to Sulla (in civil bloodletting) and
precedent for Cassius (as antagonist to Caesar); but such irony is far
from Valerius' purposes. With Caesar, and not Pompey, imported into
the story, the anecdote is brought to a safe conclusion; imperial vanity
is consoled when praise of Caesar forms the rhetorical closure. For Valerius, in many respects, Caesar is the foil to what has come before, to
those two prior generations of civil strife. Cassius, far from being celebrated as the last of the Romans, is not allowed the melodramatic and
proleptic fiction of judgment by Pompey; rather he and his exemplum
properly give way to Caesar.

31. Suetonius reveals that, by vote of the senate, the Ides of March was re-
named *Parricidium* (*Divus Julius*, 88). The designation "parricide" was, thus,
part of the official (Augustan) version of these events, and so I have not translated it with the (comparatively) neutral "murder" or even "destruction of one's
country."
32. Plutarch, *Brutus* 9.

The imposed, arbitrary nature of this seal is more clearly seen in 9.15.5, an episode that has no connection with Caesar. Here Valerius relates one of the abuses of Sulla's reign: a usurper has ejected the son of a Roman citizen (Asinius Dio) from his home. Valerius does not, however, then tell of the fate of the pretender or of the legitimate heir. Instead comes a rather obfuscating phrase: "but Caesarian equity, after it had restored the Republic from Sullan violence, with a more just first citizen guiding the helm of the Roman empire, revivified the protection of the public."[33] Caesar is not said to have reinstated the rightful son— perhaps Valerius did not know the actual outcome, and certainly chronology argues against Julius Caesar as the actual restorer. The mention of Caesar's justice is important to the shape and understanding of the chapter, both as foil to the outrages of civil strife and as transition to the next (the first foreign) exemplum, where a woman of Milan, an inheritance hunter, is checked by the "unbreachable constancy of Caesar." The contrast of the new age with the old, with special emphasis on the Caesars' roles, has been a recurrent theme in this chapter. The first exemplum, after passing (in a *praeteritio*) over the case of Equitius (the pretended brother of the Gracchi), relates Julius Caesar's banishment of the pretended grandson of Marius. Valerius then moves from the *divinae Caesaris vires* (9.15.1) to the *divi . . . Augusti . . . numen* (9.15.2), which does not suffer an interloper into the imperial family. Augustus would no doubt have been delighted—with his epithet and with the celebration of himself as champion and restorer of the family. The historian is not so pleased as, in lieu of the complicated series of events intermediate between Sulla's dictatorship and Caesar's final years, Violence gives way to Equity.

Valerius' abiding interest remains with individuals and not with the course of history, however imagined. Details of chronology, the progression of events, the role of institutions, men's various motives are of no interest in themselves. These are not unknown to Valerius, but he does not deviate from his search for category and illustration—for the outstanding and unusual as displayed by famous and infamous

---

33. Valerius 9.15.5: *verum postquam a Sullana violentia Caesariana aequitas rem publicam reduxit, gubernacula Romani imperii iustiore principe obtinente in publica custodia spiritum posuit.*

men. And yet his composition is not everywhere so simple. The Caesars, most famous of men for this Tiberian author, have required special treatment. The examples of Cassius and the usurper of Dio's household have suggested the outlines of a technique of praising the Caesars on mention of their foes. Valerius is perfectly consistent in this technique; the figure of Pompey repeatedly demands from Valerius comparison with Julius Caesar. Pompey's achievement will be measured and then, like all of the "history" intermediate between Sulla's dictatorship and the Ides of March, capped by this comparison. Additionally, material that is ostensibly prorepublican will either be similarly sealed by final allusion to Caesar and the new age, or so categorized as to lose all political resonance.

Pompey in defeat, in humanity, in his omens, and in his debts is great in himself, no match for Julius Caesar. On the day following the Battle of Pharsalus Pompey had retired to Larisa where, according to Valerius, all the citizens came to honor the vanquished general. In this grand illustration of "Modesty" (*Verecundia*) Pompey bids the people pay this reverence to the victor. In assessing the republican general Valerius adopts a rhetorical posture of doubt, the posture of uncertainty as to the proper interpretation of this action: "I would say, 'not deserving of being conquered,' except that he was vanquished by Caesar" (4.5.5: *dicerem, non dignus qui vinceretur, nisi a Caesare esset superatus*). Pompey is bested off the battlefield as well; Caesar has outstripped him in the very quality here exemplified. Valerius' claim in the opening sentence of the following exemplum makes this claim: "the exceptional quality of C. Caesar's modesty was frequently displayed, and it was attested by his last day" (4.5.6: *quam [verecundiam] praecipuam in C. quoque Caesare fuisse et saepe numero apparuit et ultimus eius dies significavit*). Caesar not only outdistanced his one-time rival for power but seems to have belonged to a different category. If the reader has any doubts about Caesar's standing after hearing of Caesar's numerical lead (*saepe numero*) in instances of modesty, the familiar elements of Valerius' panegyric ensure that Pompey is vanquished. Caesar's murder is again an act of parricide: he is "pierced by the daggers of the numerous parricides" (*compluribus enim parricidarum violatus mucronibus*); and his death is an epiphany of the divine: "his divine soul was separated from the mortal body. . . . in this manner men do not die, but the immortal gods return to their home" (*divinus spiritus mortali discernebatur a corpore. . . . in hunc modum non homines expirant, sed di immortales sedes suas repetunt*).

The agonistic treatment and climactic juxtaposition of Pompey and Caesar are found also in the final Roman examples of the chapter "On Humanity and Clemency" (5.1). In a series that has begun with the senate's and developed to Roman generals' acts of kindness to conquered foes, Pompey is depicted raising the fallen King Tigranes (5.1.9). From this act of humanity conferred, Valerius moves to the humanity not received by Pompey—his betrayal and death in Egypt (5.1.10). This reversal of fortune, a favorite theme in Valerius, is the more attractive as it leads to an even greater act of humanity: Caesar's grief for Pompey and his care for his son-in-law's remains. Pompey's peculiar fate and indeed the entire chapter lead up to this grandest exemplum of all, the illustration of "the clement soul of the divine prince" (5.1.10: *mansuetus animus divini principis*). Valerius then tacks on a similar moment:

> On the news of Cato's death, Caesar said that he envied Cato's glory and that Cato had envied his, and he preserved Cato's patrimony, intact, for his children. And by god, the preservation of Cato would have been no small part of Caesar's divine deeds.[34]

Caesar's words seem a bit odd. They are more pungent in Plutarch,[35] who has Caesar envy Cato's death, Cato Caesar's sparing of his life, and in Cassius Dio,[36] who has Caesar angry because Cato begrudged him the glory of sparing his life. Valerius' version, with its mutual, undifferentiated envy, has lost some force to achieve its terse expression. Valerius' simplification is to make the two men have something in common; antitheses of thought, character, and action are here dismissed. In addition, Valerius has tried to make two *sententiae* from this incident and, finally, to slant the episode to Caesar's favor. The reader

34. *Catonis quoque morte Caesar audita et se illius gloriae invidere et illum suae invidisse dixit patrimoniumque eius liberis ipsius incolume servavit. et hercule divinorum Caesaris operum non parva pars Catonis salus fuisset.*

35. Plutarch, *Cato* 72.

36. Cassius Dio 43.12.1.

is not told Cato's glory stems from his death; though this is clearly the point of Plutarch's and Cassius Dio's anecdotes, Valerius will not express so positive a republican sentiment. The author remains intent upon Caesar the ever-clement and will not allow his hero's glory to be shared. Cato like Pompey is here chiefly as foil.

Julius Caesar, coming last or nearly last in a series of exempla on a particular theme, is imagined as the greatest exemplar of that theme. The Caesars as climax in any series or indeed in history is hardly a surprising conception. Panegyric demands exaltation. The contemporary universal history of Velleius Paterculus shares this panegyrical tendency: history rushes along so precipitously to reach its pinnacle—Tiberius. The unusual element in Valerius' composition is not praise of Caesar but the pattern of imperial panegyric, its appearance upon the mention of certain other figures. One curious effect of this presentation of history is that the more modern can supplant the more remote. Loyal apologies, occasioned by a favorable mention of Cassius or Pompey, develop into a more than balancing praise of the Caesars. Julius Caesar's humanity not only rivals Pompey's but as the apogee of this quality tends to replace it as the definitive exemplum.

This sort of replacement or, more properly, displacement—where mention of Pompey is closely succeeded by greater eulogy of Caesar—occurs also at 6.2.11 and 1.6.12–13. In the first instance, the replacement is no longer figurative: Pompey's unpaid debt to Servius Galba is made good by Caesar:

> Now, the demand of Servius Galba was full of effrontery: he dared to make the following interruption when the divine Julius was deciding cases in the forum after the consolidation of his victories, "C. Julius Caesar, I guaranteed a loan for Cn. Pompeius Magnus, your onetime son-in-law, in his third consulship, and now the note is called in. What should I do? Should I pay?" By clearly and openly reproaching Caesar's sale of Pompey's property he deserved to be ejected from the court. But that heart softer than clemency itself ordered Pompey's debt to be repaid from his own treasury. (6.2.11)[37]

---

37. *Iam Servi Galbae temeritatis plena postulatio, qui divum Iulium consummatis*

In itself the paying of this debt is not the strongest proof of "displacement." Caesar as usual receives the highest praise Valerius can manage: he (or rather, his heart) is described in terms of a moral abstraction as "softer than clemency itself." The convincing evidence that Caesar is here meant as a cap to Pompey is to be found not only in these terms but in the position of this exemplum: penultimate in the series of *Libere Dicta aut Facta* and the first Caesarian subject after a string of exempla that, in some detail, presents dissent to Pompey. The problems of Pompey's rule, formulated by Valerius as a tradition of Liberty's outraged responses to this implied tyranny, are succeeded by Caesar's liberal action. The metonymic connection, from liberality of speech toward Pompey to monetary liberality in lieu of Pompey, is the formal tie that asserts the transition between exempla. Cato and Caesar had shared envy; here Pompey and Caesar share liberality. But both cases redound to the credit of Caesar.

The theme truly corresponding to liberality toward Pompey is dissent toward the Caesars. This liberality of speech does occur in the next (and final) exemplum:

O, how dangerously stubborn was Cascellius, a man famous for his learning in civil law! For he could not be moved by anyone's influence or authority to formulate a legal principle for any of the things the triumvirs had conferred; in his judgement all their grants were extralegal. When the same man spoke too freely about the times of Caesar and his friends advised him not to do so, he answered that the two things that men thought most bitter allowed him this license: old age and childlessness. (6.2.12)[38]

---

victoriis in foro ius dicentem in hunc modum interpellare sustinuit: "C. Iuli Caesar, pro Cn. Pompeio Magno, quondam genero tuo, in tertio eius consulatu pecuniam spopondi, quo nomine nunc appellor. quid agam? dependam?" palam atque aperte ei bonorum Pompei venditionem exprobrando ut a tribunali summoveretur meruerat. sed illud ipsa mansuetudine mitius pectus aes alienum Pompei ex suo fisco solvi iussit.

Valerius is retailing a curious incident otherwise unknown, although a letter of Cicero (*Ad fam.* 6.18.3) states in passing that Galba had guaranteed a loan for Pompey.

38. *Age, Cascellius vir iuris civilis scientia clarus quam periculose contumax! nullius enim aut gratia aut auctoritate conpelli potuit ut de aliqua earum rerum, quas triumviri*

The thematic connection to the preceding exempla, the parallel to Pompey and the previous exemplum, is left unexpressed. Instead, the final example is made to fall within the chapter's compass as an instance of liberal (excessively free) speech (*liberius loqueretur*). The more natural parallel of event to event is not suppressed but differently and diffidently handled and is itself displaced. Valerius has not ignored the republican tradition of dissent—here the learned jurist Cascellius' candid remarks about the times of Julius Caesar—but tacks it on at the chapter's end, after Caesar has been seen as Pompey's generous rival and victor.

Pompey's glory is not denied but, like Cato's, eclipsed by the brighter imperial light. The historical rivals for power fight a very unequal battle for commemoration. A final illustration of the success of Pompey's displacement and of Caesar's celebration is drawn by Valerius in the famous (borrowed) scenes of heaven's foreboding. Pompey's and Caesar's deaths come in succession as the climactic close to the Roman examples of the sixth chapter of book 1. Passages 1.6.12 and 13, respectively, present omens of defeat for Pompey, death for Caesar. The anecdotes are commonplace (Cassius Dio has bees swarming about Pompey's standards, much as Valerius does)[39] and do not augment Suetonius' picture of the events.[40] To the marvels accompanying Pompey's departure from Dyrrachium, Valerius has spliced the omens before Pharsalus. The juncture may be novel; the material is not. He has taken this second dose of prodigies, with slight alterations, from the original account in the third book of Caesar's *Civil War*.[41] The death of Julius Caesar in the subsequent exemplum similarly offers no novel detail, yet

dederant, formulam conponeret, hoc animi iudicio universa eorum beneficia extra omnem ordinem legum ponens. idem cum multa de temporibus Caesaris liberius loqueretur, amicique ne id faceret monerent, duas res, quae hominibus amarissimae viderentur, magnam sibi licentiam praebere respondit, senectutem et orbitatem.

39. Cassius Dio 41.61.

40. Suetonius, *Divus Julius* 81.

41. Caesar, *B.C.* 3.105. Valerius preserved the order of the sites of the prodigies (Elis, Antioch, Ptolemais, Pergamum, Tralles), although he omits the name but not the substance of the first, and has at times followed Caesar's diction.

Valerius' introduction and conclusion are quite distinctive in their creation of original linkages. The stories of the two exempla are not presented as separate, rival displays of the gods' unheeded admonitions, as would be the proper treatment in a chapter meant to exemplify prodigies. Instead, Valerius gave the first exemplum a pointed introduction, which does double service. The exemplum is thereby connected with what follows while the reader is provided with a specific divine agent, omnipotent Jove, and a ready moral: "Even omnipotent Jupiter gave frequent warnings to Cn. Pompey not to rush into a final trial of war with C. Caesar" (1.6.12: *Cn. etiam Pompeium Iuppiter omnipotens abunde monuerat ne cum C. Caesare ultimam belli fortunam experiri contenderet*). Repetition of the same point closes the exemplum: "by which omens is revealed heaven's intention both to assist Caesar's glory and check Pompey's mistake" (*quibus apparet caelestium numen et Caesaris gloriae favisse et Pompei errorem inhibere voluisse*). For Valerius, once Pompey is the instance of a category, Julius Caesar demands an immediate entrance into the text.

Valerius' certainty as to the designs of the divine before the Battle of Pharsalus is thin flattery compared with the invocation of the divine Julius that begins the final Roman exemplum:

> Supplicating your altars and your most holy temples, divine Julius, I pray that you may benignly and favorably allow the slaughter of such great men sanctuary under the guard and safekeeping of your own example; for we are told that on the day on which you sat clothed in purple on a golden throne (lest you seem to spurn an honor zealously conceived and conferred by the senate), before you presented yourself, a spectacle much desired by the citizens' eyes, ready to attend to religious ritual, to which you were soon to be transformed, the heart was not found in the sacrificial ox, and the haruspex Spurinna interpreted that this sign pertained to your life and plans, both of which the heart contains. Then broke out the parricide of those men who, while they wished to remove you from the body of men, have added you to the council of gods. (1.6.13)[42]

---

42. *Tuas aras tuaque sanctissima templa, dive Iuli, veneratus oro ut propitio ac faventi*

The actual incident (the failure to find the ox's heart and Spurinna's reply) is hurriedly told, cramped between the turgid invocation and the familiar rhetoric of Valerius' finish (*erupit deinde eorum parricidium, qui, dum te hominum numero subtrahere volunt, deorum concilio adiecerunt*). Caesar here "trumps" Pompey as the divine force that consoles Rome for the loss of her great men; he becomes the supreme instance of the category. Indeed like his heart softer then clemency itself, Julius Caesar defies categorization; he is beyond abstraction, removed from these mortal realms.

Undeniably, such rhetoric comes easily to Valerius, and yet Caesar and the imperial house are not an ubiquitous, dominating presence in Valerius' work. Though on occasion imported as the seal to the civil wars, for the most part they appear in their proper chronological period and do not form the apex of every chapter they enter. The lengthy series on "Bravery" includes two of Julius Caesar's soldiers for their outstanding service (3.2.22–23). The final exemplum (3.2.24) reserves the greatest palm for L. Siccius Dentatus, the pinnacle of Roman virtue—partly for reasons of his impressive statistics (battles fought, enemies slain) and also because of the strong authority of Valerius' declared source, M. Varro. Some aspects, at least, of Roman history are too venerable to suffer displacement, and Valerius clearly has various loyalties—to old time virtues, heroes, and history as well as to the new imperial reality. The conflict of these loyalties does not much trouble an author intent upon the continuity of the Republic with the Empire. Thus, for this author, praise of republican heroes does not imply criticism, but can demand praise, of Caesar.

An examination of the little that could be taken as criticism of Caesar confirms the conclusion that Valerius does not exclude prorepublican

---

numine tantorum casus virorum sub tui exempli praesidio ac tutela delitescere patiaris: te enim accepimus eo die, quo purpurea veste velatus aurea in sella consedisti, ne maximo studio senatus exquisitum et delatum honorem sprevisse videreris, priusquam exoptatum civium oculis conspectum tui offerres, cultui religionis, in quam mox eras transiturus, vacasse mactatoque opimo bove cor in extis non repperisse, ac responsum tibi ab Spurinna aruspice pertinere id signum ad vitam et consilium tuum, quod utraque haec corde continerentur. erupit deinde eorum parricidium, qui, dum te hominum numero subtrahere volunt, deorum concilio adiecerunt.

material but provides it with the proper frame: either a novel classification or, as noted already, comparison with Caesar. The closest to outright criticism of Caesar is the highly unflattering story of the unconstitutional arrest and attempted imprisonment of the younger Cato. The glaring illegality of this incarceration, however, receives no attention:

> Admiration for a courageous and moral life made M. Porcius Cato so venerable to the senate that, when he was taking up the whole day in the senate house in speaking against the publicans (contrary to the will of the consul Caesar) and therefore by his order was led off to prison by the lictor, the whole senate did not hesitate to follow him. This softened the severity of the divine mind. (2.10.7)[43]

Valerius, of course, devotes no more inquiry to republican law than he has to factional politics. The exemplum immediately preceding has just described Marius' lucky deliverance from the barbarian assassin. The justice or legality of Marius in or out of power has been passed over in silence while Valerius dwelt on the melodrama of Marius dragged from the swamps and saved in the house of the woman he once convicted. The introduction of Cato in the final pair of Roman exempla for this chapter on "Majesty" does not bring with it any further regard for law. Both the tale of the senate's respect and the final story of the people's regard for the morals of Cato (in 2.10.8 he leaves the theater so the mimes can continue) redound to the credit of Cato alone. Valerius retails the dramatic, visual proof of the sway Cato exercised over the people of Rome and so has couched description and analysis of the events in moral not legal or political terms. The actual historical antagonism and bitter conflict of 59 B.C. are completely absent (*invito C. Caesare consule* suffices for historical setting). This temporary failure in Caesar's political gerrymandering and Caesar's abrogation of lawful practice are nowhere evident, although such a historical reality underlies the obfuscating and abstract panegyric of *divini animi perseverantiam*

---

43. *M. quoque Porcium Catonem admiratio fortis ac sincerae vitae adeo venerabilem senatui fecit, ut, cum invito C. Caesare consule adversus publicanos dicendo in curia diem traheret et ob id iussu eius a lictore in carcerem duceretur, universus senatus illum sequi non dubitaret. quae res divini animi perseverantiam flexit.*

flexit. Unconstitutional behavior has become an abstract virtue, a severe steadfastness: the temporary failure of political violence is memorialized as a concession granted by the divine.

The second exemplum where a little historical knowledge would lead one to think that criticism of Caesar seems the natural, unavoidable conclusion similarly shifts the story from its original, political point. The historical setting is, in contrast, further developed; but this was necessary, for otherwise the incident would have been inexplicable:

> Not as famous [as the case of the consul Fabius Rullianus in the preceding exemplum] was the paternal role of the Roman knight Caesetius, though equal was the indulgence. When he was ordered by Caesar, now the conqueror of all enemies domestic and foreign, to disown his son because as tribune of the people with his colleague Marullus his son had reproached Caesar for royalist ambitions, he dared answer in this manner: "More quickly will you take from me all my sons, Caesar, than I shall strike one of them with my reproach." For he had two sons of exceptional promise to whom Caesar kept promising he would liberally grant favor and honors. Even though the greatest clemency of the divine prince guaranteed the safety of the father, who would not think that something greater than human nature had been dared, because he did not yield to him to whom the whole globe had submitted? (5.7.2.)[44]

This incident, just like the senate's trooping along behind Cato, is one of Caesar's minor setbacks; again his extraordinary, if not extralegal, maneuver has been frustrated. Both stories should belong to a series

---

44. *Non tam speciosa Caeseti equitis Romani sors patria, sed par indulgentia. qui ab Caesare omnium iam et externorum et domesticorum hostium victore cum abdicare filium suum iuberetur, quod is tribunus pl. cum Marullo collega invidiam ei tamquam regnum adfectanti fecerat, in hunc modum respondere sustinuit: "celerius tu mihi, Caesar, omnes filios meos eripies quam ex his ego unum nota mea pellam." habebat autem duos praeterea optimae indolis filios, quibus Caesar se incrementa dignitatis benigne daturum pollicebatur. hunc patrem tametsi summa divini principis clementia tutum praestitit, quis tamen non humano ingenio maius ausum putet, quod cui totus terrarum orbis succubuerat non cessit?*

of *libertas* offered to Caesar. Instead, any political interpretation for Cato or Caesetius must give way to "Majesty" and "Parental Love and Indulgence to Children," the respective chapter headings. Valerius' technique in twisting and distorting the point of these stories has not been to provide Caesar with some novel motive. Indeed, the historical figure of Julius Caesar does not emerge. His person and motivation are nowhere to be found; he has become an abstraction suitable for the flourish of rhetorical praise. The figures of Cato and Caesetius, while remaining essentially rhetorical (not in any way complete or developed), are memorialized as particular instances of an eccentric virtue—a personal virtue that by opposition to Caesar is marked not as heterodox but as extreme.

For his safe handling of the republican heroes, Valerius relies especially on the choice of theme, on a *translatio* of category. Skirting criticism of Caesar is much easier if the historical antagonist can be thrust into the mold of a traditional and so uncontroversial category. The salubrious themes are not just virtues made sacrosanct by the *mos maiorum,* but Roman social institutions. The chapter headings under which the remaining republican heroes are grouped seem at first to be love and bravery: the exceptional material appears in chapters on "Friendship" (4.7.4 and 4.7.6: partisans of Brutus celebrated), "Bravery" (3.2.14: Utica is Cato's monument; and 3.2.15: his sister's resoluteness), "The Fidelity of Slaves" (6.8.4: Cassius killed, at his wish, by his loyal slave), and "Conjugal Love" (4.6.5: Porcia again). All of this exceptional subject matter neither criticizes Caesar nor celebrates the republican martyrs. Valerius does not take up the Cato and Anti-Cato polemics, at least not on any political level. Justification for the inclusion of these historical figures derives from the Roman social institutions they exemplify: *clientela*—both that of "friends" and of master and slave (where slaves act as if they were loyal freed clients)—and marriage. Even Cato's overtly political suicide can be understood in traditional, institutional terms (the precedent is the acts of *devotio* of the Decii) compounded with a typically Valerian moral and ahistorical analysis.

"Friendship," for instance, provides the pretext for much that otherwise would not appear in Valerius' work. The third illustration of this chapter (4.7) has the true friend of Caepio—responsible, Valerius says, for the destruction of the Roman army at the hands of the Teutons

and Cimbrians—deliver him from jail and join him in flight. Little wonder, then, that Valerius can call the case of the two partisans of Brutus
"somewhat more praiseworthy" (4.7.4). Volumnius, conspicuous in his
excessive grief for his friend M. Lucullus (killed by Antony), is brought
before the victor and pleads for death. Valerius' conclusion offers great
insight into his own categories of analysis and techniques for handling
politically perilous material:

> Let Greece say that Theseus, endorsing [acting as second to] the
> unspeakable passion of Pirithous [for Persephone—the queen of
> Hades whom the two mortals tried to abduct], entrusted himself
> to the Kingdom of Death; it is pointless to narrate this, stupid to
> believe it. Look on the common blood of friends, at wounds en-
> twined in wounds, death embracing death—these are the true
> proofs of Roman friendship, those of that race facile at fiction are
> lies bordering on the monstrous. (4.7.4)[45]

A small phase of Roman civil conflict is superseded by the rhetoric
of a greater contest, that between Greece and Rome, whose prize is
fame. Greece is the enemy, literary and intellectual, common to Volumnius and Antony, Valerius and his readers, an enemy who can be invoked to distract and unite the domestic antagonists and who can be
defeated by recourse to a patriotic morality. The sum of all this is, however, that Valerius declines to pass judgment on Antony or on the partisans of the assassins.[46] Politics simply does not count for much in this
entire chapter. The first two exempla were about friends of the Gracchi,
victims of the senate. In the fifth the pro-Sullan Petronius and P. Caelius fall to Cinna's army. The sixth returns to the conflicts of Caesar's
successors: Servius Terentius, the loyal friend of Decimus Brutus,
fleeing from Mutina, with the assassins closing in, vainly tries to substitute himself for his friend. An exclusive focus on friendship unto

45. *loquatur Graecia Thesea nefandis Pirithoi amoribus suscribentem Ditis se patris
regnis commisisse: vani est istud narrare, stulti credere. mixtum cruorem amicorum et
vulneribus innexa vulnera mortique inhaerentem mortem videre, haec sunt vera Romanae amicitiae indicia, illa gentis ad fingendum paratae monstro similia mendacia.*

46. This story is not so famous that, like Cato at Utica, no Roman author
can ignore it, for Volumnius is known only by this reference.

death and the arousal of national prejudice have served in place of judgment in much of this chapter's material; the final exemplum (4.7.7) returns to a familiar technique: again, the series has a Caesarian cap. The last and the greatest examples of friendship are Laelius and Agrippa: "the first granted the greatest of mortal friends, the second the greatest of divine friends" (*alter virorum, deorum alter maximum amicum . . . sortiti*). Imperial and Ciceronian authority are here conveniently joined (much as the greatest soldier of all, according to Varro, follows two of Caesar's veterans to end 3.2). The literary authority, established by the eponymous interlocutor of Cicero's dialogue (*Laelius De amicitia*), is simply appended to the imperial, not undermined; and the series has been brought to a doubly orthodox close.

The allied theme of "Fidelity of Slaves" (6.8) presents very similar treatments. A Gracchan example (6.8.3) follows one drawn from the civil conflict of Marius and Sulla (6.8.2). As in the chapter on "Friendship," the suicide is rendered faithful service, and an attempt to save the proscribed fails. Valerius' treatment of the next anecdote—from the time of Caesar—presents a marked difference:

> A different noble family, a different madness, but a like example of fidelity. The recently manumitted Pindarus killed C. Cassius— by his command—after Cassius had been defeated at Philippi. By this voluntary suicide he so removed him from the insults of his enemies and so stole him away from men's sight that not even the corpse of the slain man was found. What divine avenger of that most awful crime so numbed the right hand, which had burned for the murder of the country's parent, that it trembled in supplicating Pindarus, from fear that by the judgment of a loyal victory it might pay the deserved penalty for public parricide? In fact it was you, divine Julius, who exacted the vengeance owed your celestial wounds by compelling the person who betrayed you to beg ignoble help, so driven by passion that he neither wished to live nor dared to die by his own hand. (6.8.4)[47]

---

47. *Alia nobilitas, alius furor, sed fidei par exemplum. Pindarus C. Cassium Philippensi proelio victum, nuper ab eo manu missus, iussu ipsius obtruncatum insultationi hostium subtraxit seque e conspectu hominum voluntaria morte abstulit ita, ut ne corpus*

This exemplum does differ, in treatment, from Volumnius and Lucullus, those republican partisans exemplifying "Friendship" at 4.7.4.
Historical details and context do not suddenly appear, but here imperial flattery is in full force. Cassius is damned as a public parricide and
depicted trembling, on his knees before his faithful freedman. Julius
Caesar (*dive Iuli*) is then directly invoked. This treatment, with its sudden infusion of panegyric, does differ from that of Volumnius and Lucullus despite the similarity of theme and the identity of the agents'
situation and politics. The stature of these republican martyrs is the
crucial difference, since no obscure partisan but one of the chief assassins, Cassius, is the subject of 6.8.4.

Pompey may often require the appended comparison with Caesar.
The armed conflict of a military foe does not threaten as the hidden
weapons of the conspirator. Valerius cannot mention Cassius without
trumpeting his guilt; the course of 1.8.8 pauses to vilify the conspirator,
"C. Cassius who ought never be mentioned without the preliminary
epithet of 'public parricide'" (*C. Cassius numquam sine praefatione publici
parricidii nominandus*). Valerius holds good on this notice: the reader is
reminded of this public crime in all the appearances of Brutus and
Cassius in *Memorable Deeds and Sayings*.[48] With the exclusion of those
passages where Brutus, Decimus Brutus, and Cassius are raised in
passing to identify a partisan and so to orient the reader, these three
are uniformly abused as the traitorous assassins. D. Brutus, for in-

---

*quidem eius absumpti inveniretur. quis deorum gravissimi sceleris ultor illam dexteram,
quae in necem patriae parentis exarserat, tanto torpore inligavit, ut se tremibunda Pin-
dari genibus summiteret, ne publici parricidii quas merebatur poenas arbitrio piae victoriae exsolveret? tu profecto tunc, dive Iuli, caelestibus tuis vulneribus debitam exegisti
vindictam, perfidum erga te caput sordidi auxilii supplex fieri cogendo, eo animi aestu
conpulsum, ut neque retinere vitam vellet neque finire sua manu auderet.*

48. At 1.5.8, a discrediting anecdote about Cassius, the charge is not repeated. Valerius has leveled it, however, in the immediately preceding exemplum, against Brutus. In 9.9.2, the error of Cassius' suicide at Philippi,
parricide is not mentioned, but its punishments are. Compare the similar diction of 6.8.4. In addition, the introductory example (9.9.1) relates the people's
mistaken outrage in killing Cinna the poet for the conspirator of the same
name. Caesar has been sufficiently praised, and so the second exemplum of
this chapter can merely allude to and not name the act of parricide.

stance, appears in his own right only in an exemplum (9.13.3) aimed
at illustrating the discreditable theme of *De cupiditate vitae* (overzeal-
ousness for living). Valerius has two exempla devoted to M. Junius Brutus: the omens before his death (which Valerius terms "worthy for an
admitted parricide") are described at 1.5.7, and his words before the
final battle are the substance of 6.4.5. From Valerius, these resolute
words elicit no praise; rather Brutus is "the parricide of his own virtues
more than of the father of the country" (*suarum prius virtutum quam
patriae parentis parricida*). Caesar's actual assassins clearly form a separate class of historical figures. Their isolation from all praise is quite
unique. No theme is capable of mitigating their censure. What can be
described as a tendency with Pompey—the recurrent balancing of any
favorable treatment with greater praise of his enemy, Caesar—has become, in the case of the assassins, a consistent technique of malediction.

Here for the first time in Valerius, the author's contemporary political reality does more than intrude, work anachronism, or distort motives. The inflexible, predetermined quality of propaganda colors
Valerius' relation of the imperial house with prior history. And yet the
most striking aspect of such treatment is its restriction to these few leaders of the conspiracy. There are, of course, any number of propagandistic sins of omission: Octavian is never mentioned; the reader would
never know from Valerius that he was one of the triumvirs; all the imperial family appears solely in glowing light. Nonetheless, with all who
might have been censured, the list is surprisingly select. The distinct
difference in Valerius' exempla of the three Caesars is not their brittle,
imagelike quality, for as in so many of the exempla, the pictures given
of these men in *Memorable Deeds and Sayings* are creations for the moment: complete in themselves, they suffice for the chapter heading but
will not sustain much further probing. And yet, to maintain a view of
the late Republic and incipient empire as a smooth continuum under
the guidance of the Caesars requires an extreme obliqueness of treatment. Omission, characteristic of Valerius for this period, is part of the
panegyrist's method. Octavian's rise to single power is not chronicled;
indeed, strikingly little, other than the deaths of the assassins, is to be
found of the events bridging the fatal Ides of March and the Battle of
Actium. The actual pictures of Augustus and Tiberius, like Valerius'
treatment of Octavian's foes, are consistent, one-dimensional, and re-

stricted. Valerius' admiration for Augustus and Tiberius does not spill over into the body of exempla: the Caesars do not assume a great portion of his pages. In assessing Valerius' attitude to the imperial house and its effect upon his work, the neglect of this period of history is as important as the hard and unreal images he substitutes, and the restriction or localization of his panegyric.

When Valerius does allude to this period—either to identify his subject or to provide it with context—anonymity as well as omission often obscure the actual historical situation. That is, Octavian is never mentioned, and the triumvirs remain nameless. So, for example, the sole indication of the time and setting for Octavius Balbus' display of paternal love is the notice *proscriptus a triumviris* (5.7.3). This is deliberate: Octavian has not so much been forgotten as willfully suppressed. So suggests an exemplum that narrowly skirts the anachronism of calling Octavian Augustus. To lead off his chapter on dreams, Valerius relates the visitation of Minerva to Augustus' physician on the eve of the Battle of Philippi. Octavian obeys her summons to participate in the battle by having his sickbed brought into the line (so states Valerius), only to witness Brutus' capture of his camp (1.7.1). Within the narrative of this anecdote Valerius refers to Octavian as Caesar, but his introduction consists of the rhetorical question, "From what place should I better start than from the most revered memory of the divine Augustus?" (*quem locum unde potius ordiar quam a divi Augusti sacratissima memoria?*). Valerius is not quite guilty of anachronism: he has carefully avoided this by calling Octavian Caesar within the frame of the anecdote.[49] Mention of the name "Octavian" would only weaken the family connections subtly built up in this chapter (1.7.2 is Calpurnia's dream before her husband's murder; in 1.7.7 Caesar's ghost haunts Cassius Parmensis in his flight from Actium). An emphasis on these family connections, the common epithet *divus,* and not such historical niceties as Octavian's name add luster to the supernatural fortune of the Caesars.

The search for indications of Valerius' knowledge of the series of alliances and conflicts leading to Octavian's final supremacy yields little of promise. Embedded in Valerius' retrospective treatment are some

---

49. Valerius repeats this practice in another exemplum about Octavian at 3.8.8.

hints of historical knowledge—for example, not calling Octavian Augustus but Caesar, or the circumlocution of the close of 7.6.6, which relates Augustus' anti-inflation measures in the Bosporus and concludes: "the care of Augustus, then free for the safeguarding of the world, dissolved this most bitter storm" (7.6.6: *amarissimam tempestatem Augusti cura tutelae tunc terrarum vacans dispulit*). Augustus is at leisure to safeguard the world because, of course, Antony has been killed. Actium is, like Philippi, imagined by Valerius as the loyal, punitive effort of the *divi filius* who then returns to his other familial duties—the care of the world.

Brutus and Cassius have been dispatched as Caesar's assassins. Antony is by contrast a most inconvenient figure; for his most famous actions belong to the years of Octavian's ascent, and his relation to Octavian is hardly clear-cut. Despite these potential difficulties, Valerius' depictions of Antony are remarkably uniform. Although he does not receive outright condemnation, like the regicides, nor the virulent abuse that the contemporary pamphleteers directed against him while in Egypt, Antony is thoroughly maligned by Valerius by being consistently presented as a murderer. A single instance may seem innocuous: at 9.15.ext.2, for example, a barbarian pretender is revealed as such because Antony was known to have killed the real King Ariarthes. When all the examples are considered, however, the effect is overwhelming. Volumnius, the republican partisan, is Antony's victim (4.7.4), as are D. Brutus and his friend Terentius (4.7.6). Antony grants Popillius the favor of murdering Cicero (5.3.4). Furius is sent by him to kill D. Brutus (9.13.3). Antony is mentioned in conjunction with Brutus' suicide at 1.5.7 and 5.1.11. He appears at 1.7.7, only to establish the context for the death of his partisan Cassius Parmensis. Antony is damned as well by his agents, both by these assassins and by his prefect Turullius, guilty of sacrilege (the violation of a sacred grove later expiated by "Caesar," i.e. Octavian) at 1.1.19. His only favorable mentions come in combination with a Caesar (Julius or Octavian): Maevius, Octavian's loyal centurion, is spared by Antony. The whole anecdote, however, is shaped to Caesar's advantage, not Antony's: Valerius celebrates the virtue of Caesar's soldier and barely records the sparing of his life. Antony's clemency is not praised; this act but adds to the soldier's and Caesar's fame. Valerius ends the exemplum—and this is the sole indication of the soldier's deliverance—with, "Antony added soundness [i.e., safety] to his virtue" (3.8.8: *Antonius enim virtuti eius incolumitatem tribuit*).

Antony's humanity toward Brutus' corpse is praised at 5.1.11, but this too is only a reflection of Julius Caesar's glory. The prior exemplum details Caesar's double humanity—toward Pompey and toward Cato. Even more than with Pompey, conjunction with Julius Caesar (and his adopted son) overshadows any positive portrayals of Antony. The effect, for the reader, of Valerius' depictions of Antony and the parricides is the same: Octavian's historical rivals have been thoroughly maligned, and the agents in the final struggles of the Republic have been reduced to one. Octavian does not emerge so much triumphant as alone, with the conflict downplayed and his opponents belittled.

Augustus and Tiberius

Valerius' picture of Augustus has hardly a reference to the struggle and uncertainty of these times: a son avenging his father replaces the historical tumult. If one considers all that a panegyrist could say of Augustus, Valerius, though consistent in his outlook, is surprisingly unforthcoming on this grand subject. This is partly the result of Valerius' practice (which he describes in the preface) of excerpting from written sources. He seldom embellishes from his own experience or his own times, and so we are without a stock of prized anecdotes that only a contemporary could give. Equally, panegyric has not spread throughout the work. Augustus does not head every list as the incarnation of every virtue; in his occasional appearances he is consistently celebrated as the champion of the family. Of the exempla directly about Augustus (and not those in which he provides context or where some one of his agents is the principal), only 7.6.6 (his price-control measures in the Bosporus) does not focus on and celebrate this, and even here his "guardianship [*tutela*] of the earth" has a paternal tone.

The remaining exempla of Augustus celebrate him as the champion of legitimacy. At 7.7.3 he restores the disinherited son of Tettius. At 9.15.2 he expels the pretender who claimed to be his nephew; in this chapter two more pretenders are deposed by Augustus, a fortune-hunting woman of Milan and pseudo-Ariarthes of Cappadocia (9.15

ext.1 and 2). Augustus appears not as the champion but the victim of lawful inheritance in 7.8.6, where the will of T. Marius Urbinas, who maintained he would make Augustus his heir, once opened, made no mention of Caesar. Since Augustus is Valerius' type for legitimate, regular inheritance, this exemplum is not simply an anecdote about the *princeps,* but is, like Cicero's rejection as a witness (eloquence incarnate defeated in eloquence's camp), the paradoxical defeat of a type within his proper sphere. And so it remains a sort of reverse exemplum that by its "negative" qualities reinforces the "positive."

Despite, indeed even in, this exemplum, Augustus remains the defender of legitimacy and the family. The great noble families of Rome had a double appeal for Valerius: they embodied the *mos maiorum* that he celebrates and certain famous families such as the Scipios and the Decii provided precedents fulfilled, exempla that their own descendants imitated. Within these families signal actions recur in different generations (e.g., the *devotio* of one Decius has been imitated by a younger generation—Decius Mus is thus both the subject matter of an exemplum and the proof of the efficacy of an exemplum). Valerius employs this feature of distinguished families to advantage with Tiberius. Indeed, just as one Scipio, occasionally and erroneously, can take on the attributes or achievements of another, so the last Caesar is at times indistinguishable from the prior two. He has become the "salubrious parent"; Valerius strives to portray him as the third in the series of Caesars. On the piety (familial devotion) of the imperial line rests each successor's claim to legitimacy. Thus, here the demands of panegyric reinforce Valerius' usual interest in Rome's famous families.

This familial element—Tiberius as the savior-parent, Tiberius as the loyal son (and brother)—recurs in each mention of Tiberius. Invoked five times in Valerius' work, Tiberius has but a single exemplum devoted to himself. The conclusion, attractive as it might be to Tacitus, that Tiberius did next to nothing worthy of commemoration is not an explanation for why Valerius tells only of his hastening to his brother's deathbed (5.5.3). Valerius is not wary of praising Tiberius; the emperor is addressed in the preface to the whole work as "O most sure salvation of our country, Caesar" (*certissima salus patriae, Caesar*) and then as muse, while his divinity is connected with Julius Caesar's and Augustus'. Moreover, in the preface to book 2, Tiberius is again invoked in

fulsome terms, and in the preface to the chapter on "Old Age," Valerius
wishes long life on this *salutaris princeps* (8.13). At 2.9.6, although the
context is not a preface, the form of address is again one that involves
the author's entry into the text: here Valerius interrupts his narrative
of the feud of the censors of 204 B.C., Claudius Nero and Livius Salinator:

> If any of the gods had indicated to these men that their blood,
> derived from a series of famous nobles, would flow to create our
> savior-prince, they, who were to leave a country saved by them-
> selves to be saved by their common descendant, would have cast
> off enmity and joined in the closest pact of friendship. (2.9.6)[50]

This aside had been suggested by the future family connection of Livia
and Tiberius Claudius and has been inserted by Valerius into the story
he took from Livy.[51]

Valerius restricted notice of Tiberius' actions to one exemplum; and
that one may have been taken from Livy, for the *Periochae* records the
fraternal visit.[52] The remaining mentions are distinctly marked as panegyric—not just by their grandiose tone but formally as an invocation
or aside. In such practice Valerius does not differ from his contemporary Manilius: imperial panegyric is essentially and formally local-
ized. It comes as a sort of obligatory obeisance at the beginning of a
book but does not direct or dominate the text. For the most part the
subject matter, historical exempla like the truths of astrology, takes its
own course.

Because of Valerius' subject the Caesars are occasionally a topic, but
they are contained in their proper time, invoked at their proper chronological place in a series of exempla. Tiberius does make one violent
irruption into Valerius' scheme. The chapter 9.11, "Wicked Sayings

50. *quibus viris si quis caelestium significasset futurum ut eorum sanguis inlustrium imaginum serie deductus in ortum salutaris principis nostri conflueret, depositis inimicitiis artissimo se amicitiae foedere iunxissent, servatam ab ipsis patriam communi stirpi servandam relicturi.*

51. From the verbal parallels, Livy 29.37 is clearly Valerius' source, though, of course, he has nothing of Tiberius.

52. *Periochae* 142.

and Evil Deeds," has a denunciation of the parricide who attempted the vilest of Roman defeats—the murder of the *salutaris princeps,* here called also a *praesens numen* and *auctor et tutela nostrae incolumitatis.* In this exemplum (9.11.ext.4) near the end of the *Memorable Deeds and Sayings,* panegyric and topic have been fused. This censure of Sejanus underscores how exceptional are Valerius' references to Tiberius. The literary notices of Livy, Cicero, and Sallust, among others, lie behind his exempla of Julius Caesar; Augustus has fewer sources (or less treatment by these authors) and consequently fewer exempla; Tiberius, needless to say, the fewest. The downfall of Sejanus does not simply offer to Valerius the material, drawn from life, for an exemplum. This is not an ordinary event or even an extraordinary event in the career of Tiberius. Had he wanted the latter, Valerius would have included some praise of the German campaigns. This attempt, as Valerius sees it, to end the series of Caesars, to violate legitimacy and prejudice Rome's fortune, belongs to the realm of panegyric, and so it is the final of the chapter's exempla, the seal on vice.

The restriction or "localization" of imperial panegyric has important ramifications for the general understanding of Valerius. Republican and imperial materials coexist not in a state of tension but of deliberate nonresolution. Valerius is thus not a "slavish" admirer, if this slavery means the constant and consistent deformation of history along Caesarian lines. The imperial is not the thoroughgoing imprint, or not as important an imprint as other thematic and programmatic concerns.

6 Valerian Rhetoric and Ideology

The present book explores how, why, and for whom Valerius wrote. The design of his work, his choice and use of sources, and treatment of historical figures and periods have been discussed. This final chapter seeks some conclusions for the fundamental question of what declaimers would find appealing and paradigmatic in Valerius' collection, in this rhetorical presentation of history. The matter for this inquiry is at first Valerius' "style"—a subject of abuse and of importance for our author who stands as the first of the Silver writers, in time, manner, and revile. Of critics' complaints we shall not write much, first, because lament is foreign to the historian; second, because a rehearsal of scholarship would only reveal the carping redundant and insistent; finally, because critiques of Valerius' style have led to nothing more than the vacuous generalizations allegedly true for all of Silver Latin.

For it is insufficient and insignificant to say this author or indeed the literature of his generation is rhetorical or that Valerius offers rhetoricized history. We are interested in what it means to say that a literature or indeed men of a certain age are increasingly rhetorical. Inquiry must focus on Valerius' rhetorics, the process of stylization and not simply his style—as if this latter existed independently of his peculiar interests and contexts. For the present study has as a fundamental tenet that there is nothing inevitable or natural about his style. Valerius Maximus cannot simply be labeled a phase in the grand sweep of Latin prose. The organic metaphor, growth and decline, is misleading in its linearity and suggestion of inevitability whether we speak of the "regress" of the Empire itself or of its people or literature. Valerius' style is then not something to be cataloged and ranked (with or without lament) among past and future stylists. Style is a matter of choice and in Valerius' case a very conditioned choice, for he stands in a self-conscious relation to his sources. For Valerius the texts of Cicero and Livy are like an earlier declaimer whose words must be surpassed in order to be suppressed. Analysis of his style and stylization and storytelling are inseparable; together they point to the intersection of Valerius' programs and reveal the nature of the paradigmatic he strives to communicate.

Unlike the declaimers, the critics have found nothing worthy of imitation in Valerius. From the fifth to the twentieth centuries the complaints are the same. Valerius' epitomator Januarius Nepotianus in his dedicatory letter recommends Valerius' information, not his style: "For he does write of things of intellectual merit but he dilates on what should be compressed and all the while makes a display of aphorisms, is addicted to commonplaces and overflows with digressions and for this reason perhaps his readership is smaller because the toil of reading him blunts the readers' enthusiasm. And so in keeping with your desire I shall abridge his redundancies and pass by very many things, some things which he neglected I shall join."[1] Modern scholars essentially repeat these objections; the earliest modern, Gelbcke in 1865, offered the following categories of analysis (and criticism): antithesis, metaphor, personification, juxtaposition of altered forms of the same word, preference for the abstract over the concrete.[2] These categories recur, for Valerius remains the earliest club by which to beat the Silver Age. Even Carter, a penetrating critic of Valerius, compared Cicero, Valerius, and his epitomator Paris to show Valerius the worst.[3] His comparative analysis is not flawed—if the purpose of stylistic analysis is to rank candidates for imitation by schoolboys or to award the prize for clarity of narration, in which contests Cicero will always take the palm. Sinclair recognized the unequal quality of these critical contests.[4] Though not an analysis of Valerius' style, his dissertation is a great improvement in the appreciation of Valerius' aesthetic. Bliss had al-

1. *digna enim cognitione componit, sed colligenda producit, dum se ostentat sententiis, locis iactat, fundit excessibus, et eo fortasse sit paucioribus notus, quod legentium aviditati mora ipsa fastidio est. recidam itaque, ut vis, eius redundantia et pleraque transgrediar, nonnulla praetermissa conectam.*

2. C. F. Gelbcke, "Quaestiones Valerianae" (dissertation, Berlin, 1865), 8–23, cited and discussed by Sinclair 1980, 17.

3. Carter 1975, 42–45.

4. Sinclair 1980, 16–20.

ready shown Valerius' patterns of inversion and variation in diction and phrasing.[5] Sinclair's dissertation offers a critical assessment of Valerius' rhetorical figures. His special contribution is his illustration of parallels of everything from diction to *sententiae* between Valerius and the declaimers of Seneca's recollection.

The present reassessment of Valerius' style will not repeat the obvious—that is, illustrate Valerius' turgid expression and lament this decline from his sources. Bliss and Sinclair have illustrated the technique and context of Valerius' aesthetic. We shall try to go beyond labeling his style "declamatory" and consider what it deemed and communicated worthy of imitation, in sum the culture it reflects, creates, and communicates. The critics have not been wrong in branding Valerius rhetorical and proleptic of the Silver Age's manner. Indeed, he provides a first glimpse at what would become, and probably already had become, the recurrent structures as well as substance of discourse. Let us begin though with some traditional categories: word choice, placement, and grouping.

Analysis of Valerius' diction only begins with a recognition of his treatment of his source. Variation of simple and compound forms from the same stem can be traced to a desire to avoid the forms of his source, but such an aesthetic only partially explains Valerius' passion for abstract nouns and expressions. The significance of contemporary avoidance of *verba sordida* and Valerius' own practice reveal his position in a contemporary critical conflict. The qualities and consequences of his variation need stating, for his contemporaries found such composition intelligible and entertaining. Similarly, his phrasing and specifically hyperbaton will not be dismissed as a mannerism common to the future Silver writers but treated as a technique of building phrases, of knitting together his composition. Again, clarity will not emerge as either guiding principle or rhetorical effect. A discussion of his colometry, with implications for Valerius' syntax, follows this section of verbal analysis and is the transition to a study of figuration, the articulation of his thought and expression. Finally, the conclusion considers the communication of the paradigmatic in *Memorable Deeds and Sayings*—neither as a rung in the ladder of corruption nor as before from the point

5. Bliss 1951, 56–102.

of view of composition alone (e.g., Valerius working colon by colon from Cicero). The chapter's conclusion moves from an analysis of the formulaic nature of the Valerian exemplum to questions of its effect, the combination of recognition and surprise and the varying pair of impressiveness and intelligibility.

Diction

The declaimers of Seneca's *Controversiae* and *Suasoriae* come closest to Valerius' style. Peculiarities of *Memorable Deeds and Sayings* may not be Valerius' contributions or coinages but the common fare of declamation. While this declamatory context must be borne in mind and will prove important for the analysis of Valerius' diction, his relation to the texts of Cicero and Livy needs to be stressed; in the realm of diction the importance of this relation can be clearly illustrated.

The only monograph devoted to Valerius' diction, Ehrenfried Lundberg's dissertation "De elocutione Valeri [*sic*] Maximi," ignores both the declamatory and literary contexts.[6] As with most of the works on Valerius' style this is not an analysis but a collection of categories and instances. The implications of these are misleading. Lundberg has listed words, divided into parts of speech and organized under such categories as Valerius' coinages, words avoided by Cicero and Caesar, poetic words, words used with meanings different from Cicero's and Caesar's. What vitiates his labor is Valerius' practice of composition. A word employed by Valerius need not imply a change in language, either spoken or written, just as a change in word order (inversion of noun and epithet for instance) does not imply a change in the language's phrasing since, as Bliss has shown, Valerius varied his model's diction and phrasing in these ways.[7] Valerius' use will often differ from Cicero's. He will

---

6. Lundberg 1906.

7. For simple inversions of noun and epithet Bliss (1951, 58) lists, for example, Valerius 1.1.1, *Apollonis praedictiones:* Cicero, *Har. resp.* 18, *praedictiones Apollonis;* 1.1.ext.3, *bonitate eorum: De nat. deor.* 3.83, *eorum bonitate.* Bliss documents Valerius' practice with compound pairs as well, for example (p. 59)

employ simple for original compound verb or noun, or he will vary prefix simply to distinguish his treatment from the original. This practice cannot be taken as evidence for the evolution of the language since Valerius' use of one word signifies not the obsolescence of another but this single author's attempt in a particular passage to achieve a novelty of expression. One cannot argue for example for a change in meaning or usage when Valerius varies Livy's *filio quoque adulescente per idem tempus* (5.32.8) with *eo tempore quo . . . iuvene filio* (5.3.2a) or *desponsa uni ex Curiatiis* (1.26) with *Curiati sponsi* (6.3.6).

Valerius' attempted variation of his source must be considered when evaluating his diction or any other aspect of his style, for he varies grammatical case, diction, word order, and syntactic structure. Sinclair too has seen this well; he reminds that Carter's objections to the "ugly rhythms and sound effects" of *sed sacraria aedificanda sacrificiaque facienda* at 6.5.1 should be traced to Valerius' insistent variation of his source: "Cicero (*Verr.* 4.23) had already juxtaposed *faciundum* and *aedificandamque*, and Valerius is simply doing him one better."[8] It is of course significant that Valerius does differ, that Cicero's diction did not cast a binding spell but rather impelled variation. From the elder Seneca's excerpts of the declaimers we expect this to be the case: imitation of Cicero's diction is eccentric.

Conclusions about Valerius' style cannot depend on observation of his diction alone; its difference from Livy and Cicero does not result from an unmediated composition. We may easily conclude, for example, that Valerius' style is characterized by an increasing distance from the spoken language, but this means only that an intentional variation of the texts of the late republican and Augustan authors guides his word choice and phrase making. To this extent his language is increasingly literary. But what were the sources of his variation of diction? Variation, a desire for novelty, is after all only the spur to difference. The range of the admissible is really what distinguishes Va-

---

1.6.ext.2, *in os grana tritici: De div.* 2.66, *tritici grana in os.* Inversions also occur with change in case, and with the substitution of a synonym: 1.1.1, *vetustissimam Cererem: Verr.* 4.108, *Cererem antiquissimam,* or 2.3.3, *celeri motu delabi,* and Livy 26.4, *desilire perniciter* (p. 58).

8. Sinclair 1980, 37 n. 3, referring to Carter 1975, 45.

lerius' diction and the declaimers'. Valerius has apparently coined new words: *delibamentum*, for example, at 2.6.8 and *duramentum* at 2.7.10. In the latter case the impetus to the coinage or usage is clear from a parallel first observed by Morawski: Valerius' *humanae igitur imbecillitatis efficacissimum duramentum est necessitas* seems a variation of the declaimer Votienus Montanus' *necessitas magnum humanae imbecillitatis patrocinium est (Contr.* 9.4.5).[9] Similarly, Valerius' *delibamentum* may be a variation for the usual *libamentum* (used by Cicero, and by Valerius at 2.5.5). We cannot possibly reconstruct all of Valerius' sources, the points of departure for Valerius' diction, and hence we cannot begin to reconstitute Valerius' motive for each coinage. Instead, we can focus on two aspects of his diction: its supposed poeticizing tendency and the avoidance of common words for common things. This latter embraces more than what the declaimers meant as *verba sordida* and offers significant insight into the choice and play of words in the *Memorable Deeds and Sayings*.

Valerius does not allude to the Roman poets,[10] nor does he quote Latin verse. The supposed poeticizing quality of his diction has nothing to do with poetic allusion.[11] Indeed, his admission of poetic words has different motivation. The misnomer "poeticizing" arises simply because the declaimers' speeches have not survived, for this context, and probably not the influence of Ovid, directs Valerius. Sinclair has pointed out the correspondence of Valerius' *adnominatio* on Pompey's siege of the Calagurritani, *quoque diutius armata iuventus viscera sua visceribus suis aleret* (7.6.ext.3) with *Metamorphoses* 6.651, *[Tereus] vescitur inque suam sua viscera congerit alvum.*[12] Sinclair did not limit Ovidian influence to diction or just this figure: his examination of apostrophe in Valerius concludes, "Valerius, perhaps in reaction to a stimulus emanating directly from Ovid, eschewed the norms for prosaic apostrophe in favour of its poetic counterpart."[13] Ovid certainly extended

9. C. Morawski, "De sermone scriptorum latinorum aetatis quae dicitur argentea observationes," *Eos* 2 (1895): 8, cited by Sinclair 1980, 166.

10. He mentions Ennius' statue in the tomb of the Scipios at 8.14.1.

11. The case of the declaimer Fuscus is altogether different, and exceptional. For analysis of his attempted Virgilian diction and rhythms, see Fairweather 1981, 246–51.

12. Sinclair 1980, 39.

13. Sinclair 1980, 88–89.

the use and scope of apostrophe, but evidence of his direct influence on Valerius is altogether lacking. The gory pun on *viscera* may be Ovid's invention and may have passed from him to the declaimers; it certainly would have appealed to their taste for the bizarre, bloody, and antithetical. The parallel of *viscera* may point to Ovidian influence or to just how declamatory this school-trained poet was. Sinclair has argued that the frequency of the rhetorical figure *adnominatio,* the form of the supposed reminiscence of Ovid, reflected a declamatory context: "what had been a practice with Cicero became in the schools and halls of declamation an absolute mania."[14] Valerius is not seeking a poetic manner but following the practice and tastes of the schools.

Again, in matters of diction, variation from his source and not reminiscence of the poets is the surer principle of selection. Valerius' variation of his source's diction has been studied by Bliss, whose data on Valerius' substitutions are particularly important here: "Of almost 600 synonyms collected from the parallels between Cicero and Valerius, in only two or three cases does Valerius use the same synonym twice." In fact, Valerius has fourteen variants for Cicero's *dico.*[15] The search for such variants inevitably drives the composer beyond the pool of Ciceronian or even Augustan prose vocabulary. Thus his selection of a word has an almost inverse relation to its canonicity. Because Cicero has used *comprehensis (De div.* 1.36), Valerius uses *adprehensis* (4.6.1).[16] This does not mean that Valerius' diction is exotic or colloquial but only that his choice of gloss tends to be uncanonical. In fact, a canon is not being avoided; rather the context provides a word to be avoided.

Undoubtedly, Valerius' choices are meant to be understood as synonyms; there is no change in meaning just as the substitution of *iuvenis* for *adulescens* is simply a formal variation. Valerius' diction then will not reveal changes in spoken or literary language but rather illustrates the range of the admissible. I use admissible deliberately, for there can be no question that Valerius' substitutions are easy or natural, that is, a reflection of usage. Languages admit synonyms, but a native speaker's

14. Sinclair 1980, 42.

15. Bliss 1951, 70.

16. See Bliss 1951, 75–76, for a list of changes of prefix (including omission of prefix).

understanding of these does not imply their currency. Of Valerius' diction, the words he chooses to replace Cicero's and Livy's, Bliss concludes, "In the choice of synonyms Valerius seems to be looking for three things: first, a different word, second, a colorful one, and finally, one that he has not used recently himself."[17] Valerius' substitutions will not always be for the better; indeed, he sometimes replaces Cicero's or Livy's original with a drabber word (especially when he replaces a concrete with an abstract noun).

Valerius' diction is more varied than the prose of a generation or two earlier; but how does it compare with that of his contemporaries, and how would it have been judged by this audience? Seneca the Elder's comments on the faults of the declaimers offer considerable insight into the quality of Valerius' vocabulary. Seneca's discussion of diction is almost entirely negative; he faults and gives examples of vulgar diction, *verba sordida*. While anachronism is also censured, obscenity and these words from common life are the leading vices of diction.[18] The potential preciosity of the latter is not lost on Seneca: "The schools eschew certain things as if they were obscene and they cannot abide anything a little common or everyday" (*Contr.* 4.pr.9: *quaedam enim scholae iam quasi obscena refugiunt nec, si qua sordidiora sunt aut ex cotidiano usu repetita, possunt pati*). Tacitus' periphrasis for spade provides the *locus classicus* for the fastidious extremes of such avoidance: *amissa magna ex parte per quae egeritur humus aut exciditur caespes* (*Annales* 1.65). Seneca lists some of the words he finds objectionable. At *Controversia* 7.pr.3 he names examples of *res . . . omnium sordidissimas acetum et puleium et ‡ dammam et philerotem ‡ lanternas et spongias*. In *Controversia* 9.2.25 Rufus Vibius is censured for referring to *soleae* in a description of the praetor Flamininus' execution of a captive. *Controversia* 7.5.9 identifies *rivalis* as a colloquial word. Valerius is not obscene, though he does write of adultery and devotes a chapter to "Luxury and Lust." He does not fare so well with common words.

Valerius does not mention sandals in the story of Flamininus but elsewhere has *ansula* (8.12.ext.3), the loop for the sandal thong, and

17. Bliss 1951, 71.

18. I am indebted to Fairweather (1981, 191–200) for her full discussion of *verba sordida* in the declaimers and the ancient critics' proscriptions for diction.

his work is full of the sort of everyday word Seneca would have thought sordid: *horreolum*, a small barn; *strigimentum*, offscraping; *tabernula*, a small shop; *omasum*, bullock's tripe; *everriculum*, a kind of net. Valerius' work is not peppered with such mundane terms. These he might defend as necessitated by his broad subject. Some can be excused since they are used in negative exempla (so the tripe of 8.1.damn.8). But clearly Valerius does not feel that he needs to elevate his tone by excluding the humdrum. He includes much that is more "vulgar," to the Roman palate, than tripe. Humble or un-Roman occupations bear mentioning: an ass driver, a groom, and an eye doctor, although for all, the foreign and, for the first two, the famous contexts excuse the lapse (the *asinarius* is the man almost executed by Alexander the Great and the groom, *equiso*, is the intriguer who brought Darius to power, 7.3.ext.1 and 2 respectively). Nonetheless, Valerius' cast of characters, especially certain women, are not appropriate: *faeneratrix*, a female moneylender, and *obstetrix*, a midwife. While mentioning a whorehouse (Valerius uses *lupanar* and, metaphorically, *stabulum*, 7.7.7, perhaps after Cicero, *Phil.* 2.69) does not in itself constitute vulgarity, the use of *sputum, uber, abdomen,* and *uterus* (though the last is metaphoric) is clearly not the chaste style prized by some in the schools.

In the terms of his contemporaries Valerius avoided obscenity, Grecisms,[19] and vulgarisms. Everyday words he certainly employed. His diction can, however, be analyzed in a more positive manner. Simply by considering the groups of nouns that Lundberg had listed, more positive criteria emerge, at least for coinages and novel usage.

Many of the list of words with meanings different from Cicero and Livy are metaphorical, metonymic, or synechdochic usages—for example, the use of *ferculum* at 9.1.1 to mean not the platter but the food served in the dish. The hunt for synonyms exerts an inevitable pressure toward such metaphoric usages. The nouns in the list of words not used by Cicero and Livy fall into *verba sordida*, and abstract and agent nouns. Valerius' general tendency to abstraction will be discussed later, but here too the search for varied diction propels the author to use abstract for concrete. Variation of diction and style is not the sole instigator of

19. Valerius entitles 7.4 "Strategemata" but apologizes for this Grecism with the avowal that he cannot find a Latin synonym.

Valerius' generalizing bent; in a *sententia* an agent noun helps the transition from the particular subject of the exemplum to the general moral; like an abstract noun the agent noun can be a vehicle of induction, moving the reader from the particular to the general. These are some of the considerations that produced terms like *professor, praesultor,* and *propulsator.*[20] *Faeneratrix, obstetrix,* and no doubt *professor* are not simply proof of Valerius' tolerance of *verba sordida.* An agent noun is a kind of abstraction, tying the subject to a class, but is also a label, like *consul* or *praetor* or *uxor Scipionis Aemiliani*; and, as we have seen, Valerius is constantly concerned with what heading, by what category something is to be spoken of and understood. All these considerations direct his diction.

Valerius' reworking of the texts of Cicero and Livy is then not so mechanical as the technique of variation suggests. He does not simply rearrange the words of his source and substitute some glosses. He often modifies event, emphasis, and phrasing to make a discrete exemplum from a narrative. And the narrative that Valerius creates in this process is usually a single central sentence with rhetorical juncture and closure tacked on. He does vary his diction with the technique described by Bliss, but his reworking is not simply verbal transformation. Diction and phrasing do not issue from some machinelike converter of forms. Indeed, Valerius' composition is far more the building of sentences or, like an epitomator, the reconstructing of his sources' sentences into a single sentence. This too has important consequences for the understanding of his style. Like the choice of words, their arrangement in Valerius must be understood in context of variation and with the intended effect of stylistic distinction and suitability for declamation in mind. In part Valerius is illustrating in his book how students are to treat the texts of the classics and the words of their declamatory competitors so as to achieve distinction, so as to be recognizably and memorably different.

20. Again, Valerius' coinages should not be seen as reflections of usage, including Valerius' own. *Praesultor* is made for this particular occasion as Bliss (1951, 88) has shown: "The word for 'public dancer' is *praesul* in Cicero, *praesultator* in Livy, and *praesultor* in Valerius. The word used by Cicero is apparently the normal term for such a personage."

Word Order

This difference affects word order as well as diction (the imprint of the declaimer must be thoroughgoing). To substitute synonyms produces occasional obscurity, certainly unconventional even difficult expression, but to vary word order, even in a highly inflected language, promises more drastic changes in emphasis and greater sacrifices of clarity. The inevitable reaction of the first-time reader, except those with a taste for sententiousness, is befuddlement or queries: "why does he avoid the subjunctive? why is he so difficult?" The sources of greatest difficulty and perhaps those two points on which Valerius would have most prided himself are the *sententiae*—especially those called *adnominationes,* which depend on the reuse of a word—and the sentence structure. The obscurity that follows from the first is easier to isolate: epigrammatic brevity dependent on the repetition of the same or similar word (which may well involve a pun) makes a difficult combination. The order and rhythm of Valerius' prose merit discussion before a review of his use of rhetorical figures. Phrasing in Valerius has two special considerations: the pattern of variation of a source's diction and word order and the insistent structure of Valerius' exemplum: lead in sentence (juncture), narrative sentence, closing *sententia.* Just as the closing *sententia* has a recurrent structure (the figure *adnominatio* most often, the thought most often a resolution of antithesis) and the introductory juncture has a rhetoric of its own, the narrative sentence has, in its most developed form, an almost formulaic structure. Clarity—that is, immediate intelligibility—is neither the effect nor, as we shall argue, the intent of this artifice.

Again Seneca the Elder's collection provides the material to gauge Valerius' contemporaries' judgment of faulty word order and sentence structure. Fairweather writes of the declaimer whose style seems to have most bothered Seneca: "Faults of *compositio,* castigated by ancient theorists, which may frequently be detected in samples of Fuscus' more flowery prose include the unnatural use of hyperbaton (see Quintilian 9.4.28); the stringing together of too many short words in succession (see Quintilian 9.4.22); and the contrived repetition of the same rhythms (see Quintilian 9.4.55–56)."[21] The last may be the customary

21. Fairweather 1981, 201.

stipulation that prose is to be rhythmical, not metrical. The first two certainly are faults since they fail to knit together prose: excessive hyperbaton does not bind a colon together but draws attention to its own artifice. An overly long series of short words will also fall apart. In both of these cases the prose is not bound together in convincing and deliverable units. So the critics said, even if some of the declaimers practiced otherwise. Valerius does not follow all these faults, though his use of hyperbaton parallels Fuscus'; but the characteristics of his composition, whether they be vices or virtues, are comprehensible only in the same terms—heavily contrived techniques to articulate long cola and long, perhaps complex sentences. These are characteristics of Valerius' narrative sentences, for the *sententiae* and to a lesser degree the introductory sentences, while they do not avoid hyperbaton, aim more often than has been acknowledged at brevity.

First, the caveat applied before analysis of Valerius' diction needs restating here. Word order in Valerius is often the direct result of inversion of the word order of his source. Bliss has demonstrated that Valerius inverted both simple pairs of words and more complex phrases. The patterns and consequences of this variation merit further inquiry as do two of Bliss' conclusions in particular: first, that Valerius does not prefer any specific order in inverting noun and epithet and in rearranging whole phrases (Bliss' own sampling of these inversions reveals Valerius' preferences). Second, Bliss observed that Valerius' rearranging leads to more complex phrasing and sentences; this pattern of "variation" has greater significance.

To begin with the smallest scale, Valerius' variation of pairs of words seems to prefer no particular order. So just as with diction, the scholar should draw no deductions of actual usage from Valerius' patterning of, for example, noun and modifier. The examples already given demonstrate this well: Cicero's order of adjective or genitive and the noun modified, or vice versa, is simply reversed in Valerius' *Apollinis praedictiones* and *bonitate eorum* and *vetustissimam Cererem*. These simple inversions can accommodate synonyms and words other than noun and modifier: Livy 26.4.5, *desilire perniciter,* and 2.3.3, *celeri motu delabi*; Livy 29.37.10, *Item M. Livius,* and 2.9.6, *Salinator quoque.*[22] Bliss also dem-

22. Bliss 1951, 59.

onstrates Valerius' inversion of larger phrases: Livy 7.2.9 *puerum ad canendum ante tibicinem cum statuisset,* and 2.4.4, *adhibito pueri ac tibicinis concentu*; Livy 2.7.7, *populo summissis fascibus in contionem,* and 4.1.1, *fasces . . . in contione populo summittendo.*[23] Valerius' rearranging seems more complex as the phrases lengthen: Livy 29.37.8, *cum ad tribum Polliam ventum esset,* and 2.9.6, *ut est ad Polliam ventum tribum.* Valerius at times seems to be postponing the verb of his source: consider his final placement of *summittendo* in the previous example and the following rearrangements of Cicero: *De natura deorum* 3.83, *ornarat . . . tyrannus Gelo,* and 1.1.ext.3, *tyrannus Gelo . . . ornaverat*; *Brutus* 90 *tum igitur nihil recusans . . . pro sese,* and 8.1.abs.2, *pro se iam nihil recusans*; *De divinatione* 1.72, *immolaret ante praetorium,* and 1.6.4, *ante praetorium immolaret.* In fact, Valerius does not always transpose the verb to the end of his colon. But is his rearrangement simply inversion of the original? Bliss maintains that no pattern of modifier and noun can be deduced in Valerius—that is, his word order is due to inversion. Here Bliss has erred in part because he focuses on the verifiable evidence for inversion and thus neglects the majority of Valerius' prose and specifically that prose, Valerius' prefaces, which had no model. Bliss observed that "In the simplest type of inversion we find 26 cases in which Livy has the order noun-adjective and Valerius the opposite. There are on the other hand only 8 cases where Livy has the order adjective-noun and Valerius the reverse. In both cases the proportion of emphatic to unemphatic usages seems about equal."[24]

Bliss offered the same conclusion for the inversions of Cicero (26 cases of noun-epithet and 16 epithet-noun). First, Bliss's conclusions clearly do not follow from his data. He tries to buttress his argument "that Valerius makes no fetish of the emphatic usage" by considering the placement of the possessive and reflexive pronouns.[25] In fact he considered only *meus, tuus,* and *suus,* but the data are all but irrelevant. The preponderance of the customary position of these words should elicit no surprise. These cohere so closely with their noun and are such weak or uncolorful modifiers that they fail as hyperbata, and hyper-

23. Bliss 1951, 62.
24. Bliss 1951, 69.
25. Bliss 1951, 69.

baton is clearly Valerius' conscious aim as the means to achieve an involved and cohesive style. If we reconsider Valerius' variation of the units larger than simple pairs, his effect will come clear. Further, take up *Memorable Deeds and Sayings* and open it at random and the insistent pattern of modifier and modified, the so-called emphatic usage, unescapably harries your reading. Even from Bliss's statistics this was predictable: neutral (unemphatic) word order predominates in Cicero and Livy. If Valerius is to vary them, the conclusion is clear. This tendency is not limited to passages that vary Cicero and Livy; it especially marks Valerius' prefaces.

Phrasing and Colometry

At this point we can reconsider the point and effect of Valerius' word order. First, his transpositions of Cicero's and Livy's larger units has a decided effect, which is not simply to delay the verb. Valerius' word order tends to split up discrete rhythmical cola so that they may be articulated in longer rhetorical cola.[26] In the example from Livy 2.7.7, *populo summissis fascibus in contionem,* Valerius has fractured the ablative absolute so that its subject and verb may contain the other elements of the grammatical phrase: the grammatical constituents and the rhetorical colon are thereby one: *fasces . . . in contione populo summittendo* (4.1.1). More often Valerius achieves this effect by making the original into an ablative absolute: Livy's *puerum ad canendum ante tibicinem cum statuisset* (7.2.9) becomes in Valerius' hands *adhibito pueri ac tibicinis concentu* (2.4.4). The important point is not the emphatic position of Valerius' genitives: their placement has nothing to do with the addition of emphasis but is occasioned by the separation of noun and modifier (*adhibito* and *concentu*), which has made a Livian clause of several discrete cola (two separate prepositional phrases and the separate, final articulation of the dependent conjunction and verb) into a single rhetorical colon. Discrete cola in Livy and Cicero are often so rearranged into more cohesive if complex cola. Valerius prevents the material of his source from fragmenting into small units.

26. For this distinction, see Habinek 1985, 10–11.

Fuscus, it will be remembered, was criticized for having series of short words, a criticism in effect of loose-knit prose. Valerius' prose may seem overly knit, but his purpose of subordinating the material of his source into a single central sentence in part requires this. He is aiming at a periodic style, but his style must outdo the periods he found in Cicero. Semantic postponement clearly marks his sentences. The prior position of modifiers is a principal means of carrying the reader along in a complex sentence, of binding together what were originally discrete cola and clauses into single cola that are more easily subordinated.

Valerius' sentence structure is actually quite simple. The narrative sentence usually begins with the subject's name (often but not necessarily the grammatical subject); title or some apposite follows; next is a relative clause sometimes interrupted by a subjunctive clause; the main predicate is last. The reader is carried on, just as in the smaller units understanding is delayed and cola fashioned by the final placement of, for example, the noun of a hyperbaton.

That such hyperbaton is difficult to follow, even clumsy is undeniable. Even in a sentence such as the following where we are given the main predicate early (though the interesting point of the exemplum, the motive of the tribune, is reserved until the end), the separation of noun and modifiers, meant to avoid subordinated syntax, may lose the reader as it pulls him on:

> *L. Manlio Torquato diem ad populum Pomponius tribunus pl. dixerat, quod occasione bene conficiendi belli inductus legitimum optinendi imperii tempus excessisset quodque filium optimae indolis iuvenem rustico opere gravatum publicis usibus subtraheret.* (5.4.3)

Valerius strives to reduce even the main clause to a more compact colon by the separation of object and verb in the idiom *diem dicere*. The use of participles is striking here as so often in Valerius. The avoidance of *cum* and the subjunctive reflects no change in Latin syntax but Valerius' interest in producing a long sentence that will not fracture into many phrases.[27] Thus we are to hear *Pomponius . . . inductus . . . filium . . .*

27. Bliss (1951, 82) has described this tendency: "Valerius likes to begin his *exempla* with a series of adjectival clauses describing his subject, and then cap

iuvenem . . . gravatum. Interlocked word order and, specifically, the extended use of the participle produce Valerius' involved style.

Construction interlocked by hyperbaton, frequently of participles, is quite typical of Valerius. Bliss calls it "this almost-mania of Valerius' for extreme synchysis" and gives as an extreme example 7.4.ext.2: *Cannensem populi Romani aciem . . . conpluribus astutiae copulatam laqueis.* Bliss further notes that the result of this arrangement is the order A-B-A-B.[28] The resulting sentences, of course, do not signal their structure by the use of subordinating conjunctions, or certainly not to the same degree that Cicero's or Livy's involved hypotactic periods do. Valerius does not limit this style to the narrative, central sentences of his exempla; it also characterizes the prose of his prefaces. Even where Valerius does employ subordinating conjunctions, he resists any linear unfolding of the sentence. For example, at 8.12.pr. a rather straightforward sentence is made more complicated by the insertion of a relative clause immediately following the subordinating *ne; separatum tamen et proprium titulum habeat, ne, cui deorum immortalium praecipua indulgentia adfuit, nostra honorata mentio defuisse existimetur.* This sentence is then made truly obscure by the use of abstract nouns, and in particular the tacking on of relative clauses and the separation of participle from (new) subject. The sentence continues, or rather starts again with a new jussive subjunctive (i.e., parallel to *habeat*). When Valerius seems to have exhausted the possibilities of prolonging his sentence by hanging phrases on relative pronouns and participles, he resorts to the addition of a final phrase dependent on an absolutely final gerund: *et simul spei diuturnioris vitae quasi adminicula quaedam dentur, quibus insistens alacriorem se respectu vetustae felicitatis facere possit, tranquillitatem saeculi nostri, qua nulla umquam beatior fuit, subinde fiducia confirmet, salutaris principis incolumitatem ad longissimos humanae condicionis terminos prorogando.* While the demands of panegyric may have dissuaded Valerius from

---

the entire period with a single main clause and verb which ties the whole thing together," and Bliss has seen one of its consequences: "This usage tends to eliminate, or at least curtail, the use of subordinate clauses, especially those introduced by *cum*."

28. Bliss 1951, 65.

penning a straightforward wish for longevity for Tiberius, such a style
is not peculiar to this passage.

Valerius goes to extraordinary lengths in avoiding normal, neutral
word order in order to bind together his lengthy sentences. Bliss has
noted, "in actual narrative Valerius is not a great deal more wordy than
his epitomator."[29] Of course, Valerius' epitomator splits up Valerius'
narrative sentences. Excess verbiage does not characterize Valerius'
narrative; his periphrases do not necessarily lengthen the original but
tend to substitute abstract for concrete expressions. In great part this
is what has so horrified stylists. Latin prose composers have been told
forever that Latin is a concrete language; they are not to use abstract
nouns and are to avoid metaphoric language. They are not to write,
"And let there be certain props as it were for the expectation of more
prolonged age, resting on which confidence may grow readier by the
contemplation of ancient good fortune and strengthen the tranquillity
of our age, the best of all, by extending the well being of our saving
prince to the most distant boundaries of the human state." Perhaps
here Valerius himself is a little taken aback by his expression; unlike
Cicero he does not usually mitigate his metaphors with *quidam, quasi,*
velut, or *tamquam.*[30] Valerius clearly has a certain disregard for the word
order, phrasing, and hence delivery of his source's text. But will this
"mania" for a new style drive him to disregard rhythm altogether? Certainly, he seeks a flow of prose different from Cicero. Valerius' prose
is bound together in ways much less discernible. Antithesis and sudden
change of view, the characteristics of the *sententia,* are accommodated
by a style that is not simply complex but whose relations are inter-
twined. The grammatical relation of his participial constructions, for
example, is "simpler" than the hypotactic structures of his source, but
this apparently straightforward joint can communicate the same causal
or temporal relationships. The relation of cola, like that of thought, is
not signaled as directly. This is an essential not just of the derivative
epitomator's compression but of a style that strives above all to be surprising, extraordinary.

Sacrifices of usual word order and even of sense are requisites of this

29. Bliss 1951, 80.
30. Sinclair 1980, 142.

style. Valerius' rhythms have also been seen as a casualty of his desire to improve his source.[31] The results of Muench, who studied Valerius' clausulae, the rhythmic endings of sentences, in book 9,[32] when compared with Cicero's practice, using the figures of Laurand for the Sixth Philippic, demonstrate an orthodox practice.[33] First, Valerius' prose is rhythmical, not metrical: he seldom uses the heroic clausula, the ending of a dactylic hexameter.[34] And the three rhythms he most prefers are Cicero's favorites (see table 6). Valerius does rearrange word order to achieve these clausulae as the placement of forms of *esse* demonstrates: *Punica classis esset oppressa* (2.8.2); *leges a se esse servatas* (3.7.1d).[35] The infinitive is postponed in the following examples for the same rhythm: *si posset averti* (1.7.3) and *rei publicae permisit irasci* (3.8.2).[36] Valerius also varies the order of ablative absolutes and the position of the reflexive pronoun *se* and employs the enclitic *que* to produce the favored clausulae.[37]

The different impetuses of Valerius' word order can collide; his insistent variation of his source does at times produce unrhythmic end-

TABLE 6. *Comparison of Cicero's and Valerius' Clausulae*

Clausula	Cicero	Valerius
‾‿‿‾⌣	31%[a]	38%
‾‿‿⌣	25.6%	24%
‾‿‿‿‿⌣	12%	19.1%

[a]Muench had included paeon and spondee (‾‿‿‿‿⌣) under instances of cretic and spondee (‾‿‿⌣). Laurand's figures for the two clausulae have been combined.

31. See note 5.

32. Muench 1909.

33. Laurand 1965, 2.160–65. See the chart and analysis of Laurand's figures in Habinek 1985, 170–74.

34. Muench 1909, 19–20.

35. Muench 1909, 35.

36. Muench 1909, 36.

37. See Muench 1909, 38–44, for Valerius' techniques of variation of forms and word order for the sake of rhythm.

ings. The reworking of Livy's *cum ad tribum Polliam ventum esset* to *ut est ad Polliam ventum tribum* varies diction and word order and has the additional advantage of an interlocked hyperbaton, but Livy's ending, a familiar variation of the double cretic (‾˘‾‾˘‾) is sacrificed (‾˘‾‾˘‾˘, a variation not even listed by Muench). Valerius could have avoided these iambs with the final order *Polliam tribum ventum,* which gives cretic and spondee, a favorite clausula, but this would destroy the interlocked word order.

Figuration

In the contest of stylistic desiderata the new has here won out over the traditional. The critics may well feel that a forced and heavy-handed manipulation of word order has replaced the subtler articulation of the phrase—the rhythmic signaling of the clause's end. But this is in part a consequence of the variation of the texts, which have made canonical such stylistic criteria and judgments. Critical language about Valerius' or the Silver Age's style, if it does not indulge in the metaphor of organic decline, speaks of the loosening of restraint. Diction has been thrown open to the words of the poets. In particular, *sententiae* and figures of all kinds abound. The phenomena underlying the metaphorical descriptions of critics are the increased density and transparency of rhetorical techniques. Sinclair wrote, "Valerius employed figurative language with a freedom and reckless abandon quite alien to republican prose."[38] Since this is the central attack upon Valerius, its importance is unmistakable, but the purpose of this study is not apology. Is it the case that restraint has flown to the winds? Is this a consequence of ignorance, tastelessness, or inability? Valerius' manipulation of diction, word order, syntax, and rhythm should make manifest that he was a capable stylizer, conversant with rhetorical conventions, and that he had far different stylistic aims. To return to the fundamental issue: is Valerius' style unrestrained? This is a curious notion implying that the earlier authors had some natural inclinations

38. Sinclair 1980, 141.

that have been checked by something, call it innate taste or acquired training. The wild animal of Latin Prose held in check by a sober generation now runs rampant. Or perhaps, the purebred creature of Cicero and the Augustans has now been tainted by new blood. Unquestionably, the late republican linguistic and stylistic criteria are no longer in evidence, but the new style's relation to these is not wanton abandon but conscious manipulation.

Instead of dilating on the loosenings of restraint or the abandonment of restrictions, the critic would do well to consider both the literary origins of this style, its peculiar relation to the texts it varies, and also its contemporary contexts and purposes. Faced with an increased density of rhetorical figures, the literary critic cannot simply label these aural titillation or literary gamesmanship. Even if declamation is deemed only a "leisure activity," if it is believed that rhetoric in its retreat from the forum is now the stuff of idle play, this playful leisure still teaches or values something. Further, we should not confuse the evidence for declamation, the writings of Seneca the Elder and Valerius Maximus, with either the oral declamation or the actual legal practice of the day. These authors present excerpts only, and these excerpts are teaching texts; they may well exaggerate techniques as pedagogic showpieces tend to do. Finally, these works are interactive texts—neither journalistic fragments nor altogether written, literary constructs. They arise from an oral performance and seek to influence it.

Valerius is exemplifying what to know of the past and how to communicate that knowledge. His book exemplifies the proper style and figuration to communicate that knowledge. A knowledge of the illustrations of the past cannot be divorced from its proper expression. Indeed, Valerius exemplifies how to write and speak, the proper subject and style. The reader is to learn not simply a mnemonic catalog of people and events but the skills of the entertainer, the pleader, and the adviser.

Valerius' postures of doubt about how to treat a certain historical figure anticipate the originality of the treatment that follows and reflect the integral role of rhetorical figures in what is being taught. The reader is to learn how to write and deliver an apostrophe or *dubitatio* just as he learns the deeds and words of Scipio Aemilianus. We shall focus on Valerius' figures of thought, not because alliteration, asyndeton, or anaphora are unimportant;[39] they too are meant to communicate the correct style, but Valerius' figures of thought shape and define his material in more novel and insistent ways. Their greater imprint on the material consequently claims our attention as it constitutes a major share of Valerius' claim to usefulness and originality.

Valerius' leading, almost insistent figure is *adnominatio,* which, in its play of two forms of the same word or two words from the same or similar sounding stem, is said to be used for aural effect.[40] In fact, it is a standard feature of Valerius' *sententiae,* a standard technique for Valerius' epigrammatic closes, and no doubt part of the sententiousness derives from the sound effects. But it must be distinguished from alliteration, for example: sound is not the object, but the sound of epigram and the suggestion of pungent thought that accompanies epigram. Valerius' *adnominationes* also involve surprise: *libertas sine Catone? non magis quam Cato sine libertate* (6.2.5). Chiastic order certainly helps here as also in *praefatus non se Catilinae illum adversus patriam, sed patriae adversus Catilinam genuisse* (5.8.5). This figure relies on saying different things with the same words just as the declaimers sought different *colores,* twists of interpretation, from the same facts. With *adnominatio,* at any rate, verbal economy and an aural effect not different in kind from anaphora or alliteration are achieved, but *adnominatio* does not simply add emphasis or jingle. Its popularity in Valerius is due to its difficulty. The difficulty facing Valerius the stylizer has always been to vary the familiar. His contribution does not come in *inventio*—his material is provided—but in the reworking of that material. His *adnominationes* succeed, as do his chapter headings for example, by stretching the applicability of words. Valerius thereby strives to contain and codify experience in verbal formulas.

Three other types of figuration demand appraisal since, while characteristic of Valerius, they represent extremes of style, at least from the standpoint of his predecessors. Along with antithesis, metaphor and apostrophe are among the most startling and frequent essentials of his

39. Sinclair has considered these and eleven other figures in his thesis.

40. Sinclair (1980, 22) follows Quintilian (9.3.66) in emphasizing its "stunning aural effect."

style. The need for synonyms has certainly driven him to some of his metaphorical expression but in no way explains the mixed metaphors that so often dazzle plausibility. The very frequency of these mixtures suggests that Valerius does not mean to create a sustained likeness. His comparative language does not present the reader with concrete images; indeed, the sustained metaphors are often the most banal. For instance the nautical language of 8.1.abs.12 is perfectly consistent: *Calidius Bononiensis in cubiculo mariti noctu deprehensus, cum ob id causam adulterii diceret, inter maximos et gravissimos infamiae fluctus emersit, tamquam fragmentum naufragii leve admodum genus defensionis amplexus.* This simple conceit cannot compare with the more improbable, unstable, and striking shipwreck of fortune: *Caduca nimirum et fragilia puerilibusque consentanea crepundiis sunt ista, quae vires atque opes humanae vocantur. adfluunt subito, repente dilabuntur, nullo in loco, nulla in persona stabilibus nixa radicibus consistunt, sed incertissimo flatu fortunae huc atque illuc acta quos sublime extulerunt inproviso recussu destitutos profundo cladium miserabiliter inmergunt* (6.9.ext.7).[41] In its flight from one fancy to the next, this metaphor could be described as yet another feature of a style meant to captivate for the moment, but Valerius is aiming at something more permanent. He aims to be remembered, to have his version of an exemplum, figuration as well as content, stick in his audience's ears and displace earlier accounts. The incongruous achieves this well.

Clearly, we must take into account the expectations of Valerius' audience.[42] Unlike Livy and Cicero, Valerius does not mitigate his metaphors with *tamquam* or *quasi*.[43] Sinclair thought this significant for two

---

41. Sinclair (1980, 145) called this the "most eccentric" admixture: "Here he begins with *puerilia crepundia*, an odd and unprecedented image, proceeds with the ebb and flow of waves, and then combines for good measure the agricultural *radices*. If this were not enough, he adds an allusion to wind, and closes, finally, with what appears to be a metaphor of shipwreck."

42. Compare the contemporary mixed metaphors of the declaimer Musa, which Fairweather (1981, 218) found farfetched: *caelo repluunt, odoratos imbres, caelatas silvas, nemora surgentia* (*Contr.* 10.pr.9).

43. Sinclair (1980, 141) points out that Valerius uses *tamquam* once (8.1.abs.12), *quasi* twice (6.9.6, 8.13.pr.), and regularly omits these when he found them in his source.

reasons: the metaphors had "increased impact" while the practice was a precedent for later avoidance of these words (e.g., in the younger Seneca).[44] Such practice certainly seeks an immediacy of impact, which the apologizing *tamquam* and *quasi* tend not to effect. These words draw attention to the metaphor and ask for the reader's or listener's involvement with the likeness. The listener hears the metaphor declared as such and is thus made ready to entertain it. Valerius' prose does not involve a reader or listener in this way. As we shall see with the next class of figures, Valerius' figures offer the reader no time for reflection, no distance for analysis. Very much like his hyberta, and cola structure in general, Valerius' figures hurry the reader along with an insistent hand.

A number of Valerius' figures seek to collapse the distance between author, text, and reader. Apostrophe, exclamation, *interrogatio, dubitatio,* prosopopoeia, and the use of the second-person singular all seek an immediacy of contact in the trio of subject, author, and audience. Valerius' apostrophes are among the most peculiar features of his style. Valerius addresses directly places, gods, things, and persons.[45] Virtues and city-states alike are invoked in exemplum-length apostrophes. Other grand entities, the Caesars in particular, receive full-length apostrophes. Sinclair sought to demonstrate, "First, that Valerius expanded in certain key respects on the Ciceronian usage. Next, that these developments are paralleled in post-Vergilian poetry." The contrast with Cicero is instructive: he predominantly apostrophized persons not things or places and his apostrophes "have no clear-cut structural function."[46] Sinclair made several important observations of Valerius' practice: Valerius imports apostrophes where his material had none; these protracted apostrophes are an end in themselves though he deemed their function as "effecting transitions"; and the apostrophes often occur in final exempla, the climactic position, where they are meant perhaps to elicit the audience's applause.[47] This is not the only consider-

---

44. Sinclair 1980, 142.
45. Sinclair 1980, 72–80.
46. Sinclair 1980, 86.
47. Sinclair 1980, 86–89.

ation Sinclair gives Valerius' audience; he maintains that apostrophe serves emotional needs.[48]

Apostrophe is, however, not simply the injection of emotion or a figure to finish off a chapter on the grandest note. Nor can we say that it represents another poetic intrusion into prose. Apostrophe is allied to the set of figures whose technique is one of pure fiction. As with the fiction of *dubitatio* or the reconstructed scenes of prosopopoeia so essential to *suasoriae,* author and reader enter the text. This is the same sort of naive rhetoric that purports to be giving words of advice to Hannibal. This rhetoric maintains that we are there to counsel the author as he searches for expression, to advise the long-dead general, to speak face-to-face with the city of Syracuse or Jupiter himself. We are not here dealing with the presence of a poet in the text undercutting the weave of his fiction. Like the absence of *quasi* or *tamquam,* Valerius' entire style does not draw attention to the fictive or fickle nature of its construction. The author's entrance into the text may be a consequence of the self-conscious narrator Ovid but has little to do with the progress of narratology. In the figures of *dubitatio* and exclamation, attention is focused on the figure of the speaker, but the reader is to see the difficulty of the material and the manipulative skill of the speaker.

Sinclair had pointed out Valerius' occasional use of the second-person singular. He considered the practice in his discussion of hyperbole, but while it is hyperbolic, this figure is better understood as a direct address to the reader, a technique akin to those others described previously that import the reader into the text. Sinclair again traces the poetic genealogy of this figure and its florescence in Ovid and the declaimers.[49] Its similarity to prosopopoeia and the fictions of *suasoriae* is clear from the following examples, of which the first imagines Alexander's attempted bribery of Xenocrates, the second King Antiochus' petrified response to the senate's legate: *quid? rex Alexander divitiis [the abstinentia of Xenocrates] quatere potuit? ab illo quoque statuam et quidem aeque frustra temptatum putes* (4.3.ext.3) and *non legatum locutum, sed ipsam curiam ante oculos positam crederes* (6.4.3).[50] Sinclair tried to tie this use

48. Sinclair 1980, 81.
49. Sinclair 1980, 107–10.
50. Sinclair (1980, 107–8) discusses these examples in terms of hyperbole.

of the second-person singular to actual recitation of Valerius Maximus'
chapter. The practice certainly is not determined by any specific occasion but reflects the context for which Valerius wrote. Declamation
required this sort of intrusive rhetoric. Valerius' practice of *interrogatio,*
for example, could equally be asserted as evidence of actual performance. The melodramatic fiction of recreated repartee, however, suits
the declamatory performer and points to no particular performance.

Conclusion

In his preface to the whole work, where Valerius appealed to Tiberius as muse, he had set down an account of his methods
and aims. These have proved a most practical sort: he has culled from
written sources so that others—his readers—need not.[51] A disclaimer
then stressed that his work was not to compete with prior histories, in
scope, in learning, or in style.[52] His initial "program" defined what he
is not, an antiquarian historian (Varro), a historian and stylist (Livy),
or a great stylist (Cicero). His practice fully bears this out, although
generations of readers attest to his usefulness, his ease of access.

As a guide to his principles of selection, his favored sources suggest
that a certain canon of authors and texts at least recommended a story
to him. Valerius was not poring over the junior annalists and the Hellenistic dramatic historians. The arcane or esoteric, in subject and in
sources, never draws him as does the orthodox and mainstream. The
consequent duplication of information (e.g., the familiar material of
Cicero's speeches rehashed in Valerius) does not trouble this author,
whose stated aim is not originality of subject but his reader's conve-

51. *Urbis Romae exterarumque gentium facta simul ac dicta memoratu digna, quae
apud alios latius diffusa sunt quam ut breviter cognosci possint, ab inlustribus electa
auctoribus digerere constitui, ut documenta sumere volentibus longae inquisitionis labor
absit.*

52. *nec mihi cuncta conplectendi cupido incessit: quis enim omnis aevi gesta modico
voluminum numero conprehenderit, aut quis compos mentis domesticae peregrinaeque
historiae seriem felici superiorum stilo conditam vel adtentiore cura vel praestantiore
facundia traditurum se speraverit?*

nience. After all, Valerius has a claim to originality simply in filling those guiding rubrics, his chapter headings; the difficulty of ancient books, Greek and Latin, in this respect (without tables of contents, footnotes, or indexes) is quite manifest.

For whom and for what is this collection convenient? The answer is, most immediately, for declaimers and declamation; this does not preclude a readership of lawyers who, Quintilian claimed, should prefer the unbiased examples drawn from history to witnesses (10.1.34). Declamation, perhaps later refreshed by the reading of Valerius and Seneca the Elder, was a stage of the Roman lawyer's education preliminary to actual practice. While the rhetoric of his proems and his junctures creates the illusion of a seamless whole, Valerius' pages are not suited for continuous reading but for memorization and insertion into the competitive oral performances of declamation, which are a characteristic literary activity of Augustan and Tiberian Rome. The discrete arrangement of chapters and the clear signaling of these sections by both rubric and preface attest to Valerius' own desire for ease of access. This context and purpose have important consequences for Valerius' methodology and presentation. Contradiction is not surprising in a work whose contents will be used to illustrate either side of a debate. Nor has the inclusion of republican material seemed odd since Valerius is not occupied in creating, *ex nihilo*, an imperial panegyric but is rather, at least in part, engaged in summing up the materials of a declamation that has evolved immediately from the daily practices of Roman schools and only remotely from Greek rhetorical and pedagogical theory.

What is new in Valerius is essentially what is new in the Roman declaimers. The forms that the exempla take reveal this novelty. Without new material (the fruit of further antiquarian research), a new arrangement and understanding (the *exaedificatio,* which is Livy's boast and which Valerius like Velleius did not attempt), or a superior classical style, what does Valerius offer? The matter-of-fact answer is that again and again he demonstrates category and illustration—just how a category (a particular theme) can be richly embellished with recognizable subjects in striking settings. The surprise of his readers is a conscious aim; the difficulty of stringing together resistant material, whether republican and Caesarian, Greek and Roman, or a traditional story in a new classification, is an opportunity for the declaimer's skill. This is why, too, the inversion of situation and paradox of all forms so appeal to Valerius. With a number of speakers performing back to back on the same, familiar theme, distinction comes from the novel twist. In making his textbook, Valerius has rooted out the various instances of various abstract classifications, but his interest in and contribution to the subject does not stop with this. Valerius is especially taken with paradoxical subject matter and with novel classifications and junctures because these stretch the rhetorical and verbal category. His greatest contribution is not the materials ferreted out but the subsuming rubric and the connecting juncture. Thus he delights in the rhetorical figure of *dubitatio*—the postured doubt as to whether Sulla is *felix* or *fortis*.

The usual complaints directed against Valerius' work arise from the two fields of contest that he explicitly disavows in the preface: history and literature (learning, composition, and stylization). The "style" Valerius adopts rivals his plundered sources but not on their grounds.[53] Having reduced these narratives to serviceable, though somewhat abstract, declamatory units, Valerius recasts them with new diction, sentence structure, and perhaps above all new figures. In this fashion he does not simply provide a "Reader's Digest Guide" to exempla but the very stuff of declamation—complete with his own diction, if ultimately pirated at least varied, and novel lead-in and closure. The embellishing details are left to the speaker's invention. Valerius' "style" and its inseparable relation to his sources are cannibalistic and combative.

Throughout, constitutional query animates Valerius. His steady concern is "What does such and such a story exemplify? Is it an instance of this or that?" The obfuscation and abstraction that Valerius does fall into and for which he has been faulted is ultimately a product of this exclusively verbal analysis. Though not in any grand fashion, Valerius is engaged in inquiry into the applicability of words. His innovation and that of the declaimers comes in pushing the limits (the meanings) of abstract categories. This is yet another technique of defying his audience's expectation.

Valerius' is, therefore, not a superficial treatment of history, just as

---

53. Seneca the Elder heaps ridicule on the only one of his generation to attempt such imitation, Cestius, who thought and taught that he could improve on the whole of a Ciceronian speech.

his work does not result from slothful compilation. He does enlarge and change the received categories. The boundaries of the classical (e.g., Cicero's illustrations for "Friendship") are not subjected to any analytic reevaluation but are instead changed, made novel or different, by having these include unexpected instances. Behind this process is a system of constitutional query first documented by Antiphon. Only a narrow set of readers will be angered by a response to the question "What is friendship?" that gives examples (and these often common-place) and not definition.

By Valerius' time this rhetorical habit had long been established in Rome's schools (as is clear both from Cicero's *De inventione* and the *Rhetorica ad Herennium*). The pedagogic tradition took especial delight in controversial, overlapping cases where the abstractions conflict—for example, "Is an accidental death an instance of manslaughter or mur-der?"; "Should an oath to a pirate be fulfilled?" (here "Fidelity" and "Rightful Vengeance" collide). The result of this historical process was not a hierarchy of abstractions, a philosophical ordering of vices and virtues, but a plethora of arguments and examples. Valerius presents his readers no systematic analysis of these distinctions. However, he too is twisting the applicability of categories, and his work, while venerating a canon of authors, changes and even distorts the point of those stories he has found. To ask what name should be given a particular person or event is to depart from a received vision. Valerius does not make heroes of villains but does seek new categories, sometimes with the re-sult that he suggests more than the material will bear. Here form seems to have run away with substance, for in the desire to see paradox, con-flict, or novelty, a resonance alien to the material is imported.

This is a sophisticated composition. Valerius must draw invention in the pursuit of praise and blame from a traditional set of characters. The vilified and the exalted do not shift. For Valerius, the moral and intellectual universe is studded with these figures—with precedents, not arguments. His purpose is to produce from these the slight bewil-derment that gives way to a knowing amusement when the familiar, couched in some novel form, is recognized afresh.

Such may have been the immediate appeal of declamatory perfor-mance. The paradigmatic that Valerius' exempla communicate in-volves more than this immediate appeal. Valerius' recurrent dramatization of his pedagogic program takes the form of references to his proposal (*propositum*) and declarations to the reader of how an event or figure is to be understood. Valerius does not evoke his audience's emotional or intellectual response; these he supplies. We are told how to understand events from the past, what face to put on, just as we are told of the proper public behavior and demeanor of the bereaved father who was also the Republic's magistrate. The skills prized and communicated by Valerius are in part verbal dexterity within a system of categorical thinking. The Valerian curriculum offers a fare of famous Romans, which the student makes his own by memory and by a technique of variation and abstraction. Historical context and clarity of motive or of style are not taught. Valerius evades the issues of historical causation, a characteristic to be expected in a community without history; but the Rome of Virgil and Livy and Augustus has historical self-consciousness, and so this is a deliberate choice. The marshaling of history owes much to Augustus in whose forum the stone procession of grand republican figures marched into the present. Valerius' seamless history is similarly manipulative, though his rhetoric calls attention to its rhetorician in ways so insistent as to be transparent. The density and transparency of technique and effect have little to do with the conveyance of points of information or the persuasion of a point of view, two of the essentials of contemporary theorizing on the ends of public speech. Valerius teaches from the past but he does not offer the clear and simple images such as Nepos' biographical sketches a generation earlier. Valerius has professed that his work is substitution for wide reading, a form of ersatz culture.

We have attempted to describe the qualities of this culture. Comparison with the texts from which it springs reveals not an obfuscating style but techniques of indirection. The attractions of stylistic indirection, it is true, have not often been recognized. The variation from a source and preference for abstraction, however, are not unconscious mannerisms. Such indirection certainly does not communicate "information" as well as the style of Valerius' sources, provided an audience values as information details of plot, event, and motive. The information that Valerius' style communicates is complex, for it communicates in part a knowledge of the source and of the present speaker's reworking of that model. It reflects and reveals a mediated composition and thereby involves the listener in the trumpeted sophistication of the speaker. Finally, this style serves more to recommend the skill of the speaker than to communicate the information of the original. To a degree never appreciated, Valerius' is a courtly style: in its indirection it is the cultivated speech of a select few. This cultivation distinguishes its practitioners as the educated. In its self-reference and self-consciousness, this style constitutes a call for attention, for recognition, for patronage. Mastery of the oblique and the ability to clothe and costume others' words and events in abstraction are skills for imperial service.

Any description of Valerius' program and purposes is inextricably bound up with the question of who is assuming the culture of the past. If the writing of one's own history marks a moment in historical self-consciousness, the writing of learned monographs marks another, though allied, moment. Pompey had to commission a manual on senatorial procedure, and the author of this was the first nonsenator to write history at Rome. A generation later and continuing under Augustus, Roman antiquarians sought not so much to understand the roots of their culture as to preserve the forms of an aristocratic culture now dispossessed. The true aristocrat does not feel the need to learn of his past through reading; his methods of acculturation are familial, institutional, and traditional. It is the arriviste who learns of the Roman through a handbook and whose anxieties about the aristocratic culture he seeks to appropriate direct Valerius' work.

Bibliography

Adams, F. 1955. "The Consular Brothers of Sejanus." *American Journal of Philology* 76: 70–77.

Alewell, Karl. 1913. *Über das rhetorische Paradeigma: Theorie, Beispielsammlung, Verwendung in der römischen Literatur der Kaiserzeit.* Inaugural dissertation, Kiel. Leipzig: Hoffman.

Alföldi, A. 1963. *Early Rome and the Latins.* Ann Arbor: University of Michigan Press.

André, J. M. 1965. "L'otium chez Valère-Maxime et Velleius Paterculus ou la réaction morale au début du principat." *Revue d'études latines* 43: 294–315.

Astin, A. E. 1967. *Scipio Aemilianus.* Oxford: Clarendon Press.

Atkinson, J. E. 1980. *A Commentary on Q. Curtius Rufus' Historiae Alexandri Magni.* Amsterdam: Gieben.

Badian, Ernst. 1969. "Two Roman Non-Entities." *Classical Quarterly* 63: 198–204.

Bardon, Henri. 1956. *La littérature latine inconnue.* Paris: Klincksieck.

———. 1940. *Le vocabulaire de la critique littéraire chez Sénèque le Rhéteur.* Paris: Les Belles Lettres.

Begbie, C. M. 1967. "The Epitome of Livy." *Classical Quarterly* 17: 332–38.

Blincoe, Mary Nerinckx. 1941. "The Use of the Exemplum in Cicero's Philosophical Works." Ph.D. dissertation, University of St. Louis.

Bliss, Francis R. 1951. "Valerius Maximus and His Sources: A Stylistic Approach to the Problem." Ph.D. dissertation, University of North Carolina.

Bonner, Stanley F. 1977. *Education in Ancient Rome: From the Elder Cato to the Younger Pliny.* Berkeley and Los Angeles: University of California Press.

———. 1949. *Roman Declamation in the Late Republic and Early Empire.* Liverpool: Liverpool University Press.

Bornecque, Henri. 1967. *Les déclamations et les déclamateurs d'après Sénèque le Père.* 1902. Reprinted, Hildesheim: Georg Olms.

Bosch, C. 1929. *Die Quellen des Valerius Maximus: Ein Beitrag zur Erforschung der Literatur der historischen Exempla.* Stuttgart: Kohlhammer.

Bowersock, G. W. 1981. *Augustus and the Greek World.* Westport, Conn.: Greenwood Press.

———. 1969. *Greek Sophists in the Roman Empire.* Oxford: Clarendon Press.

Brooks, Edward, ed. 1970. *P. Rutili Lupi De Figuris sententiarum et elocutionis.* Leiden: E. J. Brill.

Butler, Harold Edgeworth. 1909. *Post-Augustan Poetry: From Seneca to Juvenal.* Oxford: Clarendon Press.

Caltabiano, Matilde. 1975. "La morte del console Marcello nella tradizione storiografica." *Contributi dell' Istituto di Storia antica dell' Università del Sacro Cuore* 3: 65–81.

Canter, Howard Vernon. 1933. "The Mythographical Paradigm in Greek and Latin Poetry." *American Journal of Philology* 54: 201–24.

———. 1925. *Rhetorical Elements in the Tragedies of Seneca.* Illinois Studies in Language 10. Urbana.

Caplan, Harry. 1944. "The Decay of Eloquence at Rome in the First Century." In *Studies in Speech and Drama in Honor of A. M. Drummond,* 295–325. Ithaca, N.Y.: Cornell University Press.

Carney, T. F. 1962. "The Picture of Marius in Valerius Maximus." *Rheinisches Museum* 105: 289–337.

———. 1960. "Cicero's Picture of Marius." *Wiener Studien* 73: 83–122.

Carter, Christopher J. 1975. "Valerius Maximus." In *Empire and Aftermath. Silver Latin II,* ed. T. A. Dorey, 25–56. London and Boston: Routledge and Kegan Paul.

———. 1968. "The Manuscript Tradition of Valerius Maximus." Ph.D. dissertation, Cambridge.

Cichorius, C. 1888. "Über Varros libri de scaenicis originibus." *Commentationes Philologae Ribbeckenses.* Leipzig.

Clark, D. L. 1949. "Some Values of Roman *Declamatio*: The *Controversia* as a School Exercise in Rhetoric." *Quarterly Journal of Speech* 35: 279–83.

Clarke, M. L. 1951. "The Thesis in the Roman Rhetorical Schools of the Republic." *Classical Quarterly* 45: 159–66.

Clift, Evelyn Holst. 1945. *Latin Pseudepigrapha: A Study in Literary Attributions.* Baltimore: Furst.

Comes, Giovanni. 1950. *Valerio Massimo.* Rome: Signorelli.

Dalzell, A. 1955. "C. Asinius Pollio and the Early History of Public Recitation at Rome." *Hermathena* 86: 20–28.

Dorey, T. A., ed. 1966. *Latin Historians.* London: Routledge and Kegan Paul.

Earl, D. C. 1963. *Tiberius Gracchus: A Study in Politics.* Brussels: Latomus.

Eyre, E. J. 1963. "Roman Education in the Late Republic and Early Empire." *Greece and Rome* 10: 47–59.

Fairweather, Janet. 1981. *Seneca the Elder.* Cambridge: Cambridge University Press.

Faranda, Rino. 1976. *Detti e fatti memorabili di Valerio Massimo.* Turin: Unione Tipografico-Editrice Torinese.

Fiore, Benjamin. 1982. "The Function of Personal Example in the Socratic and Pastoral Epistles." Ph.D. dissertation, Yale University.

Fischer, K. D. 1980. "Der früheste bezeugte Augenartz der Klassischen Altertums." *Gesnerus* 37: 324–25.

Fleck, Michael. 1974. *Untersuchungen zu den Exempla des Valerius Maximus.* Inaugural dissertation, Marburg/Lahn.

Fraenkel, Eduard. 1952. "Culex." *Journal of Roman Studies* 42: 1–9.

Gehrmann, A. 1887. *Incunabula incrementaque proprietatum sermonis Valerii Maximi.* Programm, Rössel.

Geissler, Wilhelm. 1914. *Ad descriptionum historiam symbola.* Leipzig.

Gold, B. K., ed. 1982. *Literary and Artistic Patronage in Ancient Rome.* Austin: University of Texas Press.

Goodyear, F. R. D. 1984. "Tiberius and Gaius: Their Influence and Views on Literature." *Aufstieg und Niedergang der Römischen Welt* II, 32.1: 603–10.

———. 1982. "History and Biography." *The Cambridge History of Classical Literature* 2.32: 639–66.

———. 1981. *The Annals of Tacitus, Books 1–6.* Vol. 2: *Annals 1.55–81 and Annals 2.* Cambridge: Cambridge University Press.

Goold, George P. 1977. *Manilius. Astronomica.* Loeb Classical Library. Cambridge: Harvard University Press.

———. 1961. "A Greek Professorial Circle at Rome." *Transactions of the American Philological Association* 91: 168–92.

Gries, K. 1956. "Valerius Maximus an Minimus?" *Classical Journal* 52: 335–40.

Griffin, M. T. 1975. *Seneca.* Oxford: Clarendon Press.

Gruen, E. S. 1968. "Pompey and the Pisones." *California Studies in Classical Antiquity* 1: 160–62.

Guerrini, Roberto. 1981. *Studi su Valerio Massimo, Con un capitolo sulla Fortuna nell' iconographia umanistica.* Biblioteca di studi antici 28. Pisa: Giardini.

———. 1979. "Moduli sallustiani in Valerio Massimo. Il capitolo De Luxuria et Libidine, IX, 1." *Rendiconti dell' Istituto Lombardo* 113: 152–66.

Guillemin, A.-M. 1937. *Le public et la vie littéraire à Rome.* Paris: Les Belles Lettres.

Gwynn, Aubrey. 1964. *Roman Education: From Cicero to Quintilian.* New York: Russell.

Habinek, Thomas N. 1985. *The Colometry of Latin Prose.* University of California Publications: Classical Studies 25. Berkeley: University of California Press.

Häussler, R. 1968. *Nachträge zu A. Otto: Die Sprichwörter und sprichwörtlichen Redensarten der Römer.* Hildesheim: Georg Olms.

Haight, Elizabeth Hazelton. 1940. *The Roman Use of Anecdotes in Cicero, Livy, and the Satirists.* New York: Longmans.

Helm, Rudolf. 1955. "Valerius Maximus." *RE* 8A.1, 90–116.

———. 1940. "Beiträge zu Quellenforschung bei Valerius Maximus." *Rheinisches Museum* 89: 241–73.

———. 1939. "Valerius Maximus, Seneca und die Exemplasammlung." *Hermes* 74: 130–54.

Heraeus, W. 1900. "Neue Beiträge zur Kritik des Valerius Maximus und Nepotianus." *Philologus* 59: 416–40.

Hervieux, Léopold. 1883–99. *Les fabulistes latins depuis le siècle d'Auguste jusqu'à la fin du Moyen Âge.* Paris: Firmin-Didot.

Hillscher, A. 1892. "Hominum litteratorum graecorum ante Tiberii mortem in urbe Roma commoratorum historia critica." *Fleckeis.* Suppl. 18: 353–444.

Hofrichter, W. 1935. "Studien zur Entwicklungsgeschichte der Deklamation von der griechischen Sophistik bis zur römischen Kaiserzeit." Dissertation, Breslau.

Housman, A. E. 1900. "The Aratea of Germanicus." *Classical Review* 14: 26–39.

Jenkinson, E. M. 1955. "Further Studies in the Curriculum of the Roman Schools of the Republican Period." *Symbolae Osloenses* 31: 122–30.

Kagan, Donald. 1969. *The Outbreak of the Peloponnesian War.* Ithaca: Cornell University Press.

Kempf, C. 1966. *Valerius Maximus.* Leipzig: Teubner, 1888. Reprinted, Stuttgart.

———. 1866. *Novae Quaestiones Valerianae.* Berlin.

Kennedy, George. 1972. *The Art of Rhetoric in the Roman World.* Princeton: Princeton University Press.

Klotz, Alfred. 1942. "Studien zu Valerius Maximus und den Exempla." *Sitzungsberichte der Bayerischen Akademie der Wissenschaften* 5.

———. 1925. "Zu bellum Alexandrinum 55, 5 und Valerius Maximus IX, 4, 2." *Rheinisches Museum* 74: 234.

———. 1909. "Zur Litteratur der Exempla und zur Epitoma Livii." *Hermes* 44: 198–214.

Kohl, Richard. 1915. *De scholasticarum declamationum argumentis ex historia petitis.* Münster: Schoeningh.

Kornhardt, H. 1936. *Exemplum: Eine bedeutungsgeschichtliche Studie.* Göttingen: Robert Noske.

Krieger, B. 1888. "Quibus fontibus Valerius Maximus usus sit in eis exemplis enarrandis quae ad priora rerum Romanorum tempora pertinent." Dissertation, Berlin.

Kroll, Wilhelm. 1924. *Studien zum Verständnis der römischen Literatur.* Stuttgart: Metzler.

Lambert, M. 1970. "Alexandre vu par Valère Maxime." *Ludus Magistralis* 5. 23: 6–15; 25: 13–15.

Lane, E. N. 1979. "Sabazius and the Jews in Valerius Maximus. A Re-examination." *Journal of Roman Studies* 69: 35–38.

Laurand, L. 1965. *Études sur le style des discours de Cicéron.* Amsterdam: Hakkert.

Lichtfield, M. W. 1914. "National *exempla virtutis* in Roman Literature." *Harvard Studies in Classical Philology* 25: 1–25.

Lintott, A. W. 1968. *Violence in Republican Rome.* Oxford: Clarendon Press.

Lundberg, Ehrenfried. 1906. "De elocutione Valeri Maximi." Dissertation, Falun.

Lützen, Ludolf. 1907. *De priorum scriptorum argenteae quae dicitur latinitatis studiis scholasticis I.* Eschwege: Programm Friedrich-Wilhelms-schule.

Maire, Siegfried. 1899. "De Diodoro Siculo Valeri Maximi auctore." Dissertation, Schoenberg.

Maslakov, G. 1984 "Valerius Maximus and Roman Historiography: A Study of the *Exempla* Tradition." *Aufstieg und Niedergang der Römischen Welt* II, 32.1: 437–96.

———. 1978. "Tradition and Abridgement: A Study of the *Exempla* Tradition in Valerius Maximus and the Elder Pliny." Dissertation, Macquarie University.

Mejer, Jorgen. 1978. *Diogenes Laertius and His Hellenistic Background.* Wiesbaden: Steiner.

Moles, J. 1983. "Fate, Apollo and M. Junius Brutus." *American Journal of Philology* 104: 249–56.

Momigliano, Arnaldo. 1955. "Ancient History and the Antiquarian." *Journal of the Warburg and Courtauld Institutes,* 13. 1950: 285–315. Reprinted, *Contributo alla Storia degli Studi Classici* 67: 67–106.

Morawski, C. 1892. *De rhetoribus Latinis observationes.* Cracow.

Muench, Victor. 1909. "De clausulis a Valerio Maximo adhibitis." Dissertation, Breslau.

Münzer, Friedrich. 1963. *Römische Adelsparteien und Adelsfamilien.* Stuttgart, 1920. Reprinted, Darmstadt.

———. 1897. *Beiträge zur Quellenkritik der Naturgeschichte des Plinius.* Berlin: Weidmann.

Norden, Eduard. 1973. *Die Antike Kunstprosa*. Leipzig, 1898. Reprinted, Stuttgart: Teubner.

Novák, R. 1896. "Zu Valerius Maximus." *Wiener Studien* 18: 267–82.

Ogilvie, Robert M. 1980. *Roman Literature and Society*. New York: Penguin Books.

———. 1965. *A Commentary on Livy, Books 1–5*. Oxford: Clarendon Press.

Palladini, M. L. 1957. "Rapporti tra Velleio Paterculo e Valerio Massimo." *Latomus* 16: 232–51.

Parks, E. Patrick. 1945. *The Roman Rhetorical Schools as a Preparation for the Courts under the Early Empire*. Johns Hopkins University Studies in Historical and Political Science 63, no. 2. Baltimore.

Pearson, Lionel. 1941. "Historical Allusions in the Attic Orators." *Classical Philology* 36: 209–29.

Pease, Arthur Stanley. 1963. *M. Tulli Ciceronis de divinatione libri duo*. Urbana, Ill.: 1920. Reprinted, Darmstadt: Wissenschaftliche Buchgesellschaft.

———. 1955. *M. Tulli Ciceronis de natura deorum*. Cambridge: Harvard University Press.

Peter, Hermann. 1906. *Historicorum Romanorum Reliquiae*. 2 vols. Leipzig: Teuber.

Price, Bennet J. 1975. "Paradeigma and Exemplum in Ancient Rhetorical Theory." Ph.D. dissertation, University of California at Berkeley.

Rambaud, Michel. 1953. *Cicéron et l'histoire romaine*. Paris: Les Belles Lettres.

Rawson, Elizabeth. 1985. *Intellectual Life in the Late Roman Republic*. London: Gerald Duckworth.

Rayment, C. S. 1964. "Ancient Rhetoric (1957–1963)." *Classical World* 57: 241–50.

Reiff, Arno. 1959. *interpretatio, imitatio, aemulatio. Begriff und Vorstellung literarischer Abhängigkeit bei den Römern*. Würzburg: Konrad Triltsch.

Reynolds, L. D., and N. G. Wilson. 1974. *Scribes and Scholars. A Guide to the Transmission of Latin Literature*. Oxford: Clarendon Press.

Riposati, Benedetto. 1939. "M. Terenti Varronis De Vita Populi Romani." *Publicazioni Dell' Università Cattolica Del S. Cuore* 33. Milan.

Rovelstad, A. M. 1929. "Valerius Maximus as an Author in the High-School Course." *Classical Journal* 24: 578–84.

Sage, M. M. 1979. "The Elogia of the Augustan Forum and the De viris illustribus." *Historia* 28: 192–210.

Schnetz, J. 1904. *Neue Untersuchungen zu Valerius Maximus, seinen Epitomatoren und zu Fragmentum de praenominibus*. Programm, Munnerstadt.

Schoenberger, Hans. 1914. "Über die Quellen und die Verwendung der geschichtlichen Beispiels in Ciceros Briefen." Programm, Ingolstadt.

————. 1910. "Beispiele aus der Geschichte, ein rhetorisches Kunstmittel in Ciceros Reden." Dissertation, Erlangen.

Schullian, Dorothy May. 1981. "A Revised List of Manuscripts of Valerius Maximus." *Miscellanea Augusto Campana* 17: 695–728. Padua: Autenore.

————. 1937. "A Neglected Manuscript of Valerius Maximus." *Classical Philology* 32: 349–59.

Sealey, R. 1961. "The Political Attachments of L. Aelius Sejanus." *Phoenix* 15: 97–115.

Seelisch, R. 1872. "De casuum obliquorum apud Valerium Maximum usu, Liviani et Taciti Dicendi Generis Ratione Habita." Dissertation, Münster.

Sinclair, Brent. 1980. "Valerius Maximus and the Evolution of Silver Latin." Ph.D. dissertation, University of Cincinnati.

Skidmore, Clive Julian. 1988. "Teaching by Examples: Valerius Maximus and the Exemplia Tradition." Dissertation, University of Exeter.

Sochatoff, A. F. 1938–39. "The Basic Rhetorical Theories of the Elder Seneca." *Classical Journal* 34: 345–54.

Stewart, Zeph. 1953. "Sejanus, Gaetulicus, and Seneca." *American Journal of Philology* 74: 70–86.

Sumner, G. V. 1965. "The Family Connections of L. Aelius Sejanus." *Phoenix* 19: 134–46.

Sussman, Lewis A. 1978. *The Elder Seneca. Mnemosyne* Supplement 51. Leiden: Brill.

————. 1972. "The Elder Seneca's Discussion of the Decline of Roman Eloquence." *California Studies in Classical Antiquity* 5: 195–210.

————. 1969. "The Elder Seneca as a Critic of Rhetoric." Ph.D. dissertation, University of North Carolina.

Syme, Ronald. 1978. *History in Ovid.* Oxford: Clarendon Press.

————. 1964. "The Historian Servilius Nonianus." *Hermes* 92: 408–24.

————. 1939. *The Roman Revolution.* Oxford: Clarendon Press.

Szemler, G. J. 1972. *The Priests of the Roman Republic: A Study of the Interaction between Priesthoods and Magistracies.* Collection Latomus 127. Brussels.

Temporini, Hildegaard, and Wolfgang Haase, eds. 1984. *Literatur der julisch-claudischen und der flavischen Zeit. Aufstieg und Niedergang der Römischen Welt* II, 32.1. Berlin and New York: Walter de Gruyter.

Thormeyer, W. 1902. "De Valerio Maximo." Dissertation, Göttingen.

Wilkes, J. 1972. "Julio-Claudian Historians." *Classical World* 65: 177–92.

Williams, Gordon W. 1978. *Change and Decline: Roman Literature in the Early Empire.* Berkeley: University of California Press.

————. 1968. *Tradition and Originality in Roman Poetry.* Oxford: Clarendon Press.

Woodman, A. J. 1983. *Velleius Paterculus: The Caesarian and Augustan Narrative (2.41–93)*. Cambridge: Cambridge University Press.

———. 1977. *Velleius Paterculus: The Tiberian Narrative (2.94–131)*. Cambridge: Cambridge University Press.

———. 1975. "Velleius Paterculus." In *Empire and Aftermath: Silver Latin II*, ed. T. A. Dorey, 1–25. London and Boston: Routledge and Kegan Paul.

Zschech, Fr. 1865. "De Cicerone et Livio Valerii Maximi fontibus." Dissertation, Berlin.

Zetzel, James E. G. 1981. *Latin Textual Criticism in Antiquity*. New York: Arno Press.

Index of Authors and Passages Cited

General Index

Ablative absolute: V's use of, 52, 132, 243

Abstraction, 31; of moral categories, 32, 163, 256; disguises difficult subjects, 44, 54; applied to historical figures, 159, 160, 189, 190, 191, 197–98, 218, 219; and style, 258–59

Abstract nouns: V's use of, 48, 140, 169, 231, 246; as chapter headings, 27, 53; replacing concrete nouns, 231, 232, 237, 238, 239, 245

Acilius, C., 36

Adnominatio, 235, 236, 240, 250

Aelius (praetor), 162

Agent nouns, 238–39

Agrippa, M. Vipsanius, 221

Agrippa, Menenius, 140, 141

Albucius Silus, 193–94

Alcibiades, 21, 80, 81, 82

Alexander, 8, 9, 12, 21, 238, 253; borrowed exempla about, 98–107 passim; unprecedented exempla about, 104–5; addressed directly, 161

Alexander Polyhistor, 63

Anaxagoras, 106

Anaxarchus, 82, 83, 105

Annals, 74; of priests, 20; of magistrates, 31; used by Cicero, 37

Antiochus, 253

Antipater, Coelius, 32, 138, 139, 140, 143, 144; used by Cicero, 34, 39; cited by V from Cicero, 62, 63, 202

Antiphon, 257

Antithesis: V's use of, 231, 250; and *sententiae*, 246

Antonius, C., 121

Antonius, M. (orator), 176; and Marius, 158–59; eloquence of, 160, 179–80, 181, 182

Antony: and Cicero's death, 161, 192, 195, 196; V's depiction of, 220, 225; overshadowed by Pompey, 226

Apology, 40; used to handle difficult subjects, 40, 42, 44, 54

Apostrophe, 205, 235–36, 249, 250; to Marius, 41; to Pompey, 160; to the Caesars and others, 252–53

Appian, 96

Arganthonius of Gadis, 144

Ariarthes, 225, 226

Aristocratic culture, 11, 12, 259; presented to nonaristocratic audience, 57

Aristogeiton, 22

Aristotle, 4, 106

Aristoxenus Musicus, 63, 145

Ascanius, 36

Asconius, 135, 149, 197; avoided controversial forms of history, 147, 204

Aspines, 4

Atticus, 199; world chronology of, 18

Audience: declaimers and students, 1, 12, 16, 255; V's, 9, 14, 55; upwardly mobile, 13–14, 56, 57; of Tiberius' day, 149, 174, 186; stylistic expectations of, 237, 251, 252–53

Aufidius Bassus, 147

Augustine, 121

Augustus, 20, 113; Forum of, 143, 258; as patron, 148; and Marius, 158; not linked to civil conflict, 158, 159, 183, 186, 192; history under, 193, 259; propaganda of, 205; V's picture of, 207, 209, 221, 223–24, 225, 226–27; divinization of, 208; few exempla on, 229

Bassus, J., 196

Common words: avoided by contemporaries, 232, 235, 237; used by V, 237–38

Comparisons, in V, 157, 158, 160, 161, 169; shape image of the past, 186

Composition: method of, 39, 40, 44, 48, 62, 83–84, 132, 233; rhetorical techniques employed in, 43; use of sources for, 48, 72; associative process of, 58; by category and instance, 174

Contamination of sources, 61, 70, 77, 109; results in stylistic pastiche, 200; of Cicero and Livy as sources, 202

Controversiae, 8, 16; set at Rome, 24; labels debated in, 172

Corbulo, 147, 149

Coriolanus, 45

Cornelia, 143

Coruncianus, 134, 135

Cotta, 181

Crassus, L., 180, 181

Crassus, M. Licinius, 30, 37, 38

Crassus, P., 18, 181

Cremutius Cordus, 147, 148, 186

Croesus, 21

Crohn, H., 99, 100

Cruelty: chapter theme, 40; of foreign nations, 54, 115, 116; of individuals, 54, 150, 175

Ctelius of Cnidos, 63

Culture, Augustan: derivative of republican past, 3

Cumanus, C. Blossius, 44, 45, 46, 47, 48

Curius, M'., 134, 135

Curtius, 161

Customs, early Roman, 122

Cyrus, 21, 103

Damasippus, 49, 50

Damastes, 63, 145

Damon and Phintias, 84, 86–89, 99

Darius, 99, 102, 238

Decii, the, 5, 162; family precedents fulfilled, 227

Decius Mus, P., 227

Declamation, 12, 17, 27; core of elite education, 4, 7; as oral culture, 8, 60; required Roman exempla, 24; joined incongruous exempla, 31, 47; source for V, 62, 78, 114, 146, 153; audience for V, 114, 233; appearance of famous men in, 161, 174; promulgated Augustus' view of history, 192; influence on V's style, 235, 236, 239, 254

Decline of literature, 3, 248–49

Demades, 105, 106

Dentatus, L. Siccius, 115, 216

Dicta, 91; of famous men, 72, 99, 100, 107; oral tradition of, 100

Dictation, 60

Diction: contaminated, 52; transformed by V from Livy, 70, 75–76, 95; transformed by V from Diodorus, 90, 91; transformed by V from his sources, 98, 200, 232, 233–35; transformed by V from Trogus, 101, 106; transformed by V from Valerius Antias, 132; transformed by V from Cicero, 169; poetic, 235–36; and use of synonyms, 236–37; and common words, 237–38; and metaphoric usages, 238, 239; and *clausulae*, 248, 256. *See also* Abstract nouns; Agent nouns; Coinages, V's; Grecisms; Poetic language; Synonyms

Dio, Asinius, 209, 210

Dio, Cassius, 2, 61, 211; on Cato's death, 212; on Pompey's defeat, 214

Diodorus Siculus, 16, 63, 79–99, 138, 146; encyclopedism of, 78; not V's source, 80, 82, 83, 86, 89–90, 100; same order of stories in V, 90, 92, 93; as source on Alex-

ander, 99–100, 101–2; not V's
source on Alexander, 103, 107
Diogenes Laertius, 82, 86
Diogenes the Cynic, 105
Dionysius of Halicarnassus, 16; en-
cyclopedism of, 78; on Roman
women, 114, 124; on Poplicola,
140, 142
Dionysius of Syracuse, 87, 88, 89,
105
Direct speech, 72
Dissent: anti-imperial, 148, 149;
shown toward Pompey, 185, 213,
214; toward J. Caesar, 187; not
evident in V, 206, 207; toward the
Caesars, 213–14
Domitius, Cn., 30, 34, 38
Dubitatio, 249, 252, 253, 256

Education, Roman, 3; and advance-
ment of careers, 13; taught Romanness, 13, 186; made stories
into commonplaces, 86; and historiography, 149; context of V's
exempla, 152; source of V's categories and techniques, 153
Egnatius, 114, 125
Emphatic usage, 242–43
Encyclopedism, Hellenistic, 78
Epaminondas, 98–99
Ephorus, 81
Epigrammatic style, 196, 240; and
sententiae, 250
Equitius, 156, 209
Errors, historical, 2, 19, 39, 67, 135,
136; not proof of source, 118;
and the Scipios, 120
Eutropius, 130–31
Exempla: historical, 4, 12, 205; use
of, 6; traditional, 7; as models of
conduct, 12, 258; V's subject, 15;
divided into Roman and foreign,
17, 28, 50; collections of, 18; dehistoricized, 19; selection of, 19,
39, 40; joining of, 19, 43, 124–25,
139; ranking of, 22, 28, 32; pairs
of, 23, 105; opposite, 26; chrono-

logical order of, 28, 31; divided
into favorable and adverse, 29,
31; fashioning of, 68, 239; formulaic nature of, 233, 240

Fabius, M., 118
Fabius Maximus, 43
Fabricius, C.: and offer to poison
Pyrrhus, 127–30, 131, 132, 133;
and Epicureanism, 134, 135; as
the stuff of lore, 143
Fairweather, J., 240
Fathers, bereaved, 65, 68, 69; as a
commonplace illustration, 71, 72;
as model of behavior, 258
Fenestella, 149
Figuration, 232, 248, 249, 256; of
thought, 250; with metaphor,
251–52. *See also* Metaphor;
Metonymy
Fimbria, C., 167–69, 180
First person, 25, 41, 53; in
prooemia, 19, 54; in a citation,
143
Flaccus, Cn. Fulvius, 21, 118
Flaccus, Munatius, 49, 50
Flaccus, Verrius, 63, 64, 78n, 96,
118, 119, 138
Flamininus (praetor), 237
Flamininus, L., 136–37, 138
Flaminius, C., 29–38 passim
Fleck, M.: on Valerius Antias, 126–
27, 129–31, 136; on an annalist
as V's source, 134, 135; on
Asinius Pollio, 144; on the rhetor-
ical schools, 152
Foreign exempla: outnumber Ro-
man, 21, 24, 25; absent, 24; fol-
low Roman, 29; balanced with
Roman, 48–49; drawn from
Cicero and Trogus, 107
Forster, E. M., 46
Fortune, reversals of, 17, 23, 56–57;
as theme for Marius, 163, 174;
for Sulla, 174; for Cicero, 203
Freedom of speech, 54, 55, 56, 131

CANISIUS COLLEGE LIBRARY

3 5084 00327 8416

PA 6791 .V7 B58 1992

Bloomer, W. Martin.

Valerius Maximus & the
rhetoric of the new

CANISIUS COLLEGE LIBRARY
BUFFALO, N.Y.